Levels of COMPASSION

Copyright © 2008 Bonnie Baumgartner
All rights reserved.
ISBN: 1-4392-0436-5
ISBN-13: 978-1439204368

Visit www.booksurge.com to order additional copies.

BONNIE BAUMGARTNER

LEVELS OF COMPASSION
BOOK 16 SELF LOVE

2008

Levels of COMPASSION

TABLE OF CONTENTS FOR
Levels of COMPASSION
Book 16 Self Love

Acknowledgments................................xi
Introduction xv

Chapter 1 **VIBRATIONAL SCALE** of the
       LITTLE HUMAN..... 1

Chapter 2 Level Below zero, **Death, Addiction** 13
       SEEDS of SEXUAL ADDICTION 14

Chapter 3 Level 0. **Abandoning the self** 19
       SELF COMPASSION........................20

Chapter 4 Level 1. **Oppositional, Angry**.............25
       CORDS are multidimensional 26

Chapter 5 Level 2. **Conventional** 35
       MULTIDIMENSIONAL LANGUAGE 37

Chapter 6 Level 3. **Thriving, Inquisitive** 45
       EXPERIENCES or LESSONS 47

Chapter 7 Level 4. **Eagerness** 55
       SELF LOVE Is *multidimensional*..................58

ATTACHMENT to the THIRD DIMENSION 61
SENSORY AWARENESS 68

Chapter 8 **VIBRATION SCALE** of the
DIVINE HUMAN 77
CHOOSING ASCENSION 81

Chapter 9 Level 5. **In and out**. 89
Level 5 Awareness' 91
RESTRUCTURING 95
UNSEEN WORLD support 103

Chapter 10 Level 6. **Balancing** 109
Balance PATHOLOGY 110
HUMAN DNA by Kryon 114
Level 6 Awareness' 116
ENERGY / LIGHT 121
YOUR SIGNATURE 123

Chapter 11 Level 7. **Soaring** 129
Level 7 Awareness' 130
ONE SOUL, ELEVEN experiences. 133
ROMANCE on LEVEL 6 and 7 135
Paul. 138

Chapter 12 Level 8. **Oneness**. 147

Chapter 13 Level 9. **Completion** 151

Chapter 14 **EARTH** 153
PEACE 154
The END of ATLANTIS.

Chapter 15 FEELING and HEALING............167

Chapter 16 LAWS of the UNIVERSE 173

Chapter 17 MASTER NUMBERS..................181

Chapter 18 A—D words and concepts..............187

Chapter 19 E—H words and concepts 221

Chapter 20 I—R words and concepts................247

Chapter 21 S—Z words and concepts 285

My Book list

my website is www.mysticknowing.com
and NOW an on line **dictionary** for you.

***

ACKNOWLEDGMENTS

I have deep, deep gratitude for the divine humans that have been so kindhearted with their consciousness creativity and time.

Kelly Arbogast who brainstorms with me and shares his vast knowledge. He created and serves as the webmaster on the Mystic Knowing website. http://www.mysticknowing.com

Dan Laudicina who gives a different point of perception and fills in awareness that I miss. He helped fill out information I lacked.

Becky Beebe who sees pictures and stories to add different levels of consciousness to our thoughts and ideas.

Torben Hansen who feels, knows and shares his higher mental fields and personal knowledge. Torben facilitates other humans going through their awakening process. Torben is sensitive to the patterns we get "stuck in," and helps people to evolve out of the repetitive behaviors we use to distract ourselves with. His webmaster is Kelly Arbogast and the website is, http://www.look4insight.com

***

I am so beholden to the invisible angels, our entourage, soul, gnost and correspondents assisting us on our journey of ascension. thank you.

The Group channeled by **Steve Rother** Lightworker.com

The Brotherhood of Light channeled by **Edna G. Frankel** edna@beyondreiki.com

Archangel Metatron through **James Tyberonn**, www.earth-keeper.com,

INTRODUCTION OF

Levels of COMPASSION

Self Love and SOUL MELDING, Book 16

The Invisible Realm loves things orderly and easily measured and everything in its place. There is an emotional level or vibrational scale for humans based on the level they function at most of the time. The level dictates your perception of reality, your truth's and behavior and your spiritual awareness.

For the first time humans now have a scale for the divine human or ascension or soul melding where instead of your guides and angels being in your auric field your soul resides there.

We are humans on this planet for the purpose of gaining spiritual wisdom and compassion. Each level of wisdom and compassion or vibration needs to be EARNED by the INDIVIDUAL. Your vibrational level cannot be stolen or bought, it needs to be earned by you the human with the THOUGHTS and FEELINGS you carry and the CHOICES you make.

Remember this planet HAS always **had a dark bias.**

Each level has its unique belief system and PERCEPTIONS of reality.

When what we SEE is altered and our values and truths changed, we have probably changed levels. The levels I am mentioning are broad, there are twelve levels within EACH level I have mentioned. I have started with the lowest vibration and worked my way up to the highest compassion for a human.

MENTAL visualization, creating images in the mind OR verbalizations like chanting mantras aloud MIGHT have served you at one time. **NOW** it sends the message to the brain that you are afraid of YOURSELF and afraid of your **intuitive**, DIVINE feelings and **awareness**. Mental visualization or verbalization creates a BARRIER to your divinity. Allow the mind to step aside and YOU GO *directly to the multidimensional language* of feelings. Your RAW, **genuine feelings** and senses become available to you.

When we get a breakthroughs in awareness it is because we FELT the multidimensional language. The mind DID NOT suddenly get smarter. Anytime you have overwhelming feelings of compassion or knowingness and intuition it is your multidimensional language coming through YOUR feelings.

Faulty belief systems create barriers to healing yourself because our biology follows our beliefs. Try to feel joy and gratitude for all you DO HAVE, clear your mind of negative thought loops that depress your biology. We create what we focus on and our TOTAL BEING vibrates on the level we THINK and FEEL at.

The little human CHILD experiences and lives frequently in fear until the adult owns and releases those fears. Unless you have done work to heal the childhood wounds, FEEL them and OWN them, your adult life is just REINFORCING and repeating YOUR childhood and past life PATTERNS. The purpose of the patterns is to get you to SEE what happened in YOUR childhood. To MAKE you AWARE of the misdirection's and correct them. The human needs to notice these things, WAKE UP and stop drifting in unconsciousness!

Low vibrating UNCONSCIOUS humans USE children to satisfy their needs and ignore the child's needs. They are repeating the pattern their childhood gave them which is anti compassion.

SELF LOVE *Is a multidimensional SPIRITUAL attribute.* NOT linear.

SELF ESTEEM, self **worth** or *love* is a multidimensional attribute and NOT a third dimensional, linear attribute.

Accept and embrace ALL of your emotions.

CONSIDER your emotions as your PARTNER in awareness and consciousness raising moving you into total compassion. The more you partner with your emotions as the loving instructor and friend they are, the more you value your human self. The more self love you have the more you are brought back to your perfection.

Historically, consciousness has been a very small, DARK, limited container with very few options. The time has come to go outside the box and as we leave the LIMITS, a void is created, a vacuum. At a certain point that structure has the potential of imploding. Consciousness from old energy is being taken out of the earth at this time and filled with new energy.

A VOID or a Null Zone is established after there is an expansion outwards of energy which receives a blow or shock causing it to COLLAPSE inwards upon itself. The old established energy patterns (belief systems) are now broken and there is no way that they will ever return to the previous pattern. This would be similar to the feeling you would have after being in a hurricane or any natural disaster. This shattering creates the perfect foundation for the introduction of something ENTIRELY new to come in. To break free from old stagnant patterns and belief systems giving us the opportunity for a *quantum leap* into a deeper sector of awareness.

Release your need for CONTROL in your life, the invisible realm has things well in hand so you can celebrate and be joyful. The human is a bridge between our "soul and matter," the "divine and earth." We are to enclose and make a balanced whole of these opposites. Our ENTIRE *electromagnetic self,* layer upon layer, wrapped around and through our physical core is the bridge.

Ascension levels are discerned by what amounts of; agenda, lesson, BLAME, judgment, doubt, gossip, DRAMA, COMPROMISE, lack and karma the little human *has released.* If you decide to pull ANY of these back into YOUR life you will drop back to the third dimension. It is YOUR JOB to notice the differences so you can CHOOSE AGAIN.

Lower level vibrational luminous light or strands can represent **attachments** that others have to you or from you that are PARASITIC in nature. The attachments are to DRAIN your energy. *THE CARE taking and attachments* to THINGS or humans in the third dimension need to be released as they keep our vibration at a rather low level.

In HIGHER vibrations we communicate and SHARE, instead of feeding from our guides, angels, other humans or addictions. It is an evolutionary step for humans to harmonically interact with the **thought strands from higher dimensions.**

Soul enters matter and then creates through matter. Soul has to enter the human for there to be **a PASSION in the human.** When you do not have a passion your soul thinks something else is more important for you to DO first. So LISTEN UP to your sensory awareness.

ASCENSION is to stay in your current biology but move to the NEXT LEVEL of spiritual awareness or compassion in this lifetime. This moving to higher and higher levels of spiritual wisdom and awareness can and does happen to some over and over again.

When the voice of the inner self becomes louder than the voice of the third dimension a constant stream of self love, compassion and unconditional love is maintained. The above are prerequisites for healthy creating. Owning the truth of your thoughts and feelings keeps them in useful service to you by not letting you ignore what you feel. Staying in the present moment, facing your feelings and moving into SOLUTIONS and *resolutions* help the individual and the collective.

Conspiracy theories develop **inner fears** and humans externalize them. Believing the enemy is outside of you blocks expedient SOLUTIONS and *resolutions* for healthy change.

We left our "homes" eons ago on a mission, we volunteered to help each world we entered. Agreeing to adopt their lifestyle and ways. We teach the ways of the legion of light.

***

CHAPTER 1

<u>VIBRATION SCALE</u> of the *little human*.
 Below 0 to 4.
 Your ENTOURAGE, guides or angels reside in your auric field.

Level Below 0, **Death,** pity, blame, addictions, using others.
 No light to 15%. **light**

Level 0. **Abandoning the self,** UNCONSCIOUS no emotion.
 15 to 30% light.

Level 1. **Oppositional,** angry, in pain, hate, HALF CONSCIOUS.
 30-50% light.

Level 2. **Conventional,** traditional and cautious, 3/4 CONSCIOUS.
 50-60% light.

Level 3. **Thriving,** inquisitive, seeking, MOSTLY CONSCIOUS.
 SELF LOVE is being mastered on level 3 through 5
 60-70% light.

Level 4. **Eagerness,** cheerful, enthusiastic, FULLY CONSCIOUS.
70-80% **light.**

VIBRATION SCALE of the *DIVINE HUMAN*
ASCENSION or SOUL MELDING
Your SOUL reside in your auric field.

Level 5. **In and out,** little human 50% or less melded with soul.
   80-90% light.

Level 6. **Balancing,** biology, DNA, 80% in divine will.
   90-95% light.

Level 7. **Soaring,** little human emotions and concerns going.
   95-100% light. MARRIAGE with the SOUL

Level 8. **Oneness,** human functioning as one with soul. Human is fully melded and out of duality.

Level 9. **Completion,** of an ERA, a cycle, or a LEVEL.

VIBRATION SCALE

The EMOTION or **VIBRATION** the human displays the most determines the level they are vibrating at. The word emotion or vibration has the same meaning to the invisible realm and are used interchangeable. Every entity has a very specific energy balance and particular RESONANCE or vibration explaining to others who and what they are all about.

The true indication of *your vibration LEVEL* is WHO and what comes into your life. Things and people are drawn to you that share your vibration level.

The universe sends or offers you people and things that you have a strong emotion for. The universe looks for things and people in your vibration and does not judge anything as **negative** or POSITIVE, it just IS. Whether it is passion or rage you feel in the moment, those emotions both mean strong focused desire passing through you. Anything that affects your vibration affects your overall experience and your THOUGHTS about THAT experience.

We are souls having a human experience on this planet for the purpose of gaining *spiritual wisdom* or experiences on behalf of the legion of light because they are unable to do it themselves. We are full of emotions that serve us and our purpose. Many of our emotions do not serve us.

***

EACH VIBRATION ON THE vibrational scale has its own particular set of;
BELIEF'S and PERCEPTIONS of reality.
TRUTHS

BEHAVIORS
PURPOSES
CREATOR ABILITIES
SPIRITUAL CONSCIOUSNESS or awareness

There are **DIFFERENT** purposes and spiritual wisdom in each vibration. We **choose** the vibration that resonates with the level we are on.

Movement into lower or higher levels on the vibrational scale can be done one level at a time. Moving into higher levels can be done *CONSCIOUSLY by taking control of your THOUGHTS and EMOTIONS* and moving them to the highest level you are currently in. Then, step by step move your thoughts and emotions to the bottom of the level just above you.

SOME TRAPS

Focusing on something **NOT wanted** lowers your vibration and ability to create. Higher or lower vibrations are placed by the degree of HARMONY or *discord present in them.* The degree of harmony YOU HAVE in RELATIONSHIP to all other things.

Each level of vibration needs to be EARNED **by the individual** and not by their mother or lover. Your vibrational level cannot be **stolen** or bought. Your level is earned with the THOUGHTS and FEELINGS you carry and the **CHOICES** you make on a daily basis.

When our perceptions are altered and our values and truths changed, we have probably changed levels. The levels I am mentioning are broad and have twelve different levels within EACH level I have mentioned. Remember this planet **HAS had a dark bias** which has only tipped to a light bias in 1987.

***

EACH LEVEL on the VIBRATIONAL SCALE CARRIES a percentage of Light to **DARK** commensurate with the way the little human thinks and feels. PLEASE know that the light and dark of the human and the levels they function in move within a range. The smaller the percentage of light the human has, the smaller their ability is to be flexible.

Love and compassion are multidimensional emotions!!!

BELOW level 3, the human is too dense to feel love and compassion from the invisible realm. From other humans below level 3, humans consider being cared for as love and compassion.

AT THIS TIME

Those hovering at the ratio of 50% light to dark are considered fence sitting because they are not moving up or down the vibrational scale. The invisible realm is making it hard to stay at 50% and are nudging people to pick a direction. At the time of the GREAT SHIFT, if you are 51% or more dark you will not wake up after the 3 days of darkness. That could be a third to two thirds of the population. If you are vibrating at 51% or more darkness your biology is NOT being upgraded either.

This planet and the humans on it are in the process of evolving spiritually back to our natural ANGELIC state of being. Angelic beings create and recreate. The more imperfect the world appears to humans, the harder humans work to perfect things and in that process they perfect themselves.

When the human acts as the participant and the observer their experience is enriched and their knowledge is enhanced. All our lifetimes are both original and sequential in this illusion.

THOUGHTS

Our **thinking and thoughts** are the fastest energy in the universe and infinitely faster than the speed of light and the ability of humans to travel through the dimensions. At a certain speeds, thinking interacts with the physical propulsion system allowing it to be projected forward by its propellant AND THE thinking of its participants.

The nature of our reality is BASED on thought.

Our true nature is biology and electromagnetic, luminous pulsing. We have luminous strands of electromagnetic light that is extended to many different realms and places. Each luminous connection can be described in terms of its vibrational resonance. We are spiritually linked by observable, vibrational strands to other realms and our soul family.

ATTACHMENTS

Lower level vibrational luminous light or strands can represent **attachments** that others have to you or from you that are PARASITIC in nature. The attachments are **to DRAIN energy.** *THE CARE taking and attachments* to THINGS or humans in the third dimension need to be released as they keep our vibration at a low level.

In HIGHER vibrations we communicate and SHARE, instead of feeding from our guides, angels, other humans or addictions. It is an evolutionary step for humans to harmonically interact with the **thought strands from higher dimensions.**

When the voice of the inner self becomes louder than the voice of the third dimension a constant stream of self love is maintained. Unconditional love, allowance and acceptance are a prerequisites for healthy creating. The greatest good for all concerned fosters spiritual growth.

In old energy we have CONTROL through **fear.**

CONSPIRACY theories increase our **inner fears** and externalizes them. Believing the enemy is outside of you distracts the human from developing SOLUTIONS and healthy *resolution* of their fears. When you talk to your fears, instead of resisting them, you learn from them and you are able to redirect the energy.

DRAMA prevents the human from feeling *their OWN feelings*.

Our **true feelings** are in service to us. Owning the truth of your thoughts and feelings keep them in useful service to you by not letting you IGNORE what you feel. Staying in the present moment, facing and owning your **feelings of fear.** Moving into SOLUTION and *resolution* assists the individual and the group.

Drama and pretend emotion is a substitute for AUTHENTIC emotions. Drama keeps the cycle of fear and overwhelm feeding itself. Pretending or philosophizing on a higher mental plane cannot substitute for real feelings.

Accept and embrace ALL of your AUTHENTIC emotions. Think of your emotions as your PARTNER in awareness and consciousness raising moving you into total compassion. The more you partner with your emotions as the loving instructor and friend they are, the more you value your human self. The more self love you have the more you are brought back to your perfection and the next cycle in love.

What emotion and thought comes through the human goes out to the entire planet and beyond. Honesty of feeling and thought in your relationship with yourself allows passion and excitement to flow through you increasing your magnetism to attract higher vibrational matches.

Allowing others the same freedom to feel and exist in their own love, focused on what they WANT and NOT consumed with taking care of and feeding another is the higher vibrational attribute. Allow other humans to experience with you detached and having no agenda.

One piece and particle at a time we are working with the new energy and consciousness. Be fully aware that you have expanded your consciousness in ways you're not actually aware of yet. The resources, energies and aspects of our future self and potentials are here to enhance our self love and joy.

It is a beautiful thing to have a biology on earth.

It is a time for gentleness as we are all going through healing and a great deal of change. Fear will lead you away from your heart without your awareness. Fear will keep you away from your dreams and aspirations. Fears will stop the love from flowing. You must allow your heart to decide where the love is to flow.

Light waves and energy don't always move in a straight line. Light can be manipulated by other forces and other energies. Around 2005 some fear energies have started to bring INTERFERENCE ENERGY between the human and higher vibrations leading some humans into a "little human direction of having not enough" and away from their spiritual wisdom and direction. Discernment is more important now than it ever has been because of the interfering energies.

Just stay with your feelings they will guide you.

OUR FEARS START IN CHILDHOOD.

The little human child experiences and lives in fear until the adult owns and releases the fear. After that you move to past lives to remove those fears you FELT like that in this lifetime.

During the days of Lemuria and Atlantis we knew how to create our reality. We were great healers and mystics and knew how to bend and change reality.

Our consciousness today is much lower than it was in Atlantis, Lemuria and Egypt several thousand years ago. True consciousness is all about the relationship inside ourselves with all our aspects working with each other.

During childhood we are so soft, gentle and tender, so vulnerable and easy to wound. An argument close to a newborn child is all it takes to wound a child and create fear within it. That fear will freeze and always radiate a reality in your life. The inner emotions become external manifestations or issues. This fear can also come from a family member or an ancestor. The entire family can have the same fear living in a low level lack of acceptance of the self.

Where does anxiety START?

The bottom line is that we copy our parent's relationship patterns. That relationship is imprinted within us and underneath that we look completely different.

The psychic magnetism and gravity of this dimension is so strong it pulls even the most evolved soul into this very dense reality and causes them to forget who they are and they immerse themselves in it.

By immersing fully into the psychic magnetism and gravity of this dimension you actually can then remember your angelic, divine self. We will bring love to this planet because we want to bring love to ourselves. A completely new world and shift in energy is happening at this time.

Our planet has its challenges and difficulties, but these are illusions. Fear is an illusion that plays into the grand beauty of life that many humans are missing. Running from fear is not helpful. Death has beauty in itself, honoring and thanking the biology in your last moments for the great ride and experience. You release the biology and move into a more spiritual state.

So many humans are in psychological disorder and or physical imbalance and or spiritual chaos. You know it is the spiritual awakening process when you begin to question things that you have never questioned before. You question the authority in your life you never questioned before. You question WHY you are here on earth and what does it all mean and what is it that you should be doing right now.

THE AWAKENING IS RIGHT HERE!
RIGHT NOW! And so it is.

***

CHAPTER 2
BELOW ZERO

Level Below 0, **Death**, pity, shame, blame, addiction, using others. Usually trying to **DESTROY** *their awareness* and / or their biology in some manner. This is too low a vibration for angels to attend to the biology. **No light—15% light.**

***

When you isolate the emotional or vibrational range you operate in most of the time, it is easy to determine the other predictable behaviors that are found in that range. Each level has a **UNIQUE belief system** and **PERCEPTION of reality**. The low vibrating human is INFLEXIBLE with very rigid NARROW belief's. They tend to feel POWERLESS and persecuted. They VICTIMIZE others that are smaller or more dependent than they are. When they get frightened, which is *much of the time* they can and will vent on others ALONG with SUBMITTING to let others control them. When they get wounded they *move into that pain* and become even more unstable and irrational, fearful and easier to control. YOU WOULD BE FOOLISH to TRUST anyone at below zero with anything, person or task. Whatever you trust them with will get twisted or perverted and possibly destroyed.

FOR AN EXAMPLE

An individual who is living in self pity, blame or addiction, no matter what their situation or environment, regardless of their education or intellect or position in life will twist reality. Their choices and decisions are made from the most extremely limited point of perception of *despair and hopelessness.* They are **incapable of SEEING** other options or directions because they are in extreme despair.

Addictions and despair are used to avoid awareness of and belief in more constructive things and behaviors.

***

SEEDS of SEXUAL ADDICTION

"I have always been afraid to really enjoy sexual activity, yet I engage in it frequently."

I fear getting caught in the trap of LUST and the sexual virus, **FEEDING** and being FED, all the **DRAMA** and loss of CONTROL.

Loss of control of my essence and free will or choice.

"I have always been afraid to really enjoy the sex act." Sexual activity triggers me and I dissociate and become the victim once again, powerless against my own need to feel loved.

Fearing sexual activity and the loss of your personal control of your biology would be an appropriate reaction as a result of the childhood misuse of your biology by your mom. As a child you had up close and personal experience with sexual addiction and the addicts dissociating or going into a hypnotic state while abusing you. Your essence LEFT because it knew it was being controlled and forced and was helpless to do anything about it. The biology got used and forced. This is not the act of a loving caretaker. This is one biology or bit of matter controlling another biology or bit of matter. It is the creating of fear, suffering, loss of control of the biology and pain in the little one.

"I fear getting caught in just sex and lust with no HEART." Just as all my family members have done.

DOESN'T THAT DESCRIBE exactly what did happen? When, as a small child your mother took you to bed with her? When even today, engaging in sexual activity you reenact what you WERE FORCED to experience and mom reenacted what she was forced to experience in her childhood. The gift that keeps the addiction flowing from one generation to the next.

ADDICTION comes *through sexually stimulating the biology* pleasure centers and creating a physical release with no satisfaction or warmth and comfort. A real chill of *despair and FEELING of hopelessness* if you are at all conscious and aware of your feelings. This is not an expression of love in any way shape or form! This is one biology controlling and forcing another biology. Where is the LOVE in that, abuse is a very sad thing.

We have sex with powerless children wearing adult biology.

Adults abused in childhood fear their biology being "TAKEN OVER," and/or emotionally shamed into becoming the small powerless, GUILTY biology victim they were again. When they had to abandon their biology by dissociating during the abuse they were powerless to stop.

As adults when sexual activity gets started the dissociation is automatic. When two people having sex are dissociated you have two adults regressed back to their abusive childhood's. When only one is dissociated the aware one is having sex by themselves. The dissociated one is avoiding RELIVING the betrayal and pain once again.

SEXUALLY ADDICTED young and old.

The sexually addicted behaves in the same manner they observed sexual activity in the earlier episodes or their being controlled and forced. The victim is horrified by

THE TRANSFORMATION of the predator. The predator dissociates and the child can't figure out where their TRUSTED PROTECTOR went or how to get them back. Then the predators breathing increase and they are TOTALLY IN their own world. Totally unaware of and insensitive to the little biology they are using. This creates great confusion, **fear** and GUILT in the little biology about what happened and what to do about it. Most humans tend to increase their level of fear, worry and depression when abused.

When a predator puts the victim down or blames the little child, or "a separate personality" or an ASPECT comes forward to handle the perceived LIFE AND DEATH STRUGGLE and the essence goes away, FREQUENTLY to the fifth dimension for comfort from the angels. This is called LEARNED helplessness or a survival technique, a coping behavior or dissociation is used to cope with the trauma the human has experienced.

Anytime a bully makes someone small or guilty or regresses them to a much younger age and powerless state, the bully **puts them in fear**.

We put someone in fear so we can feed off their fear.

The child victim ALWAYS feels *guilty and responsible* for CAUSING the predator to do what they did. The child ALWAYS blames themselves. When a child is used sexually, they are told in many different ways it is THEIR fault and they believe that, they OWN ALL THE BLAME. How low is their self worth going to be? How evil and unlovable do they think they are?

All judgment **comes from FEAR**.

Ask your guides or angels to give you a slideshow of the original episodes of you being the victim of an older, stronger, more manipulative biology you trusted with your very existence. Ask for the episode WITH the feelings you had at that time. When a little biology has been abused by many and /or frequently. The first memories will be of the gentlest abuses.

Accepting your true, deep emotions and thoughts breaks through any fear or resistance and dissolves the emotion or thought into compassion and self acceptance neutralizing the dark energy and low vibration. Then you can refocus on the rich experience you had and **YOUR perfection**. This helps you sort out all that cannot go forward with you to the next cycle and higher energy of love.

Talk to the fears inside you and gather their wisdom.

The aspect YOU created to have this experience needs comfort, LOVE and acceptance from its creator, you. Tell your aspect how sorry you are for not being able to protect them but you can do that now and want to do that. This aspect has only experienced biology and aspect abuse. Embraced and melded it has the love and compassion it has always wanted from its creator.

The symptoms of the sexually abused are many and diverse, victims many be confused, foggy, unclear, shy and introverted, have health issues and pain in the gut and they are unable to create much in their life. Not being able to create, sucks the energy of joy right out of our human existence.

After we left All That Is, we were lonely and stared to exchange energy with other angels to get to know the self better. Learning to take energy from others made us feel better for a short bit of time and then we were looking for more. Angels started having energy exchanges first. Then they went from energy exchange TO energy stealing and then TO energy abuse. THAT abuse created an imbalance and then led to addiction. We steal energy especially from those close to us. Addictions hold you in place and stuck.

To avoid addictions, the human needs to stop feeding and love the self FIRST. When there is sexual conflict present in you because you have been sexually fed on do what you need to do to heal that wounding. To make you independent to the point that you handle your sexual needs alone without feeding off others. Give the gift of sexuality to the SELF first.

Be sovereign and hold your own space, not burdening others. Let your feelings be your guide and comfort.

Shutting down your feelings is shutting down your soul.

Humans feared they could pollute the DIVINE. That is not possible. The divine human aspect of us wants to know how it feels to take a shower, go to work, loose a love and a place to live, the divine human aspect of us wants to know all about caring for human basic needs.

Our divine human aspect does not see LACK in ANY bit of our life. The divine human aspect of us never compares what YOU have to what another may have. Our divinity is thrilled that it exists and breathes.

To receive and share our light is what we are all about.

There is no light with out dark present also.

Laughter is the the language of angels.

The third and fourth dimension is being cleared and disharmony is being cleaned up and all is getting harmonized. The rebuilt crystalline grid is on line and working.

Trust yourself, for we are the healers of ourselves. Healing requires you to take **total responsibility** for being both a victim and an abuser. And it requires you to love yourself for experiencing and gaining the wisdom.

WE ARE the LIGHT.

***

CHAPTER 3
LEVEL ZERO

Level 0, **Abandoning the self,** these humans are UNCONSCIOUS with little to no emotion and vibrating low. The angels and guides may no longer tend to the biology and it is frequently on it's own. On the higher levels of unconsciousness they are experiencing PAIN and lashing out. They are the insensitive person only aware of THEIR pain. They are the victim and please others to avoid pain. They are sad or in terror, numb or dissociated. Their sins are of omission and not handling their existence very well. They are unbalanced and dwell in their past wounds real or IMAGINED. They do not perceive love when it is offered to them. They are the passive aggressive ones.

15-30% **light.**

***

At this low vibration the guides or angels can be of little help because they can't exist in this low vibrational range and the human is unaware of them anyway. Never trust anyone in this range with children. Never trust what they say as they twist meanings. They believe if no one catches them DOING WRONG then it is OK to steal or abuse. They have no ETHICS or INTEGRITY. They believe what they say and their deceptions because **that is THEIR reality.** It is true for them.

They use other people because that is why other people exist, to be used. A child used as a "thing" to satisfy what ever need the parent is currently having. They learned this behavior from their parent, **it is a tradition handed down to the next generation**. The parent VENTS their anger and frustration about never being in control of their own existence or being in charge of their own life.

The sins and omissions of the parent fall on the child. The child is not nurtured physically, emotionally and socially. A child desperately trying to EARN LOVE from an angry frustrated parent living in a past wound is NEVER pleased or happy unless they are doing the tormenting of someone else because they are so wounded. Tormenting others distracts them from their pain.

The child filled with rage at a childhood of being forced and controlled, never able to PLEASE anyone, grows to be an angry frustrated adult finding other adults like its parent to please and earn love from. They are never successful at doing what is IMPOSSIBLE to do. BECOMES an adult that gets angry and frustrated when they try to "RESCUE" another that is angry at their parent and vents on the one looking to EARN love. On the low vibrational levels the thoughts and emotions about your experiences will be low and possibly depressed with an inability to view things clearly and have a **low level of truth and integrity**. With this type of low vibration and limited vision you are VERY prone to misdirection of your energy.

SELF COMPASSION

Earth had a dark bias before 1987.

The ratio of dark to light of the earth on the day of our birth was put into our DNA. So all born before 1987 were born with a dark bias of **compassion** and **self worth.** The skills we arrived with at birth to love the self is implanted in our biology. Then add the high probability your parents were unconscious, meaning they had little or no compassion for themselves and you have a VERY challenging almost impossible set up for loving the self.

Our self worth dictates our **ability to RECEIVE** and GIVE love and compassion. The people in our first FOUR years of life **TEACH us how THEY feel about us** and the child tends to own that information as black and white **TRUTH.** When in reality, the adults are only PROJECTING their feeling of worth ONTO the child. Which has EXTREMELY LITTLE to do with the value of the child itself. The parent reflects to the child the adults sense of worthlessness.

Now if these people are unconscious with only 50% or much less light, I can tell you with GREAT CERTAINTY you were not treated well and developed **very low** self esteem and self compassion by living with those people. So things went rapidly down hill after your birth.

That is WHY the human needs to *go back* **to the childhood** to correct the MISINFORMATION they came in with, and gathered from parents unable to love themselves. The human needs to address the wounds and misinformation created in them at birth and from the environment they grew up in. Going back to the events and the feelings that go with the major events in your life ALLOWS you to see and own them. Owning PUTS YOU into CONTROL and allows healing and releasing the FALSE TRUTHS your family offered you with great care, concern and their own personal fear.

When YOU HEAL **your childhood** wounds *with your awareness and feelings,* the adult wounds of the same type heal automatically. Healing the EARLIEST wound on your chain of similar wounds releases the rest or takes the emotional charge off them. Your entourage can supply all the information and feelings you need to heal yourself. Your job is to accept, feel and own what your entourage offers you. Owning allows you to increase your spiritual wisdom and the options and awareness in your life.

Unless you have done work to heal the childhood wounds by FEELING them and OWNING them, your **adult life is just REINFORCING and repeating** YOUR PATTERNS developed in your childhood.

As an adult you are now in control of the amount of compassion and self love you give yourself.

The patterns you learned in childhood and in your past lives are a teaching tool. The purpose of patterns is to get you to SEE what happened in YOUR childhood. To MAKE you AWARE of any misdirection and correct it. The human needs to notice these things, WAKE UP and stop drifting in unconsciousness!

Low vibrating UNCONSCIOUS humans USE children to satisfy their needs and ignore the child's needs. They are repeating the patterns their childhood gave them which is *anti compassion and self love.*

FOR EXAMPLE

The child is used by one adult to spy and tell on others.

An adult is lonely and the child is FORCED to be their friend.

The adult or sibling is ANGRY, and vents on the child.

An adult loves to CONTROL others to calm THEIR feelings of powerlessness, so the adult CONTROLS the child and greatly limits the child's freedom, development and choices.

Little humans love to please so they comply.

The weak ADULT wants to vent on the abusive spouse, but is afraid to do that so they vent on the child they do not fear and own.

They torment the child they do not fear.

The adult is jealous of a thing or attention the child gets from others. The adult takes it away or torments and rejects the child trying to make the child as unhappy as the adult is. Those that care for children vibrating at below zero, zero and 1 are not able to love or have compassion for themselves OR any child OR anyone else. Below zero, zero and 1 are only aware of what THEY need or want and how the child or another adult can supply that to them. That would include sexual activity.

Humans tend to get exceedingly dependent on each other. The dependency reaches out even into death, following them into lifetime after lifetime. There is this odd sense of needing to be with someone and making commitments to them to make them feel better.

At this time honor ONLY commitments to yourself.

When you can love YOU first, then you can honestly love another.

No matter what strife you may have in your life, remember it is only lesson. **All drama is lesson**. The lessons from your own game plan with the answers already built in.

***

A LARGER VIEW

From this point on, imbalances in resources will be felt around the world as we are all globally connected and we are all beginning to feel the connection. The millennium shift was an energetic shift. We are beginning to feel nonphysical energies shift. When we are near a person of lower, darker vibration we are aware of that. The more divine light that reaches us, the more isolated pockets of extremism are being brought into the light and exposed.

Lying reduces your vibration as well as negative criticism and unwanted judgments do. Engaging in these negative activities will become clear and definite to us and become PAINFUL. On the other hand, remember to let good deeds go with quiet grace and do not look for stroking and recognition or negative karma is released.

It is becoming easier to make higher level decisions.

Each material release gives a physical sense of release as well.

Below our conscious awareness our biology constantly recalibrates itself to integrate higher energies and more awareness.

2012 is a shift in dimensions, a much anticipated landmark. Everyone is expecting something magical to happen and of course it will. We are living firmly in the fifth dimension and you are even starting to learn how to use that in your daily life. You will realize that a lot of what you have created has already been present. When many humans gather expecting a miracle, they create one and this miracle will be multidimensional.

When a time sensitive mission is activated in us, our soul guides our passion when you let the soul lead you by opening doors in front of you OR by closing them in front of you.

The teacher stands in a very bright light because other people need that direction. Now we are stepping into higher vibrations and moving into our power. We are being activated.

Humanity is ready to hear and know.

***

CHAPTER 4
LEVEL ONE

LEVEL 1, **Oppositional** and HALF CONSCIOUS frequently leaving their biology or living in past time. Those on level one, are satisfied to indifferent or bored and are able to create some good things for themselves. They are limited by their beliefs and fears and are irrational much of the time with limited vision. They are frequently in anger or pain, hate, self absorbed, gossipy and fearful.

They twists facts to defend their half conscious reality. To feel better about them selves they try to undermine other humans reality. Always competing they love to argue and are not always truthful. They enjoy manipulate others into CONFUSION and **self doubt.** They blame, what ever happens is always someone else's fault. They are cruel and complain bitterly. Level ones are abusive bullies and hypocrites but are using their awareness to control their environment some.

30-50% light

***

Having the wish and ability to change your dominant emotion from negative or painful to pleasant and enjoyment is a reliable indicator of increased spiritual awareness and compassion for the self. The more confident and competent you become in the way you create your life, the easier it is to handle your many life experiences.

A human's attitude and behavior about love and sex is dictated by the level of their vibration. Low vibrating humans want to **RECEIVE care** and protection. Once someone has given that to them they consider it love and **they WORRY** about losing it. Their fear then becomes about "loosing their care and protection provider." They also believe that they don't deserve the caring and protection they do get. Most will fight to the death to keep what they have, the person they have obtained. These humans need CONSTANT reassurance and will even destroy the person caring for and protecting them with their constant need for PROOF they are loved, loyal and faithful.

The oppositional or angry are NOT capable of true affection, but will try to imitate it when it furthers their purpose. They charm, betray and undermine those caring for and protecting them. By undermining those caring for them they educate the other into adjusting to their ways of sucking the life out of you. They override and dominate at home or at work by controlling others with blame, guilt, dissociation and cruel invalidation's.

***

A review from my last book, "Spirituality." On this level there will be feeding cords that need addressing.

CORDS are multidimensional

CORDS are strings of energy or a vibration of **electromagnetic energy**. These strands of energy are found EVERYWHERE humans have a low or negative emotional vibration because they are FEEDING from others energetically. The cords are **visible** to the invisible realm and some humans. Cords are

LEVELS OF COMPASSION

grown and developed by humans connecting to everything and everyone they have an attachment to or are feeding from. There are cords from us to our BELIEFS, events and other humans we have known in this life time *or past life times.*

Maybe there is a cord to the waitress you verbally assaulted or the child you were cruel to. You created the DRAMA energy strands so you could FEED from them and feel alive.

The **size** of the cords shows you the depth of YOUR attachment or the amount of energy that flows through the cord. You could have many little cords to the same person or activity or a very large one.

The **location** of the cord on the body speaks volumes about your relationships with that person, event or place you are in relationship with.

Cords connect you and and what you feed from or what feeds from you energetically. Cords contain the *energy* that goes *back and forth.* Energy of all kinds, black, white and all the shades of gray energy going back and forth from you and to you from what or who is at the other end of YOUR CORD. It could be the energy of fear or control and sexual addiction or love and compassion. Strong and often reoccurring beliefs or concepts can have a thick or thin cord coming out of our physical body or ANYONE of our etheric bodies, the emotional, mental or spiritual body can all have different cords.

Cords help you stay *connected* or keep you **STUCK** in an emotion or thought pattern of energy that served you in the past. It was important to our survival to know who we could trust or not trust.

When you look for your cords you will see many different types. Sometimes you might see or feel a **ball and chain,** or a **package,** or dark **cloud,** or a **syphon.** These things can represent: FEAR, anger, BETRAYAL, regret, GUILT, a *shared* *negative belief* or low, depressed vibrating energy. This is a way to hold one's negative beliefs all together into a bundle. Hanging on to your belief's and emotions, ties up some pretty intense energy.

HOLDING that packet of negative energy triggers the law of entrainment which in turn creates a pattern of being stuck in a particular vibration.

***

LAW OF ENTRAINMENT

The law of entrainment requires two resonance's existing in the same location MUST adjust and combine. On a scale of 1-10 if one individual or object is at a 3 the other is at a 7 the law of entrainment requires they are both at the level 5. Unless one is an overpowering resonance and pulls the other to their level.

You carrying someone else's DARK ENERGY can postponed your ascension by holding you in a negative range, especially if you are care taking and protecting them. Return any darkness you carry for another so they can transmute it to another useful energy. Learn what you can from that experience, forgive both of you and grieve the loss of the entrainment. *It will alter you.*

We are a gigantic energetic creature. Every thought we have creates energetic ripples. The rising energies or vibrations on Gaia are forcing us to clear and purify all of our four bodies. The toxins or any illness patterns in any of our four bodies need clearing. The emotional and mental blockages are all low density imbalances rising up at this time to be cleared. Drink plenty of water to flush out cellular debris. We are clearing out low density energy damage that used to be normal for us to be carrying around in third dimensional energy.

LEVELS OF COMPASSION

Our body anchors our energetic layers that fan out in ever-widening circles of vibrating frequency. Our auras touch each other at six feet from the biology. That is why it makes us feel uncomfortable when a stranger stands too close. They are standing in our dense etheric bodies of emotion, mental and spiritual energies. As our auras become more sensitive it can become downright painful to have a disgruntled or unpleasant energy in your spiritual, mental or emotional space. Our energetic bodies grow more dense and real to humans as they connect to the higher frequencies brought to earth.

***

I am writing about cords and the law of entrainment because I think our awareness of these things can help us understand the way things worked in this "reality." Our reality is changing as our biology is changing, we are remembering, the way things used to be and will be in the future.

As the photon energy comes in and the vibration on the planet gets higher, little by little the energy **feeding cords are DRYING up** or disappearing from humans. Those doing the largest amount of feeding are in the greatest amount of ANXIETY and CONFUSION at this time because they have to master feeding themselves in a spiritual manner, in a rather short period of time and they do not want to.

Cords are generally "feeding tubes" to take energy. When energy is TAKEN from you and not shared, it leaves you hungry and looking to feed. A cycle you might want to work on short circuiting. When your energy is out of balance or not equally exchanged you need to understand the why of it. Just understanding and releasing the feeding can make some cords dissolve.

Awareness of what is traveling through your cords might be very helpful. I have found siblings carrying pain or suffering for each other the way our pets and plants carry pain or suffering for their humans. Siblings carry guilt or fear and EVEN when you no longer have contact with that individual you are still carrying their darkness. I recommend you cut the cord and give them back their darkness.

ANOTHER EXAMPLE

You can be sending white energy and receiving dark gray energy in return for you to transmute or carry. In the third dimension we call it codependency or being passive aggressive and taking the other OFF their spiritual path. Is that what you want to continue to do? Or allow others to do to you?

Cords are about **energy exchanges** with anything or one you have interest in. You can have an interest in or be attached to failure, experiencing the depths of what failure **feels and looks like**. You could be very intrigued with the dynamics of self sabotage or self loathing and keeping that awareness from the human. Anything you have a relationship with, and are EXCHANGING energy with, creates a cord of one type or another.

Cords carry ALL the human emotions, like fear, pain, and worry.

If and when a cord or a relationship holds you back, or **DRAINS your energy** or keeps you stuck, you might want to gather all the awareness you can about that relationship and cut the cord.

When you have been in a romantic relationship and want to terminate the relationship, cutting the cord that binds is a very helpful way to break a habit or *old energetic pattern*. You could also break a toxic relationship with a parent or any relative or friend.

When the person or thing at the other end of your cord finds it advantageous to stay connected to you, *or you do NOT release the attachment on you end* the cord will REATTACH. The cords can be reattached IN THE SAME OLD WAY or over and over again in new and different ways. Remember the cord is a **string of electromagnetic energy** that YOU feed with YOUR emotional or mental energy and that is WHY the cord exists.

There was an individual that was feeding on me and I cut the cords over and over again which were large and eventually got smaller. And then the cord would sneaked up on me. It got so I could feel the syphon of varying sizes latching onto different parts of my body. The syphon, towards the end of this felt like a pin prick or a mosquito bite, eventually this attachment went away.

CUT cords will reattached when or if you START to EXCHANGE ENERGY again.

A RECENT new DEVELOPMENT

When you cut the cords created in *old energy* you can reconnect to the same person, addiction or interest in a new way if you wish to form a new energy string or cord of electromagnetic energy. Cutting the cord removes the old energy patterns so you can view the relationship with a more UP TO DATE clarity and new and different awareness. It is tragically common for humans and their habits to operate with others in old STUCK belief patterns.

FOR EXAMPLE

You are an adult NOW and mom treats you like she did when you were a SMALL child and nothing you do makes you grown up in her eyes.

ANOTHER EXAMPLE

A person you started a relationship with five years ago hasn't noticed you are not like that any longer. And you haven't noticed all their changes they have made either. tsk tsk

CORD CUTTING

When you cut a cord put the "cut piece" into your heart to heal or PULL the energy from the cord back into you to TRANSMUTE the energy into something useful for yourself. Cords can come from past lives or this life, remaining with us until they are relinquished. Cords are frequently unhealthy and **VERY limiting**.

SILVER CORD

We are spiritually tied to the cosmic lattice and cosmic intelligence or universal energy which comes through our soul to the human. This energy knows where it's going and what it's going to do and who it will affect. Cosmic intelligence or love and compassion shines on humans to help them see clearly. The cord that is seen from our biology to the cosmic intelligence appears silver because of its luminous quality. This cord does not take energy from the human but does support the human while we have a biology.

The silver cord is smooth, very long and bright, about an inch wide. It is attached to one of several possible locations on the physical body. During the dying process the silver cord becomes thinner as it is stretched to its limit and becomes severed.

After we disconnect our cords (not the silver one) and stop feeding on others we move to communicate using the cosmic lattice, a sharing and not a feeding. When we master functioning mostly in the higher vibrational range of positive emotion with our soul, we use *the cosmic lattice or intelligence to communicate with other humans.* Many humans have a number of

LEVELS OF COMPASSION

DARK ascensions to move through before they reach the half light, half dark ascension. Then they move into increasingly higher vibrating light ascensions.

***

CHAPTER 5
LEVEL 2

Conventional, traditional, cautious and follows the rules and are very proud of that. They upset themselves when others do not follow the rules. At times they work on being more CONSCIOUS and aware humans. They function emotionally at boredom, disinterest or are content. This is when the little human is rational most of the time. They DO tend to squelch the enthusiasm and inventiveness of others. They are followers, not adventurers and want to be entertained.

50-60% **light**.

***

The key to staying connected to your angels and guides and their guidance is to stop when you realize YOU have dropped out of the flow and connection they are having with you. Allowing the little human to run things and your life is old energy and one dimensional.

Only a lower vibrating person and some religions, think there is something HONORABLE about **sacrificing themselves** or being victimized or struggling on behalf of others.

The human that decides which direction their life is moving is better able to create the life they choose to have. Instead of wishing or waiting for someone to do it for them, that is old energy, they do it themselves. Taking ACTION to control their EMOTIONS and THOUGHTS and allowing others to do the same is the direction of new energy. One of the secrets of success is knowing how to relate to those in your personal space and WHEN it is harmful to you, then you **disconnect** from them physically and emotionally.

To raise your level be alert to your DENIALS or what you are suppressing awareness of. SUPPRESSION or DENIAL of any emotion will keep you stuck in the emotion you REFUSE to OWN. By owning something **that you have PERSONALLY experienced,** you have the power to change it by looking at it from a different point of perception.

When you feel like crying, *CRY* or the suppression or denial of that emotion will hold you in apathy until you acknowledge it.

When something is fearful being *frightened is appropriate.* AVOIDING, **suppressing** or DENYING you are frightened gets you stuck in your FEAR. Denial of your awareness of your fear by trying to ward off all future fears certainly makes your world smaller and smaller and scary. Take action and own you are having frightened feelings. THEN change your reality or point of perception to learn from what your fear. Hear what that fear is telling you. Integrate and use that information and move on in another direction.

Release your anger when someone is doing something objectionable to you, express your feeling immediately, do not let it build in you. Voice your complaint at the time you experience it. Holding off your anger until it is uncontrollable makes it generally destructive when it sneaks out on you. The more you deny your feelings, the lower you drive YOUR vibrational level.

When someone is taking advantage of you don't worry about hurting their feelings. It is a crime to let them continue hurting you. Predators think they **are ENTITLED** to continue doing what they do because no one wants to "upset" them or say NO, to them. Mostly, no one says anything to the predator because they supply money to the household or the person in control of the child and they do not want the loss of the "hush money" the predator provides. Many adults prostitute THEIR children for perks and OR money.

When the media or news or friends and family make you feel hopeless quit reading or watching or listening to them. When you're talking with someone and the conversation drops lower then you are comfortable with, change the subject or just leave.

Take action, you ARE NOT a victim **unless you choose it**.

YOU are creating the life you have by avoiding or taking affirmative action. When others give only bad news, criticism, lies, gossip or arguments stop associating with them. If you wouldn't tolerate people dumping their trash in your kitchen, why let them empty their mental waste basket in your brain?

***

MULTIDIMENSIONAL LANGUAGE
Or COMMUNICATION with the invisible realm.

Historically, those with the lowest self-esteem and smallest amount of compassion for the self, are the ones in touch with their entourage, their guides and angels. Working with or talking to the invisible realm made other humans judge you as "crazy." Being immersed in an energy or environment that *does not* support you tends to create low self worth. Constantly being in a non supportive energy is rather uncomfortable and being a human we can be seriously effected. The new energy is here and evolving to support us.

MULTIDIMENSIONAL LANGUAGE or the THIRD LANGUAGE is the way the invisible realm, soul or our entourage communicates with humans. This communication happens slowly and naturally INSIDE us. It can be our OWN voice we hear, or a **smell** or TASTE or the shivery feeling we get when our entourage is in agreement with something we have said, done or thought. *IT IS the feeling* that washes over us like a tingle, shiveries or a touch on the head or cheek or any place on the body. That feeling means we have reached a point of awareness that we are feeling the *energy of compassion.* We are activating communication with our entourage energy. This is a spiritual interdimensional language that is **NOT linear** and crosses all of time and space.

When you present your soul or the invisible realm with questions, concerns or issues to increase your clarity or spiritual wisdom it is important to be AS PRESENT in the now moment as you possibly can. HEALING and GUIDANCE can be the **same thing**. Channeled guidance can relieve and release CONFLICTS within you *that block the flow of your wisdom*. Practice the guidance you get **WHEN you get** it or the guidance fades and diminishes. Reality is changing so rapidly now that what you were told a few days ago may no longer be relevant.

Blaming the invisible realm will not get you desirable results and will encourage the unseen world to shut down communication. Blaming others, human or not prevents you from OWNING what YOU have created in your life. Humans are in lesson and NOT victimhood.

Speak with gratitude and softly to hear more.

Logic and reason found on the third dimension can **HIDE** or deny multidimensional **wisdom**. When an entity wanting to communicate with you it will meld with your energy and through telepathy or whatever channel the human has open you get the information. The current energy of earth NOW allows communication IF you **WANT** to hear, sense or feel what is being relayed to you.

A way to ascertain information through multidimensional language is to ask aloud your question, the same question, three times.

The first time it will tell something to please you.

Ask again and you might get a different answer.

Ask a third time and that answer will be the right and honest one.

In the past, to communicate with the invisible realm took massive preparation to prepare the human biology for the higher vibrational energy coming into it. We were too dense to feel the loving compassion of the invisible realm. Co-creation requires synchronicity. For synchronicity to happen in your life you need to LISTEN and DO as your soul or entourage are recommending you do. That is the only way you will align yourself with those creating with you. Humans need to be an ACTIVE team member or NOTHING will happen. The invisible realm is no longer doing it FOR ANYONE as they did in the past.

Don't move too fast, answer with LOVE and be PATIENT.

We FEEL the communication of compassion.

All the tools a human may have mastered can leave or change but the cosmic flow of love and compassion is forever and constant.

During the winding down of energy the last few months of 2007, some humans lost all connection to the invisible realms. This was an **interdimensional, spiritual** event, NOT a linear thing. At that time all our gifts and tools were brought back to zero.

Some of the things we really count on from the cosmic flow, like a sweet countenance and wisdom were not available to us. Our gifts, tools and connections were getting RECONFIGURED so that in January 2008 they could get back on line fresh and clean all renewed and more powerful.

Interdimensional and spiritual energy IS NOT an upgrade or new energy added to old energy, it is all new.

The invisible realm wants humans to understand **the WAY of interdimensional and spiritual energy** so humans **refrain** from blaming themselves for doing something wrong. We have done nothing wrong it is just the way things ARE NOW as we move into multidimensions. So there is no need to change your path. Just be cautious and careful and slow to anger. Relationships with extended family and other countries often require wisdom. Wisdom creates an ability to hold your tongue at the right time. As we start understanding multidimensions and the way they function we will become more comfortable with the process.

Answers from the unseen world will be clearer and more reliable now.

Multidimensional reasoning enables us to see the planning and potentials we have available to us, in a way that third dimensional LOGIC never allowed us to see. In third dimensional logic the answers do not make sense, SO all you have to work with is your FAITH. The support we have always wanted is coming. More humans on earth are starting to see the bigger picture.

In the OLD ENERGY that we have been in for thousands of years WHILE walking a spiritual path and learning lessons, the human was unaware how they were doing until they reached a point of needing help and the **solution was** DELIVERED to the human.

In the NEW ENERGY the larger picture is the human SEEING beyond the small "in your face" issues, that humans are always working on. Now we can dabble in many more realities than JUST the past OR future. We, will be playing in NOW time and ourselves in other realities. In now time we are better able to anticipate what comes next and what options we can choose from.

Invisible realm likes a celebration or at least an acknowledgment "out loud" from the human that we have gotten or understood something each time we do, because that lets the soul know the human got it and understood. When you say it out loud it makes it real. Out loud to another person is even better. That way it can come out of the ethers where you keep it and work on it when you sleep. Out loud brings it into this reality and awareness. That is good interdimensional etiquette.

***

When you do not hear words or see pictures, there are other ways for invisible realm to communicate.

If you consider the left side of your body as your past.

Right side representing our current life.

And Louise L. Hay says;

ARMS—represent the capacity to hold our experiences in life.

LEGS—carry us forward and living life is for ME.

Jan felt shiveries on the bottom of her left arm and had an awareness that ALL her past lives shared with Tim showed up to be embraced and to sort out his and her pieces or aspects. Jan took that to mean she was holding her life experiences with some grace.

A short time later Jan felt shiveries on her lower left leg and had an awareness that the embracing and sorting enabled her to move forward and let her biology know that living life was for her.

AN EXAMPLE of a **ball of desire**.

Tim and Jan had too many lifetimes together to count with the same theme over and over. He denied his love and concern about her to HIMSELF. During one lifetime as a high religious figure, he EVEN allowed her to burn as a witch instead of leaving town with her to save her life.

All these lifetimes together created in Jan, her own ball of DESIRE that one day or lifetime Tim would OWN his feelings for her. This small ball of desire grew each lifetime and eventually had the name of Hector, a relationship guide. Hector smelled like smoke and that was how Jan knew he was present and he would tell Jan whatever she would like to hear, but what he said was seldom true and she would be surprised each time that it was not true.

In this lifetime Jan made a little headway in getting Tim to own his feelings. Jan worried about Hector always lying, was he a dark entity or what. Jan consulted with her friend, her friend said Hector was really a **THOUGHT FORM of all** her desires around Tim. Jan realized it was time to embrace and meld with Hector, her **ball of desire** and release trying to force and carry Tim's darkness. Jan's desires are inside her now and redirected, no longer outside of Jan lying to her, trying to please and give Jan what she wanted and never got from Tim.

A short time later Jan felt the shiveries on her lower left arm and was at a loss to make sense from it. IT was Tim's past lives were letting her know and to acknowledge that

Tim acknowledged that he had cared for her, to himself only. Jan needed to acknowledge and own that. So she embraced that. A few hours later there were shiveries in the left leg. Jan embraced her aspect in relationship to Tim moving forward. Then shiveries in the right leg—current life was consciously aware, but too stubborn and fearful to do more. Awareness is good.

I only wrote briefly on the emotional scale from below zero through 3 because I feel I have covered it in detail in my earlier books.

***

CHAPTER 6
LEVEL THREE

LEVEL 3, **Thriving**—inquisitive, seeking, and present in their biology. They are CONSCIOUS and aware most of the time. Level 3 is actively interested in subjects about survival and well being. They use logic and thought much of the time rather than using emotional blackmail or manipulation. At this level comes the introduction of the multidimensional aspect of **SELF LOVE**. This is an important mastery skill on level 3 increasing in level 4 through 5. Self love increases the amount of light you ARE ABLE to carry as a human.

60-70% **light.**

***

The EMOTIONAL vibration we DECIDE to dwell in will determine how we perceive our life and reality and the point of perception we view our experiences in the rising energies. The rules and belief's WE created for our self in order to survive on each dimensional level will **prevent** our taking the next steps forward into spiritual development if we cannot release the truths of the level we were previously on.

FOR EXAMPLE

We need to release old energy beliefs no longer true in the new energy. Like life is hard work, in new energy it can be joyful. The legion of light wants us to suffer, they never have wanted us to suffer. Take care of everyone else first was a way to control us. Care for yourself FIRST. I am justified in putting you down if I have more money than you because money makes me important. Money is all that matters, that is only true for the little human.

The truths and vibrations are changing. Instead of *right or wrong* evolve yourself to, for **every action** there is an EQUAL and OPPOSITE reaction. With each level change the truths change. Truths are an evolutionary process. Our EMOTIONAL state, our truths and our vibration are all in transition. It is time to honor and love the self and take care of YOU first. Start owning and enjoying your abilities, your biology and your grandness.

EMOTIONAL INTUITION **or awareness** happens as we allow communication and connection from our entourage to flow through us. The entourage brings the higher vibration or cosmic flow and peace to the human. We are jumping many vibrational levels at once and moving through many levels simultaneously consequently our energy tube is carrying a A LOT MORE energy than ever before.

At level 2 you get a mixed bag of all the shades and tints of compassion or being used.

The vibration on level three has some SELF LOVE coming from your guides and angels which increases on level 4 and gets stronger on level 5 because the human can **FEEL the love** from their entourage and a **peace** another human cannot give.

To grow SPIRITUALLY *deep within* the self, you must vibrate high enough to FEEL the compassion, love and sympathy for the self coming from the invisible realm.

NO ONE else CAN SAVE YOU.

YOU MUST SAVE YOURSELF.

Deep breathing IS the **first step** toward SELF LOVE.

LEVELS OF COMPASSION

You CANNOT breathe deeply when you don't love yourself. DEEP breathing opens up an AWARENESS of very deep-seated issues and angers you need to address now.

Lack of love for the self is an IMBALANCE of YOUR sweetness. Lack of self love prevents awareness of the sweetness life has to offer the human. We have an **inability to** *accept love* from others when they lack love for themselves. Those that lack self love will accept support for their basic physical needs to stay alive but block love coming their way because they do not feel worthy. You can recognize them by their depressed, anorexic, unhappy, dysfunctional anti survival behavior.

They HATE and BLAME themselves so much they will reject and deny love from another human, just as they reject and deny the self. Love offered by anyone is considered a *deception of one sort or another.* They consider you STUPID because you can't see they are UNLOVABLE. They are unable to go **WITHIN** to get love from their guides and angels. They are between a rock and a hard place without any compassion for them self.

Your self-love suffers or leaves when you **lie, avoid, deceive, doubt or compromise.** Those behaviors reflect your judgment of yourself and your disapproval of you. **Lying, avoiding, deceiving, doubting or compromising** the self is judging and rejecting the self and being anti compassionate.

EXPERIENCES or LESSONS

Our ENERGY STAMP (experiences) or our DNA is a record of all our experiences. When the soul decides to keep an energy stamp it gets stored in the cells of our DNA that is ready to be triggered the next time it may be used to master a life lesson. Most of our energy stamps are never brought into play because they do not get triggered during the course of our life.

Normally during the FINAL stage of our life the soul **resets** its own energy stamps in preparation for the next lifetime. The soul keeps energy stamps or experiences that may be useful in future lifetimes and releases those that no longer need to be experienced. The awareness of an experience we had NEVER leaves us. Only **our strong emotional reaction** we had to the experience leaves us when the soul takes that out of your DNA. When the human wishes to release the stamp it can be done at the time it comes into play in your life and you get THE WISDOM and no longer need that experience to help you master a life lesson.

When your soul and you choose ascension your soul removes the energy stamps which had put an emotional charge on your experiences.

FOR EXAMPLE

Say you had 30 energy stamps and you decided to work on avoiding judgment of yourself. You succeeded in doing that for a bit. Your soul would support you by taking that energy stamp or emotional charge out of your DNA. The soul will take the STRONG emotional reaction you used to have when you "failed." With the emotional reaction to having failed is taken away it is MUCH easier to curb that misdirected energy. This makes it much easier to slip on up to the higher vibration of discernment in the fifth dimension. Then you have only 29 other energy stamps to work on mastering with your guides and angels.

When you have an energy stamp on the outside of your energy tube it restricts your ENERGY FLOW. Just as stepping on a garden hose restricts the flow of water. So when you push the energy through a blocked hose, it hurts some and is FELT in the emotional body.

LEVELS OF COMPASSION

Tragically many humans **DENY the pain** they experience. Others avoid the pain by choosing NOT to run energy through their tube or choose NOT to feel, and hold all the energy. Some humans create little magical tubes on the outside of them to run energy through to reroute it and avoid feeling it.

THE BRAVE HUMANS

SOME HUMANS bravely step up and do WHATEVER it takes to heal the wound and gain the spiritual wisdom.

Our ENERGY TUBE is affected by vibrational changes, especially the shifts going on now. The vibrations in our biology and our guides and angels can and will trigger emotional releases in the human. The tube needs to *stretch* with the large amount of energy coming in now and when it does the scar tissue (old trauma) does not stretch at the same rate causing the GIFT of PAIN and AWARENESS. Old issues start coming up when you least expect them. The energy tube is the **seat of human** EMOTIONS and runs from the finite biology to the infinite soul simultaneously.

HUMANS MOVE ENERGY through their energy tube *every second of every day.* Our biology is the *bridge between soul and matter* and the bridge between the EARTH and DIVINE ENERGIES. For the *first time ever* we do have the opportunity to integrate our awareness and CHANGE the *energy tube itself.* We can make it larger and less painful.

Many are beginning to channel and that will continue to happen because of the stretching of the energy tube. So when we rework and embrace our scar tissue we create an opportunity to move to the next level. New experiences trigger whole sets of new or OLD emotions and they are NOT **SETBACKS**. Perceive them as **opportunities to advance**. Embrace them and run with them.

When you can LAUGH or count *your painful experience as a BLESSING* after getting devastating information you are doing well. "Celebrate, celebrate dance to the music."

Everything humans have made started first as a **thought form** IN THE ETHEREAL realms or mental body and had NO substance. When HUMANS bring it through the tube that runs from the ethers through our biology in front of the spine down our legs into the earth we create something that has substance and mass. We ground it which is actually a miracle. We take things having no substance and give them substance. Our biology is beautiful beyond description.

The capacity to produce and create, to stimulate creation is some of our natural identity that we are striving to reclaim.

Release your attached to acquiring THINGS, people and **objects** in the third dimension, that does not serve us any longer.

Our 90%er put in a time lag between having a thought and the actual creation so we could learn cause and effect. As our vibrations rise the time lag gets shorter and every thought we hold starts the creation process. This means creating things in this transitional period we probably want to get rid of. "Be careful of what you wish for, you might get it."

It is not possible for humans to only have energetically positive thoughts all the time. We designed the earth experience with negative energy to better understand positive energy. There will always be negative thoughts entering our mind. When you claim them or attach yourself to them, they become your reality. Our emotions travel through our emotional body and thoughts travel through the brain.

CHANGING your HISTORY

When you have changed a behavior or emotion in present time it is possible to go back into your multidimensional history and change or alter that aspect of all your previous life times. We are doing a lot of that now. Our magnetized vibration attracts the creation. When you observe the same creation in another way, and in a third way you have the illusion of a physical three dimensional object or hologram. Multiple beams of light vibrating and intersecting at one point creates the illusion of real three dimensional objects.

All of life is nothing more than an illusion.

The universe and earth started their existence as a hologram of light.

Love confuses many. Love is a form of energy within the spectrum of light.

A hologram created with light can also be created with love. Love is the act of balancing the unbalanced. On level 3 and 4 we are slightly out of balance with some parts of our energy. So we seek others that will compliment and help balance our energy.

With the new crystalline energy coming in and humans becoming one and balancing their own energy there is a great potential for deep, lasting, relational shifts. When two or more humans come together forming a connection and one individual looks into the other's eyes they see themselves through the feelings of the heart.

Humans have worked with conditional love very well in the lower vibrations. As you move forward, you move out of conditional love into unconditional loving. Conditional love is a unique human invention and it is NOT possible to make a hologram of conditional love.

When you have a meaningful relationship a THIRD vibration gets started, the harmonic of the two, the relationship. Many are attached to the idea or concept of the relationship and not the love of each other. As you evolve you will release the attachment to idea or the concept of conditional love. This is the first movement into unconditional love. At some point when one or both start to grow the relationship starts to grow apart. When you can start the hologram of love, it moves into a multidimensional level which will make all of these transitions as a human easier to flow with.

Relationships are built and not created.

UNCONDITIONAL love make a space for the best of relationships. Humans are multifaceted with different parts of them inside different dimensions of reality. When you fall in love with the different dimensions or aspects of another it creates a fuller, deeper connection that will get stronger as you move from one level to the other.

A hologram of love works best when you release restrictions like fear of being hurt and searching for the different parts of the person you can fall in love with. The more unconditional love you bring in from different points of perception, the deeper and easier communication will be. Seeing these LOVE aspects in others allows you to see a unique view of yourself, and that will facilitate you falling in love with yourself. As you love the self that releases the need for love to come from outside yourself.

The best point to build a relationship is from two sovereign beings walking side by side support each other unconditionally. The more unconditional love you can bring into any relationship enhances all. Focus on the pieces that reflect you well and amplify them. This gives you a strong foundation of unconditional love you can move to higher vibrations with.

As humans we are experiencing love from our soul and the soul is experiencing human love.

The more we play with love and see through someone else's eyes we learn to love ourselves unconditionally, without expectations or agendas. The possibility for joy is a real potential while we have fun creating many holograms of light and love to see our reflection in so many ways.

***

We are going through an awakening process right now and it is a very challenging adventure we are experiencing. You know you are in the awakening process when you become aware of the fact that things have stopped working as they always have in the past.

You have evolved unconsciously into being more insular, rejecting external activities and drama. The old beliefs and truth's are not seeming to be so true any longer. Things that mattered a great deal to you before do not any longer. You are not sure WHAT really matters any longer.

Things that we held near and dear seem to be getting lost. This is a natural process during awakening and may appear to be disorienting and confusing because we are actually allowing the illusion of what and who we thought we were fall away. Our divinity is emerging which means all the answers to all our questions are FOUND within us. The answers can be discovered in the quiet moments with yourself and your entourage that are always present to help you.

This is a death of CONSCIOUSNESS, not the biology.

In the new consciousness **all things change.**

The human is going through an *incredible transformation process.*

Look at the food you eat in a new way. View your finances, your prosperity and wealth in a new way. Consider power and control in a new way, does it have a place in you new consciousness?

Being imbalanced will no longer work. There is new understandings of the sciences, math, education and technology.

The awakening process can be VERY dark and sad. Awakening is a lonely, lonely path because it is about rediscovering YOU. The illusions of duality are departing and being replaced by knowingness from multidimensions of awareness and thought.

Look at places where there are earthquakes and other disruptive weather patterns. The disruption is striking in places where the energy has been suppressed, distorted and frequently misdirected.

There are also places were more human related activities of disruption and upheaval are taking place like bombings, riots, terrorism and things like these that are all in service of the awakening process.

Time to change our points of perception.

***

CHAPTER 7
LEVEL FOUR

LEVEL 4, **Eagerness** and cheerful enthusiasm, they are functioning mostly in present time. They are FULLY CONSCIOUS and emotionally in joy and awareness. This is when the little human is rational most of the time. They are lighthearted and flexible and are quietly enjoying their biology and their creations. Their emotional reactions are appropriate to the situations that occur in their life. Being pretty sovereign they operate from personal conviction and do not feed off other humans or drama or the collective unconscious. They function in integrity and are problem solvers. They uplift others emotionally without carrying them or their darkness. They are balanced givers and receivers.

SELF LOVE is multidimensional and an important mastery skill on level 3 through 5. Self love increases the amount of light you ARE ABLE to carry. Self-love involves recognizing you are CONSTANTLY evolving and growing to become a more compassionate and loving human, starting with yourself. You are *no longer in service*. You are now in service to you and developing your love and compassion for yourself. It is not possible to give others what you have not given yourself first.

70-80% **light.**

***

After self love and awareness has been mastered the new energy romantic relationship is no longer made up of incomplete humans joining together to create a whole. Higher vibrational love is based on two sovereign humans coming together in strong friendship with constructive purpose. At work or at home they have excellent COMMUNICATION, they understand what is said or needed and they share similar values. Higher vibrational love is conscious and aware. When we feel free to speak our mind to another human the relationship thrives. Communication and awareness is present and not just exchanging pleasantries or tolerating drama assists others to RAISE their vibration.

Any activity a human thoroughly enjoys will bring up their vibration and increase their light.

The higher vibrating human does not ABSORB or pass on all the bad or negative thoughts or information. They *take action* and CUT those lines of communication because they know there is no benefit to continuing negative communication.

It is vital to reach a **balance** between what we contribute and what we receive. That is true for all areas in our lives. Always helping others and taking nothing in return is doing them a disservice. Find a way for others to repay you. When taking a great deal from someone else like food, shelter or services find ways to return the flow or you drop YOUR vibration to being victimized.

The new energy is being experienced by MOST entities.

The slower vibrating humans are feeling the higher vibrations as stress and painful discomfort, or as DESPAIR, **fear** and *self-doubt* or JUDGMENT.

Don't wait for others to give you a pat on the back for something you did. Give it to yourself and move on to the next job. Take action and direct yourself toward what YOU consider a worthwhile purpose, something VERY interesting to you.

When you need to use tremendous effort to do something, consider if it's really the right action for you. If it is a tremendous effort to you, change your point of perception, consider if it is worth doing. Look at the larger picture to become aware of the higher purpose or positive attribute of the task.

We are masters of energy, NOT VICTIMS.

Create what you want today, BECAUSE you are the only one who can.

Always it is important to get enough **rest**, pure WATER and nutritious food, exercise and have good health as prerequisites for anyone wanting to increase their vibration. Caring for your biology is LOVING yourself.

With the higher vibrations our human sense's are SHARPER and *more sensitive* than they have ever been.

Along with all our other changes our biology is changing its relationship to the **food we ingest**. IT IS TIME to be fully conscious of WHAT you eat and WHY. There are many *layers and levels of ENERGY* in the things we eat and drink. We can converse with all we put in your mouth. Honor what enters our mouth because that unlocks some of the levels of awareness and nutrition available to us from our food. Regardless WHAT, when or **how** we eat, the essence of the energy in our food is the same.

There are many LAYERS of consciousness added to our food as it goes through its entire life cycle before we get around to eating it.

Currently the energy on earth is going through MAJOR transitions, people are awakening and events are changing rapidly. Use your DISCERNMENT and take what resonates with you.

Do not give away you energy.

Choosing the highest and best expression of your OWN, INDIVIDUAL path all the time serves you well. PERCEIVE another reality for yourself, experience the deliciousness of each moment of life.

***

SELF LOVE

Is a multidimensional SPIRITUAL attribute and NOT linear.

Our self worth is a large subject and has many aspects and outcomes. SELF LOVE is the FIRST STEP to lasting changes in the human. As you have gathered from the last chapter, self love has to be **created by the INDIVIDUAL human** FOR THE same **individual HUMAN**. The soul and entourage are waiting to help but the human needs to INITIATE thoughts and behaviors that would indicate that they loved themselves. Simple things like caring for your biology, respecting it and keeping it healthy. Staying clear of drama and judgment of the self and everyone else. No gossiping or belittling the self.

Accept and embrace **ALL of your emotions.**

Think of your emotions as your PARTNER in awareness and consciousness raising moving you into total compassion. The more you partner with your emotions as the loving instructor and friend they are, the more you value your human self. The more self love you have the more you are brought back to your perfection.

Staying CONSCIOUSLY present IN your biology is a must. Know how the biology is feeling and know what it needs. Stop distracting yourself with excessive busyness or game playing or gossip. Release the games of victimhood, judgment and blame raises your self love and consequently your vibration.

Own your life EXACTLY where it is NOW.

Consciously take control and responsibility for all your wonderful and all the painful experiences and all the experiences in between. Consciously choose the direction you want to move in now.

Remember your biology is only 10% of all that you are the 90% is invisible so mastering multidimensional conversation would be pretty important. Become aware of and aligned with the unconditional love and compassion your 90%er lavishes on you ALL THE TIME. Learn to *receive* the good things you FEEL. The human needs to BE CONSCIOUS of being a strong contributing member to all phases of the process of self love and multidimensional SPIRITUAL communication in the now moment at all times.

It absolutely is, **your job** to be aware of what is going DOWN in your life. Controlling your thoughts and emotions. Reducing and eliminating JUDGMENT and **drama**. Stop wasting time and your light in DOUBT or COMPROMISE because that lowers your vibration and ability to create and communication multidimensionally. We are angels experiencing matter to gain insight about the way it functions and now we are raising matters vibration.

Realign with the flow, feelings and agenda of your soul. With OUR focused thoughts and emotions we can create JOY and success or PAIN and suffering in our lives, always our choice. Victimhood is a choice. Our greatest **responsibility** AND opportunity in the new energy is to have fun.

FEELINGS are **important SIGNALS**.

Even the feelings labeled negative like anger and fear are important signals. They ALERT us that something needs to be looked at NOW and a new course of action might need to be crafted. Quantum physics and psychology offer proof that **our thoughts CREATE** our reality. Giving ourselves the highest truth we can own is important to our on going evolution.

Historically there were many times in life that choosing limitations served us well. Being weak, sick, or helpless is a way to get ATTENTION or HELP or to appear NON THREATENING to someone that is insecure and needs you to be weak for them to trust you and feel strong. What compromises have you made to get acceptance, attention and love from others and yourself even?

At the 4th vibrational level we are building on what self love and awareness we have already gained so far. Our wisdom is collected and we always have it available to us. Learning as a human is **a SPIRITUAL unfolding.** A mystery or like a puzzle we only get ONE piece at a time. This awakening awareness we are experiencing is not linear, it is spiritual and therefor multidimensional.

Continually our entourage and our **FUTURE SELF** sends us holograms of awareness, guidance or assistance from the other realms to help us along our path and increase our wisdom. Sometimes we are aware of the holograms but many times we are not. When it manifests itself in what appears to be physical form, that is because that is what your senses perceive best. They are frequently messages of assurance telling you everything is fine and progressing well. A message of love and encouragement to remember to love and have compassion *for yourself.*

At the start of this new ERA we are living in a constant state of flow and change. So, when you decide something on tuesday it could easily need changing by friday. Our soul knows and understands the changes. Little human doesn't't really understand what is going on and is made uncomfortable with the tremendous changes happening all the time. Our perspective is actually changing and so our choice made on tuesday needs changing by friday.

We are *gaining wisdom* with our FREEDOM of CHOICE and change. Choices about abundance or health are very, very three dimensional things to upset yourself about.

All this flow allows the little human to practice *conscious choice* and we can then demonstrate **our flexibility** to ourselves. There is no need to get locked into ANYTHING, we are rapidly losing touch with our linearness.

***

ATTACHMENT to the THIRD DIMENSION

Attachment to THINGS or *people* and the REALITY of the third dimension is old energy. Attachment to another because you NEED them or are addicted to what they may supply you with, like a reason to live or endless drama or you need their SERVICE to YOU to love yourself *leads you to* FEAR of THEIR loss, **jealousy** and possessiveness or the shadow energy of GREEDINESS. The little human wants to store, hoard and gather more and more so they are never without or in lack. Very old energy.

To avoid jealousy, greed and the fear of loss TRAIN YOURSELF to RELEASE YOUR FEAR of loss. Being able to store and hoard people or things does not bring the peace and comfort to the human the way communication with the soul and the invisible realm does.

ATTACHMENTS

Lower level vibrational luminous light or strands or cords can represent **attachments** that others have to you or from you that are PARASITIC in nature. The attachments are **to DRAIN energy.** *THE CARE taking and attachments* to THINGS or humans in the third dimension need to be released as they keep our vibration at a low level.

In HIGHER vibrations we communicate and SHARE, instead of feeding from our guides, angels, other humans or addictions. It is an evolutionary step for humans to harmonically interact with the **thought strands from higher dimensions.**

When the voice of the inner self becomes louder than the voice of the third dimension a constant stream of self love is maintained. Unconditional love, allowance and acceptance are a prerequisites for healthy creating. The greatest good for all concerned fosters spiritual growth.

In old energy we had CONTROL through **fear** of loss.

CONSPIRACY theories increase our **inner fears** and externalizes them. Believing the enemy or problem is outside of you distracts you from developing SOLUTIONS and healthy *resolution* of your fears. Our fears are not external they are internal. When we talk to our fears, instead of resisting them, we learn from them and are then able to redirect the energy we had tied up in fear.

DRAMA distracts and prevents the human from feeling *their OWN feelings,* owning them and directing them.

Our **true feelings** are in service to us.

Owning the truth of your thoughts and feelings keep them in useful service to you by not letting you IGNORE what you feel, messages from the invisible realm. Staying in the present moment, facing and owning your **feelings of fear.** Moving into SOLUTION and *resolution* assists the individual and the human group as well.

LEVELS OF COMPASSION

Of late, humans are grabbing back things and people they have released or are trying to release. The changing energy is raising fear levels in some and in an effort to move back into a zone of comfort, **that no longer exists,** we are trying to grab back things and people. This is what happens when we cling to the illusion of the THIRD DIMENSION and stop reaching for our soul connection. Knowing full well that the third dimension and money are only an illusions and not fulfilling or peaceful and compassionate.

Humans are grabbing at;
Money and control
Illness and confusion
Doubt and inadequacy
Being competitive
Judgment, blame and drama
The VERY FAVORITE one is,

Blaming the soul or invisible realm for not RESCUING the human. FEAR of LOSS, *any loss, even your long hair* is a third dimensional path and the above choices cement you to that third dimensional path. You are just **"not into" the fifth** dimension. You aren't getting it.

When there ia a FOG of LIES around a person or thing, why embrace it?

Death is a natural part of life rejoice over the person transforming back into reality and infinity. Grieve YOUR losses and move on. When looking for another awareness or experience use your FEELINGS to find it.

HUMAN CONSCIOUSNESS

On earth at this time is very delicately balanced.

There are angelic beings helping humans on all the different emotional levels. Not all humans WANT to hear what is happening, they have chosen others voices to listen to.

Consciousness for all is changing as a result of the desire to change in the general population. Humans as a group want to EXPAND and GROW to increase the number of options available to them. The light and higher vibration is having a positive affect on us all.

Historically, consciousness was in a very small, DARK, limited container with very few options, it is time to go outside the box and as we leave the LIMITS, a void is created, a vacuum. At a certain point that structure has the potential of imploding. Consciousness from old energy is being taken out.

A VOID or a Null Zone is established after there is an expansion outwards of energy which receives a blow or shock causing it to **COLLAPSE *inwards upon itself.*** The old established **energy patterns** (belief systems) **are now broken** and there is no way that they will ever return to the previous pattern. They have been IRREVOCABLY changed. The energy of a Null Zone feels *jagged and raw*. There is much hurt and pain, grieving for the "good old days" and cutting of MANY CORDS and attachments.

While in a void you find most EVERYTHING irritates you, even other people breathing is irritating. It's the shattering of a world or a belief system, a long-held desire, or sometimes an important relationship with yourself or another. You experience the FEELING with your **heart first**. LATER the brain processes the experience and all the changes. The old closely held belief gets shattered and you are liberated from its limits.

This would be similar to the feeling you would have after being in a hurricane or any natural disaster. This shattering creates the perfect foundation for the introduction of something ENTIRELY new to come in.

LEVELS OF COMPASSION

The potentials are enormous. Null Zones or voids **AMPLIFY** and *destabilize* whatever inherent **DISCORD is present** in the surrounding areas. They actually occur to help us *break free from old stagnant patterns and belief systems* giving us a unique opportunity for a *quantum leap* into a deeper sector of the unknown.

While in the void a lot of MENTAL and EMOTIONAL processing is done. The void is a **womb to birth the new** awareness. Generally voids last a few months or can be a few weeks. **The Void** is also the nothingness outside of All That Is. The consciousness we ventured into to discover *something **new** for our SOUL.*

There are enough energy workers on earth that understand the delicate balance of the old and new energy enough to keep everything from imploding violently in on us.

Some are getting sucked back into their "care taking" others are taking themselves **OFF THEIR spiritual path** because the little human wants to feel powerful once again. Some are worshiping at the "money alter," because the little human wants to feel better than you and more powerful and secure in the third dimensional reality that is RAPIDLY vanishing.

Going within and TRUSTING their SOUL is just too scary for them.

Seduction means to DRAW IN or to manipulate and that is happening NOW on a mass consciousness level on earth. The seduction is the emptiness of our old consciousness wanting things back the way they were. Old energy does not want the illusion of old wants, needs, desires and identity to slip away.

Seduction of YOUR consciousness will automatically gravitate to your weakest or most imbalanced area FIRST. It will seduce you first into feelings of **fear and lack** making you unbalanced and easily controlled. **Your wisdom within,** your soul KNOWS there is NOTHING to fear and the LACK is an illusion. There is a GREAT DEAL of manipulation of the news and markets, and the illusion of lack. Old energy based its power and control on **your BELIEF in lack.** This is an **internal seduction** or SELF DECEPTION happening around the world. The time for choice is absolutely present, RIGHT NOW, right here!

Cling to the third dimensional illusion or move into the higher vibration of the fifth dimension with your soul. The choices left at this point in our reality is how hard you plan on making it for the human to move into higher vibrations?

When in doubt your choices will be made on your behalf.

Money or your *misconception of abundance* is a bad excuse for staying trapped in the third dimension and its hypnotism. Release your need for CONTROL in your life, the invisible realm has things well in hand so you can celebrate and be joyful. Humans are seduced and CONTROLLED *by control,* not seeing how limiting, tedious and boring control is. Not to mention that it **does not** fill that empty spot we have that only connection with our soul fills.

The old energy has been invited to join the new energy but is *NOT BEING allowed* **to control** or dominate new energy.

SEDUCTION SYMPTOMS

Number one symptom of seduction is **sugar,** it is on the *Most Wanted list.* Sugar is a temporary relief and a **lower vibrational choice** from ALL the upheaval going on in our reality. Excesses of sugar get the biology all twisted and rather unbalanced during the time of changing over to a crystalline biology and vibrational structure.

Your biology knows exactly what you need to eat each day and when to eat it, if you are willing to listen and HEAR as our biology acclimates to the higher vibrations. Foods that are overly heavy or overly processed and having been pulverized, overcooked and beaten to death are **EMPTY calories** having no nutritional value for your biology. Human biology prefers raw foods. The biology, loves to do its own refining, because it knows the best way to work with food energies.

Lately the dental areas, jaws and teeth are getting hit very hard, as are the sinuses. Sleep patterns are fluctuating. We wake in the middle of the night feeling tired and worn out. You can feel unfulfilled, empty, disoriented and confused when allowing the little human to be "in control." Being pulled back into the third dimension comes through family, friends, the news and the internet WHEN you ALLOW that to happen your metal is being tested to see how strong *your resolve* is to move into the new energy and spiritual awareness.

When you ACTIVELY RESIST *any energy* you create opposition and duality along with a **large pool of STUCK.** A pocket of density for the invisible realm and the "All Love, the Brotherhood of Light" to clean up. What are you thinking? Just feel everything and decide if you want it. The energy is REAL and present because our **shift** in consciousness is creating a VOID.

Conscious breathing needs to be a regular activity from when we get up in the morning. We breathe to choose life, love and the self. Water is very important to drink, because water carries a great deal more than its chemical compounds. Water is an essence and flow of consciousness. Water is a wonderful way to cleanse and flush out the biology. Most of us are very dehydrated. With the very intense energy we're working on now, we need two to three times more water than before.

WE feel energy in our biology first, and then it is felt in the mind.

***

SENSORY AWARENESS

Feeling is sensory awareness and NOT emotions.

True feeling or SENSORY PERCEPTIONS go away when you try to *CONTROL or STRUCTURE them*. Actually most things and people go away when you try to control, force or structure them. Feeling deep, real, GENUINE feelings humans are not too comfortable DOING generally. Feelings are awareness' and sensitivities about the self, others, situations and places.

Historically when humans feel their feelings they might FIGHT them or get **confused** by having a true consciousness. Many fear the power of their feelings. Many fear the energy would overwhelm them. Feelings can throw **old systems out of whack** with the new energy. Feeling your feelings ALWAYS makes you FEEL very alive.

There are many, many energies present in our space at this time. The human mind has been trained to shut down when it starts to sense many feelings or energies as a survival tool. The MIND associates *sensory awareness with **pain*** and or **confusion**. Mental activity is quantifiable you can document it, measure it and record it. Anything else we feel is not real according to our TRAINING and our BRAIN that has the job description, to keep the biology alive.

Feelings are the method humans USE to **arrive at INTUITIVE knowledge** or divine wisdom. You can't go from third dimensional human knowledge, the brain, to divine knowledge in one step. The multidimensional language process of sensing divine wisdom starts with you feeling it. Knowledge of YOUR larger SELF, your 90%er and ALL you are, come SLOWLY through OUR SENSES.

MENTAL visualization, creating images in the mind OR verbalizations like chanting mantras aloud MIGHT have served you at one time. NOW it sends the message to the brain that you are afraid of YOURSELF and afraid of your **intuitive**, DIVINE feelings and **awareness**. Mental visualization or verbalization creates a BARRIER to your divinity. Allow the mind to step aside and YOU can GO *directly to the multidimensional language* of wisdom and feelings. Your RAW, **genuine feelings** and senses.

When we get breakthroughs in awareness it is because we FELT the multidimensional language. The mind DID NOT suddenly get smarter. Anytime you have overwhelming feelings of compassion or knowingness and intuition it is the multidimensional language coming into us through OUR feelings and awareness.

Sensory awareness can be VERY difficult to sense at times, but as you adjust and acclimate to allowing feelings to come through, you discern what comes from your INSIDES and what is circling around in your environment, invading your space. Many feelings come from your insides or your soul self that has many feelings to share with the human. It is becoming easier and easier to KNOW what is yours, what is soul's and what is not. Humans know how to take *sensory perceptions* into the brain and biology and that is multidimensional language or communication.

EMOTIONS belong to the LITTLE human and are easily MANIPULATED or controlled and go off into misdirected energy. Our emotions positive or negative, are the energetic glue that hold our pockets of **dense matter** in our aura. Releasing emotions tied to people and events allow you to move forward into the now with all of your pieces and parts fully present. Emotions are the fuel that HAS propelled our behavior and creations for good or bad.

When you AVOID, **deny** or *suppress* your SENSORY AWARENESS there is a price to pay. Fun things like *mental disease*, confusion, HUMAN DEPRESSION, **anxiety**, issues of overweight or any of the other ADDICTIONS.

When humans deliberately shut down SENSORY AWARENESS they CRAVE excitement because they feel so dead inside. Feelings or senses are pulses of life and they are MEANT to be experienced. When we don't have sensory awareness' we get irritable or start blaming. When a human feels less or nothing from their soul, they will create a crisis of one sort or another. They will spend money for a temporary thrill and then crash to enhance their HUMAN EMOTIONS. They try to apply emotions externally to fill the void left by BLOCKING their true feelings or their multidimensional communication from the invisible realm and their soul.

Our intuitive feelings are at the core of us.

Intuitive feeling is your soul SHARING with you at a high consciousness level and some humans are trying not to hear what is being shared.

CORE of EARTH

There is vibrational activity in the core of the earth that has not been there before and our biology is having SENSORY AWARENESS about it. We are blessed to feel it in the neck, shoulder, low back along with an inability to sleep. Trying to run from the SENSORY AWARENESS will not succeed because you cannot. It is not in your best interest to run from your feelings. You DO want to be SENSORY AWARE and **able to feel everything** BUT not in the biology or brain. Move the feelings you are getting to a higher consciousness level. Move the energy out of the brain and biology to your spiritual body.

Our SPIRITUAL BODY is the fourth body out from the biology and has walls between the different dimensions now. The spiritual body is on a different plane and the walls go the length of the body and extend above and below or perpendicular to the earth. The spiritual body extends out about one half to one foot from the body and is amorphous and composed of clouds of color more beautiful than those of the emotional body. They are the same colors as those of the emotional body but each color is infused with the rose light of love. The heart chakra of a loving person is full of rose light. When people are in love beautiful arcs of rose light connect their hearts and a beautiful rose color is added to the normal golden pulsation.

As we move to the next level of SENSORY AWARENESS we won't have to use crude systems like the biology or the mind to be aware. We are moving into a higher end system. Don't *keep* your SENSORY AWARENESS in your biology, it creates disease. Don't keep it in your brain it causes confusion. Feeling with only the physical or mental is primitive. Pass your SENSORY AWARENESS out to your spiritual body and the cosmic flow. Do not resist the feeling or SENSORY AWARENESS we can welcome it in a new way by feeling it at the intuitive, **sacred level**. The feelings are intensifying because consciousness is intensifying and changing.

Old energy and *old consciousness* are being sucked into the new era, kicking and screaming and causing some FEAR and **emptiness** that we all sense. Feel it from your spiritual body so you do not get sucked into it.

Historically consciousness has been a challenge and a part of the culture for a very, very long time. Now that our sensory awareness is waking up to the duality all around us there is tension around the core values that humans have held. A sorting process is underway, what to keep and what to release.

Most homes and countries around the world have the energy or the resources they need but the resources are not being distributed **APPROPRIATELY** or fairly. That is why there is so much upheaval on the earth now because resources are being redistributed.

CREATING

Within your energy field there are **four lines of vibration** used for creation. These FOUR lines are always sent out as a UNIT. The unit is a representation of your energy field as a whole.

The four lines are:

* What you SAY, *your talk.*
* You **ACTIONS** to *match* your talk.
* What you *THINK* and CHOOSE to dwell on.
* Your **BELIEFS** the *truths* you hold in the NOW moment.

When one or more of these vibrational lines do not match the others, the vibration sent out gets *foggy or unclear.* When ONE line of vibration crosses the others that cancels them out and sends a rather **distorted** signal. What you get back from a blurred vibration is rarely what you wanted. CONFUSION can cause SELF DOUBT which *blurs* a humans overall energy even more than it was previously.

Vibrational integrity is needed on all four vibrational lines. When you do not SEE which of your lines is out of sync talk it over with an objective friend, or someone that KNOWS you well. Maybe they see something you are blind to or are dissociated or in denial about. Ask your entourage what you refuse to own or do not see.

LEVELS OF COMPASSION

All vibrational lines are MOVABLE so they can stay adjusted to our **current** individual **frequency**. In rising our dimensional levels our PERCEPTIONS of our reality change. What we SEE is different and altered. Our values and truths change on each level we move to. These energy fields or vibrational lines have **always** been our personal communication and interactions with the invisible realm.

In **lower** vibrations like the third dimension and negativity, only what we SAY and DO are easily perceived by other humans. All of the four lines are easily perceived in the invisible realm, our **talk, action, thoughts and beliefs** are all seen as a unit in higher vibrations like the fifth dimension. They all should be the same.

There are no SECRETS and there never is any secrets on the higher vibration levels where we will ALL HAVE ACCESS to each other's **energy fields**. Aka, each others secrets, dissociation and denial. Prepare for that now and the transition will be less traumatic and your integrity will rise.

Secrets are a product of duality and low vibration. I guess there is LITTLE to recommend about having and keeping secrets. In my experience secrets protect predators and other criminals and abusers.

Most everyone has finished with what they came here to do. Now we had completed all our contracts with the exception of any long term commitments you have made or are in the middle of.

When you change spiritual LEVELS your **beliefs** ALSO change to match that level. This is not something to master it just happens. It is YOUR JOB to **notice the differences**. Notice the changes.

Adopt a global attitude toward humans. Look for the SIMILARITIES. Practice the art of *harmonics on earth* by educating yourself and understanding the beliefs, habits and needs of those that SEEM to oppose you from other levels and you find the resonant harmonic strands of light connecting you to them. Then oneness is remembered.

The human has many different concurrent dimensional realities also. There are many of us existing side by side in slightly different dimensional realities. In each one you may make slightly different choices and move down slightly different paths and awareness' levels.

Humans have so many layers of the "Me I AM" all of the "me" layers are part of our truth You are SO much more than you THOUGHT you were. To tap into all of your layers and levels go within. You have the council of you to commiserate and evolve with.

LIGHT

When the word light hits your ears a resonance starts up creating an *interdimensional* vibration that weaves dimensions together to ACT AS ONE. The true vibration of light will rejuvenate your biology and soul. The higher meaning of Light is enlightenment. Light is a powerful energy and *spans* all DIMENSIONAL LEVELS *simultaneously.*

Teachers of consciousness helping, facilitating and inspiring others through EXAMPLE of how to expand their consciousness and awareness are on earth at this time. That is why we are still in biology so we can partner with the unseen world to MOVE humans to the next level.

During experiences of sexual expression humans raise their vibratory level to match what the unseen world lives in all of the time. Although sex is not a necessity don't discard this effective tool without some serious consideration. Experiences of self-love through self-sexual expression can be used as a tool of creation that you have yet to fully discover.

LEVELS OF COMPASSION

The purpose of sex in the fifth dimension is to express unconditional love, used that way we discover the highest benefit from sexual activity. A heightened sexual experience will be more commonplace as a deeper level of communication is possible in this way.

The current shift that is underway NOW is ATYPICAL because the forces of creation HAVE ALWAYS removed all advanced life forms from the planet's surface and **then RESET** the vibratory level of the planet so another evolutionary journey can unfold. That is what happened at the end of Lemuria and Atlantis. When the great Ice ages and other cataclysmic events happened humans simply returned home to all that is.

By the time the shift arrives most of us won't care who makes it through.

You will realize that everything is in absolute perfection, and all those who don't want to go through the shifting process have the right to return to the creator with no judgment and they will return home.

***

CHAPTER 8

VIBRATION SCALE of the DIVINE HUMAN ASCENSION or SOUL MELDING
Your SOUL **now reside** in your auric field.

Level 5. **In and out,** little human 50% or less melded with soul.
   80-90% light.

Level 6. **Balancing**, biology, DNA, 80% in divine will.
   90-95% light.

Level 7. **Soaring,** little human emotions and concerns going.
   95-100% light. MARRIAGE with the SOUL

Level 8. **Oneness,** human functioning as one with soul. Human is fully melded and out of duality.

Level 9. **Completion**, of an ERA, a cycle, or a LEVEL.

***

ASCENSION or SOUL MELDING

Before you even THINK about melding with your soul certain spiritual things need to be lined up from this lifetime and past lifetimes. We have experienced the same type of challenge or lesson over and over again until we gain **AWARENESS of the pattern** that needs change to develop our spiritual wisdom.

We need to **DISCONNECT** energetically and physically from those that are more than 50% dark. That would include family, spouse, relatives and friends or alliances with jobs, organizations, religions, because if they are 50% dark or more they are **NOT heart centered**. You can no longer be in service to ANYONE but yourself. Carrying others darkness serves no one. Spiritual awareness is done individually, alone with your soul.

Levels 5—7 represent a progression of movement and development from being the little human able to control their thoughts and emotions and some SOUL to becoming *more and more soul* and less and less little human.

The soul needs to feel the little human is ready for this adventure and the little human needs to be an ACTIVE participant in this process, wanting it to happen. You need to want to become a divine human. The ascension we are offered NOW is harder than any ascension that has happened before. This transformation happens with a **LARGE number** of small daily steps taken to learn and master a view of life from an increasingly larger point of DIVINE perception.

We need a willingness to learn new thoughts and ways that are constantly evolving. The little human MUST;

Experience ALL of their emotions.

Gain increasing clarity.

Be fully conscious and aware of ALL their sensory perceptions. Gain increasing perception of energies around us and what they are.

Being **PRESENT** in their biology.

Accept that we are multidimensional and notice the movement from one dimension to many dimensions

Realize time and space are an illusion and live in NOW time.

Have *Increasing TRUST* and reliance on the soul's wisdom and connection to the cosmic flow of energy and the legion of light.

Increasing HONESTY and INTEGRITY **with the self FIRST** and then others.

INCREASING SELF LOVE and compassion for the little human that NEVER did ANYTHING wrong. They were experiencing and gaining wisdom for their soul.

Increased awareness of the flow from soul and when we slip out of it and slip back into duality and all its lessons.

Broader and broader awareness and understanding of **universal laws** and **multidimensional physics**.

***

12 STEPS on each level of MELDING with soul

On each level of 5 through 8 are 12 steps that need to be mastered a bit more on each level. These are the same 12 steps on each level and you go deeper and deeper in any order you care to work on them.

1. Humans need to master relating to other humans without **BLAME** or **judgment** or **DRAMA**. Take notice of and feel the energies and multidimensions for that is YOUR true reality. The third dimension is an illusion. Listen to and feel nature, commune with this intentional community. Know the value of life and feel how we are all connected regardless of the biology we are in. Learn the order or way of things so you can **fall into HARMONY** with them.

2. Observe and **know the cosmic order** and flow of "All That Is," so you can stay present in the flow without blame, judgment or drama. Place yourself harmoniously into the global, cosmic community, always broadening your awareness. Have faith in your infinite ability to remake yourselves and your experiences, over and over again.

3. **Connect solidly with your soul** and the invisible realm, have awareness of their presence and communication, fall into harmony with them.

4. Connect to YOURSELF know who and what you are and are NOT. **Stand in your belief's** loud and proud. Have faith in your infinite ability to recreate yourself.

5. **Side by side** you walk with the legion of light, know and honor that.

6. Humans are in community with the higher angelic realms and not the third dimension, **Know you come from and are LOVE.**

7. **ALLOWING** and **knowing** is the order and flow. This awareness happens slowly and naturally INSIDE US. It can be your voice you hear, a smell or taste or the shivery feeling we get when our soul or entourage is in agreement and wanting to reinforce our direction. We can know we are feeling the *energy of compassion,* a spiritual interdimensional allowing and knowing.

8. Knowing is first then comes action. Link THOUGHT, *dimension* and then **purpose** and a clear path emerges for you. Fall into harmony with WHAT IS.

9. **TRUST** yourself and the awareness YOU live in.

10. SELF LOVE first, you can only give what you have.

11. Compassion and Love for SELF first and then ALL else.

12. Creating and manifesting is what we DO.

***

CHOOSING ASCENSION

Basically ascension is about the choice to operate on what your soul believes to be TRUE and REAL and not what the little human thinks. If your goal is to acquire money, things, other bodies or continue care taking of others and carrying their darkness, you are following little human, third dimensional belief's so you would not be interested in ascension.

FOR EXAMPLE
The little human believes there is NEVER enough money.

The soul says, you live in abundance when you stay in the now moment with deep gratitude for all you have. All you have can be real or imagined, but you must genuinely believe and be in gratitude.

ANOTHER EXAMPLE

The little human judges their situation to be awful and terrible.

Soul says, WOW what a disaster, I am so grateful to be able to gather this deep WISDOM producing experience. I have learned so much and have been blessed to come out of this experience alive and wiser. What an adrenaline rush!

ANOTHER EXAMPLE

The little human says, If I don't help them (carry their refusal to take responsibility for themselves), who will carry their darkness.

Soul says you have just taken them and yourself OFF your spiritual paths.

***

Soul operates with the cosmic intelligence and the energy of love.

Love is the **highest vibration** which is always, always PERFECT. *Love is NOT in duality* and has no opposite. When you understand that and work WITH your soul, FEAR has no role or part to play. **In the absence of fear,** there is only love.

LOVE is the framework your soul FUNCTIONS in all the time to experience everything the soul experiences. When you let the little human control you with its MANY FEARS and **lack of knowledge** there is no room for JOY, survival is as high as the little human is capable of going.

TRUTH should guide every part of your journey and the earth is an illusion that our soul is playing in now. Going within to your knowingness, is your connection with YOUR soul.

YOU HEAR SOUL and IGNORE soul

Now, when you go within and hear your soul, WHY WOULD you **argue** or do the opposite? Is that rational on any level? You heard and went into human fear because you lack knowledge.

What do you suppose happens to you when you behave like that. **LOVE speaks** to you and **you argue.** What are you thinking? Why would you ignore an entity with accesses to all the knowledge there is, especially about YOU.

Love WILL NOT argue back.

Love is not a human thing and will not argue back.

Love always allows the little human to BE as fearful as it enjoys being. The little human ALWAYS wins, when you make it a contest. This is a free will zone. You can choose to be wise or STUCK.

You can't really damage a **being made of light**, but humans damage easily and in many ways.

***

At this time a great many beings are visiting us wearing their lightbodies. There are many types of lightbodies some look like a blob of light or ball of light or abstract shapes that do not need to eat, sleep or breathe. **Being a BEING of light,** the easiest, safest and most comfortable way to travel is in your lightbody. Humans are beings of light, as well as physical beings temporarily. A human in transit will be in some way tethered to the physical self on the planet. Humans travel in a flexible gold tube, going to teach or wherever, so we are protected and all others are protected.

WE cannot come to this planet without having had one life of spiritual mastery, so we understand and appreciate the ramifications of our responsibility to learn something we are to share somewhere else with those who may need to know it at some point and after we are no longer here.

Our journey began in other **lifetimes** and continues now as all lifetimes are both original and subsequent in now time. We order ourselves to appear as male or female a particular race, peace maker or god depending on our need or purpose.

Our LIGHTBODY means making ourselves **energetically lighter** by releasing our INTERNAL pressure. Yes, you are lighter than before. When we control our thoughts and emotions the biology can maintain its balance.

OUR MEMORIES

For memories to serve us they need to remain soft and pliable, not cast in stone, so they can be **healed without being shattered.**

Humans have a desire to assist.

Before assisting we need to link our thoughts with the appropriate dimension before our purpose begins to clearly emerge to us. It is wise to know first and act second. We are no longer following the language of need the little human has.

The song of your soul is what you sing.

The song of change, speaking softly in small and huge ways. We are moving from survival into compassion. Expect these changes with gratitude to avoid erecting a barrier of fear. Be present and responsive to your changes as resistance will create **physical pain and slow the process.** The areas being brought to **our awareness** are the ones we have not honored properly. Be innocent and open and receptive in thought because it will not be something you can anticipate.

Luminous light is a higher order of energy that is as intricate as our DNA and complex as the neurobiology of the brain. **Thought is an energy** that appears as a luminous strand. Thought is the fastest energy in the universe. To go to another dimension we can think and be there. Telepathy with thought is much faster than any vehicle.

Light comes in **packet form**, a STREAM, **particle** or *wave form*. Thought waves are luminous waves of energy and a vibrational particle, depending on your point of perception. When light streams it activates or lights up a luminous strand or wire. We are creating our connections to other realms and the beautiful fifth dimension. Our thoughts are energy strands and waves linking us to other dimensions. With our thoughts we provide a super highway of strands to other dimensions.

Humans in a **contracted energy state**, or shut down would not have many or any luminous energy waves. Those of higher consciousness and enlightenment have energy thoughts projecting into many different realms. Our luminous strands are also part of us. As beautiful and complex as our biology is it is coarse in comparison to the structure and light of our true light self.

Our mental body is etheric and in another dimension.

On earth our thinking is slowed because we are teaching and learning. Thought on earth has a built in necessity for repetition because thinking does CREATE **certain realities.**

In the fifth dimension and the ascension levels THOUGHTS create energetic luminous strands. Our thinking, and ideas open up neuropathways of energy strands connecting to other dimensions to ensure our transition to the fifth dimension. Some strands are not yet activated in everyone.

Thought strands hold a certain electromagnetic frequency like our electricity. These strands form a linked up grid work or network linked to higher planes. We are already committed to the fifth dimension. Holographically the groundwork is laid it is our destiny and in our DNA. These strands interact with our future and past self, holographically. Different tones and sounds when your soul decides you are ready activates your strands of electromagnetic thought. We feel the energy with tones. Every time we use a link that thought strand becomes larger and stronger. Our thought waves provide a foundation of connection. WE **minimize one activity** to bring on another. OR one screen goes small and another screen goes larger with a different task.

We are multitasking two or three lifetimes simultaneously.
In consciousness, multitaskasking is easy.
Our essence is formed in thought to a higher plane.
Each strand can have different levels of intensity.

Connecting from the crown chakra to our past and future self offers an ability to download energy from our future self to receive light and energy. There is a strand of huge energetic thought vibration from the Central Sun and a physical core offering.

***

In HIGHER vibrations we communicate and SHARE, instead of feeding.

When the voice of the inner self becomes louder than the voice of the third dimension a **constant stream of self love is maintained**. Unconditional love, allowance and acceptance are a prerequisites for healthy creating. The greatest good for all concerned fosters your spiritual growth.

In old energy we have CONTROL through **fear**. As we *play with choices* we MOVE UP a level and then we start making choices of consciousness with our soul. When we realize we are choosing WITH our soul we realize that we no longer really have to make choices of the human kind like feeding, clothing and maintenance because those become **incidentals.** The **choices you make on a HIGHER LEVEL** will automatically take care of what we call the lower level needs of the little human.

You release your free will to embrace divine will.

***

CHAPTER 9
LEVEL FIVE

LEVEL 5. **MELDING BEGINS**, Light ascensions start. **In and out,** little human 50% or less melded with their soul. **80-90% light.**

To ascend your THOUGHTS and EMOTIONS MUST be in charge of MATTER, your biology, and your survival in third dimensional reality. Many humans have a number of DARK ascensions to move through before they reach the *half light, half **dark*** ascension which is the marker for continued light ascensions. Then they move into increasingly higher vibrating, light ascensions.

There is the potential to move into higher vibrations into dark ascensions which I do not know much about other than that they exist. After the GREAT SHIFT those that are MORE than 50% dark will go back to their maker.

All humans ARE some ratio of "**matter** to **divinity**" and one does not last long without the other. Humans are at their best when they are in balance. Being all spiritual does not feed our miracle of biology. Being a beast lacking spiritual wisdom is not enjoyable. Working under your soul's direction gives the human the peace and nurturing we crave.

DARK ASCENSION

Carrying darkness for others generally starts in YOUR childhood. Many children arrive in biology to help an adult member of a family. The success rate of this type of venture is VERY low. When you are **CARRYING darkness** for a family member or a spouse, other PEOPLE, events or **organizations** that DEFINITELY changes your ratio of dark to LIGHT to darker. When you allow others to syphon your light, that also brings down the amount of LIGHT YOU carry.

Carrying others dark and taking care of them keeps you TRAPPED in the third dimension. Most are unaware of JUST how much they cripple their own growth and development SPIRITUALLY by supporting and carrying others dark energy for them. Generally people are unaware of the dark they hold and carry for others. Ask your soul or entourage what percentage of dark you carry for others, they will help YOU give the dark back to the rightful owner.

SECRETS

We carry OUR FAMILY *darkness and **SECRETS***. If something needs to be a SECRET it must be DARK. Family, including your parents will give the very small child or infant their darkness to carry. The child also reads the dark telepathically from family members and owns the dark as their own. Siblings give each other dark to carry. Sometimes one spouse will force the other to carry ALL THEIR darkness so they look clean and pure to other HUMANS. The only group fooled would be other humans. Invisible realm SEES the darkness. The spouse carrying all the darkness is so codependent they carry both people's dark plus their biological family darkness.

OH, That doesn't handicap them VERY much.

Work places and religious organizations can give you dark to carry when they are UNETHICAL and SECRETIVE as most are. Friends do the same. When they are more than half dark, people, video games and organizations will keep you anchored in the third dimension if you keep them close to you. *It is just multidimensional physics.* KNOW that and choose again.

When you have a lot of light and you are giving or allowing dark to syphon your light AND you want to ascend you will have dark ascensions until you have severed your ties with them and returned the dark you carry on their behalf.

Would you go to a list of sex offender's to find a baby sitter? Your soul knows you still "don't get it" when you carry others dark. You do not **LOVE YOURSELF enough** to allow them to travel their path WITHOUT you trying to FIX them. Ignorance of the universal laws is no defense! That is why we say *we are awakening and becoming aware.* Aware of what is spiritual (light) and what is NOT.

***

Level 5 Awareness'

Each of the twelve levels in level 5 are earned with the THOUGHTS and FEELINGS you carry and the CHOICES you are making daily. As our beliefs and truths change our PERCEPTIONS, values and **REALITY change** in alignment with our soul. Remember this planet HAS **had a dark bias** for thousands of years. We are humans on this planet for the purpose of gaining spiritual wisdom.

The legion of light is a being that animates matter. The legion of light is a *reflection* of the human consciousness. As ANY leader is a reflection of its followers. The legion of light is *ALWAYS creating* as an expression of LOVE.

Matter or the human, **wants to DO.**
Soul wants to BE. Being comes before DOING.
Talking to yourself or your 90%er increases.

Soul enters matter and then creates through matter. Soul has to enter the human for there to be **a PASSION in the human.** When you **do not** have A PASSION your soul thinks something else is more important for you to DO first. So LISTEN UP to your sensory awareness.

You may feel alone and removed from others *because you are*. You are walking the lonely path of spiritual awakening and **filling your immediate space with your own divinity.** You decided and now it unfolds. It is a series of choices or sequences that build one upon the other.

ASCENSION is to stay in your current biology but move to the NEXT LEVEL of spiritual awareness in this lifetime. One ascension is equal to what you would learn normally in one lifetime. This moving to higher and higher levels of spiritual wisdom and awareness can and does happen to many humans over and over again. Once you get the hang of how the universe operates, you just want more and more of it because it feels so much better than duality.

Ascension levels are discerned by the amounts of; **agenda,** lesson, BLAME, **judgment,** doubt, gossip, **DRAMA,** COMPROMISE, **lack,** karma and **spiritual competition** the little human *has released.* WHEN you decide to pull ANY of these back into YOUR life you will drop back to the third dimensional realities and truths, human beliefs and ways.

It is **YOUR JOB to notice** the differences and CHOOSE AGAIN.

We move from who we thought we were to *NO identity*.

From going through "spiritual depression" and voids now and again to embrace an ever EXPANDING identity and increase what we remember of our total being. At times this process causes MUCH sadness and doubt and sometimes compromise in us because it is new and different and we grieve for the human we thought we were.

SPIRITUAL DEPRESSION is **not** caused by the MIND and the mind is NOT involved. When we grab the hand of soul and take THE LEAP OF FAITH, or go into the *dark night of the soul,* a spiritual metamorphosis or transmutation takes place. The transition from human to becoming a **divine human angel.** You will experience spiritual NUMBNESS and feel abandoned by the legion of light at this time. The irony is your soul is as close to you as it is possible to be. Your angels and guides leave your egg shaped aura to make room for the soul to move in. You are in between, in a dark hole moving from the caterpillar state to becoming a butterfly. This is zero point energy, a complete emptying of the OLD for the NEW to move in. The final surrender of your human beliefs and ways. Do the happy dance to celebrate your deep spiritual depression.

BREATHE it in and bring LOTS of compassion in for yourself. This depression has been building up for many lifetimes and is part of the ascension process. The first time ever we have done it while having a biology. The TEARS and more tears and stories come tumbling out. Depression and ascension are an interrelated process. You are dying, moving to zero point energy letting go of the old limiting story you created in third dimension and have built on for many many lifetimes. Release those stories so the energy can be transmute and made available to you in a new expanded way.

When you breathe you start feeling, LIVING and waking UP. Spiritual depression generally lasts a year. During that time you will slip in and out of the void. Things and people start to go away as you move from the third dimensional brain to your heart and compassion. They are no longer a vibrational match to the new meld you have become. When we decide to move into this **interdimensional state** we see things through the *awareness of our soul and its immortal wisdom*. You may have noticed that humans lack *immortal wisdom*.

When the human REJECTS the spiritual depression (SOUL) the human slips into a third dimensional depression. They LOOSE their divine, their soul, they will go back to human free will, and their guides and angels and a lower vibration.

Spiritual depression is used as a FUEL for ascension.

A state of GRACE, **ascension is.**

Ascension is reached through clearing and balancing of all of our layers the physical, emotional, mental and spiritual. Along the way we learn to work and play with childlike enthusiasm and be in the now moment or present time. We release the karma, contracts and old vows of the human living in duality. Ascension is the ENERGY of the masters who walked the earth and told you that you could be just like them.

Some of us are birthing the divinity within us. A divine energy by the human who takes the hand of their soul and NEVER LETS GO. Waffling can put you back in duality. Some let go frequently and the soul waits. When we choose to ascend our free will is embraced by our divine will and we become a divine human. We give our energy (power) away to NO ONE else and we become sovereign.

The SOVEREIGN SELF is self sufficient with no dependency on other humans or mass consciousness or the planetary grids or the galactic grids or the cosmic grids. Our energetic meridians are **woven into the outer** dimensions and our nervous system is wired into our INNER dimensions. This total system woven into the inner and outer dimensions connects our **spiritual parts** to our **physical parts**. This system of connection by the energetic meridians is VITAL, we need to use it to clear our self of blocks and density so we can raise our vibration. The physical body must be clear enough to vibrate at the higher level for a full merge of the soul and its human. The clearer you are the more dimensions you can expand into being sovereign and having complete control over yourself.

To walk the path of ascension you need to be a SOVEREIGN being and enter **the void ALONE**. To go to the next step of becoming enlightened we need to detach and grieve the loss of the little human. The first new relationship humans have in the new energy would **ideally be with their soul** which makes **a sovereign human.**

***

The **entire solar system** is ascending along with the planetary ascension. Everything that happens on earth affects other planets. The entire quadrant is ascending and catapulting its effect on "all that is." Which is the legion of light's plan of expansion and growth. The legion of light is creation and all of its creation is ever expanding and growing.

***

RESTRUCTURING

We are not falling apart we are **being restructured.**

Our internal connections to the invisible realm are growing STRONGER and we are *developing trust* in our intuitive connections. ALL relationships, intimate, work, family and friends become DEEPER relationships of communication, understanding, and compassion or the relationship ends. That is how the soul is and functions. Allow and rejoice

Repressed ANGRY humans find their anger surfacing inappropriately, giving them yet another chance to choose again. Beware of YOUR misdirection's of energy and redirect yourself. OWN all you HAVE created and add it to your oneness. Wounds and old aspects come up from ALL YOUR LIFETIMES during this stage of ascension. *Not to be* repaired or fixed. The human needs to allowed them and **FEEL them** or they cannot be released or embraced.

They ALL want to be known and honored for their service.

The small child you were wants YOU to KNOW how it felt to be them. Your child aspect, wants and needs your AWARENESS of how it FELT to be you as a child. Then that aspect wants to be embraced and melded.

During times of rebalance reach out and touch others or take the hand that is offered to you in help or support. Release the codependency and care taking. Walk beside them.

There is help all around us, we don't have to do it alone.

COMPETITION

Spiritual competition and or thinking one level of vibration is better than another will backfire on you. Each level has its OWN set of **beliefs and truths.** With limited vision you are prone to misdirection of your energy. **Force** used in any context has stopped being effective and will come back at you stronger. To move comfortably into the higher vibrations balance YOUR male and female energy to attract the complementary harmonic balanced relationship in all areas of your life. There is no loser and no competition for enlightenment.

Many humans use spirituality as a COVER STORY for their **personal agendas.** THAT IS WHY you must discern what is true ALWAYS. **Large groups** of individuals may feel good together. Discern that they are not on a spiritual path as that is a **solitary** path.

POPULAR EXPERT

You are spiritual and a teacher, enlightened in many ways, but you are hiding your light under a bushel. The human and soul have connected but have you brought that LOVE RELATIONSHIP into the third dimension you live in? Have you owned that love! There is no need to hide anymore, flow it into this reality.

"I *am* a new consciousness teacher," but only the invisible realm knows it. Have you followed BAD popular experts BEFORE or been one? In a past life did you start a school of enlightenment or were you a teacher in one when it was not so acceptable to do that? Did you need to hide, were you betrayed by your students? When students become addicted to you they followed you after YOUR death and expected you to care for them. Being a popular expert historically was very painful. NOW it is safe to demonstrate your spirituality.

The new era has no popular experts or followers any longer. We have arrived at the AGE of **guidance and compassion.** Encouraging the student but you CANNOT DO it for them. YOU are only the one in process of doing it. When you have learned all of the answers you are probably at level 9, all complete with no biology.

Consciously create your own safe space on a regular basis, whenever it is needed. The safe space rebalances all of your energies and the energies outside you. If you want to move forward KNOW it's not about the little human.

Naps are safe places and very rebalancing.
CHOOSE LIFE
Life is not just neutral. Life is not boring.

No need to test the limits in order to feel alive. When you have your sensory awareness ON, full rich feelings of living flow in and all around you. WHEN you actively choose life and let your biology know you choose to live, the joy and your soul will come in.

Notice that much of your worries and cares are other peoples.

WHY are you trying to OWN them?

Any direction your soul wants you to go will be easy and effortless.

The synchronicity will start. Thrills are artificial things created outside you as a substitute for going within and feeling the joy and compassion of your soul, that is VERY intense all the time. Nothing in the third dimension is more intensely peaceful and satisfying than the love and compassion of your soul.

DNA

Our DNA is INTERDIMENSIONAL and we can go inside the DNA and work with it, your soul understands the cellular structure. Our DNA strands are being reconnected to loop form as they were in the beginning of oneness. Healing the DNA cellular structure in an interdimensional state, you move before the disease was there because that way it will not go back into disease. Learn to speak to your cells. As we work on raising our vibration and moving into ascension by controlling our thoughts and emotions our soul starts releasing the little human emotions or energy stamps around that issue planted in our DNA.

FOR EXAMPLE

You have always raged at others while driving. You start to see the bigger picture—everyone is on their path and you start to honor that. You talk yourself out of rage more and more. You are almost mellow when driving. So your soul says, "I think they have got it" and takes that energy stamp away. After that you notice your emotional attachment or drama leaves you. It is so liberating and wonderful to release all the upset and turmoil WE CREATED in OURSELVES over certain events and people in our life.

STOP USING, just say NO

Meditation, PRAYER, tools or *disciplines*, stones, chants and propitiation. These are DISTRACTING old energy. JUST **breathe and choose sensory awareness**. That is really living in a full, pure and true way. Accept yourself, every part of yourself, in the fullest way.

THROATS and HEARTS

Part of the ascension process will require that male energy open their hearts and female energy needs to open their throats and stand in their truth. Waiting and **compromising** needs to be OVER. Time for action is now. Put out and display your TRUTHS and INTEGRITY. As we move from the brain defining our truths in the third dimension to our heart FEELING in the fifth dimension.

We start **losing things that** no longer serve us. Things that are more dark than light: jobs, spouses, houses, family, friends and some video games and beliefs or vanity things like long hair to seduce boys with. In and around all of this you will have periods of cleaning and straightening the space around you. Getting rid of many things you do not use and have hung onto that no longer serve your changed self. The old things hold old energy.

As soul moves in self love increases.

TEARS

Crying and crying and crying for no present time reason. Tears are good they release old energy and CLEANSE stuck energy. Tears come when your old lifetimes come to be remembered, and embraced by their creator. As you change so do they, you are rewriting and grieving those lifetimes. We can get a bit dramatic with the tears and self pity. Check now and again with the invisible realm to see if you are cleansing or suffering.

INNER deep SADNESS

We feel a deep **inner sadness** for no present time reason. Your current and past lifetimes are coming to the surface of your awareness to be listened to, blessed, released and then rewritten. Its hard to say good bye and there needs to be grieving proportionate to the loss. The embracing of the same lifetime might come to you, again and again, for different reasons or changes on level 4, and level 6 and again on level 7.

SLEEP or **not** to SLEEP

Sleep patterns change and change again. You might awaken around 3 AM or 4 AM because of work going on within you or it is a time for your soul to get your attention and creativity can blossom. When you can't go back to sleep get up and do something.

Dreams of war, being chased or of monsters, are energies of the past that are coming to be blessed and released. Naps are a great way to cope.

STOP MULTITASKING

The biology has a hard time keeping up with all the changes and it is tired. **We forget** what we are saying and doing as we move from being brain centered to heart centered. We drop, forget and misplace things a lot. This is not a time for multitasking do only ONE thing at a time. Spending more time in nature will help ground you and calm you so you can get to know the new you and your limits.

When you have no desire to do anything, don't.

You are in the void or holding your soul's hand. You might feel suicidal because you have completed your karmic cycles. Just take time to grieve their loss. You are ready to begin a new lifetime while still in the same physical body. This is a reoccurring cycle for each level of ascension you go into the void.

The VOID or a Null Zone is established after there is an expansion outwards of energy which receives a blow or shock causing it to **COLLAPSE** *inwards upon itself.* The old established **energy patterns** (belief systems) **are now broken** and there is no way that they will ever return to the previous pattern. They have been IRREVOCABLY changed. The energy of a Null Zone feels *jagged and raw.* There is much hurt and pain, grieving for the "good old days" and cutting of MANY CORDS.

GET HELP

Get help, use all the tools available to you for YOUR body, mind and spirit. The miracles lie within us and outlast any earthly strife we are experiencing now. To minimize your stress and develop NEW options—get help. Do not look to doctors or holistic healers to heal you or FIX YOU. They can help, support, ease and facilitate that is all. Don't give away your power, in the new energy that no longer works and ultimately depletes you. Take responsibility for where you are now. Gather as much information as you can about your symptoms, and then search for tools and awareness you resonate with.

We can control our own nervous system.

We can command it to *release stress and pain.* We can take in new fuel for the body. We are able to control the pace of our heart beat, through our breathing to calm ourselves down. We have the power to control our thoughts and our biology.

Make peace with your limitations.

Find joy in each little moment it is a question of mind over matter. It is time on the 4th and 5th level to control that. All that causes YOU PERSONALLY, emotional pain needs to be CHANGED FIRST so you can then CLEAR your physical pain. Our pain is *learned* and does not reside in the soul. Many lessons were resolved and ended in this one hard life.

The human is a bridge between our "soul and matter," the "divine and earth." We are to enclose and make a balanced whole of these opposites. The biology along with its physical, emotional, mental and spiritual **layers is the bridge**. Our ENTIRE *electromagnetic self,* layer upon layer, wrapped around and through our physical core is the bridge.

SELF LOVE

Self esteem, **worth** or *love* is a multidimensional SPIRITUAL attribute and NOT a third dimensional, linear attribute. At the 5th level we are building on what self love and awareness we gained on the 4th level. There are new skills, TRUTHS and gifts available to you now as you meld with your aspects and soul. All of your past life gifts become available for use. Soul brings a new level of awareness and knowledge to the human. We get an equal amount of love to match the amount of love we **give ourselves**. We CREATE in proportion to the amount of love we are able to **receive** not more or less.

GRATITUDE

Gratefulness is recognizing, FEELING and **owning** what has been done for you. It is the wonderful feeling of emotion we get in the now moment and when we are in the cosmic flow.

Gratitude, appreciation, or **thankfulness** is a positive emotion or attitude in acknowledgment of a benefit that one has received or will receive. Just existing IN BIOLOGY and BEING ABLE to experiencing DENSITY and FREE WILL is considered something to be **very** grateful for. The feeling of indebtedness has a negative connotation. The feelings of gratitude are beneficial to **our subjective emotional well-being** and increases experiences of *positive emotion.* Having a generalized grateful personality greatly diminishes the ups and downs that humans tend to have in life. People who tend to experience gratitude more frequently than others do, tend to be happier, more helpful and forgiving. Grateful humans are less depressed than their less grateful counterparts.

Laughing is a multidimensional feeling and raises our vibration. **Compassion and gratitude happens multidimensionally also and raises our vibration.** We exist in multiple dimensions each of us being a different expression of the soul in harmonic overtones.

How many lives have we spent searching for a supreme being OUTSIDE of ourselves only to find the legion of light in *your mirror*. The challenging part of being divine is that WE are not the ONLY divinity. We need to master living together in harmony with other creators and help support them. Can you also be grateful for the opportunity to help and support all the OTHER divine humans? The GREATER our **skill** at responding to the LARGE variety of humans on this planet the greater our RESPONSIBILITY is in the **spiritual realm**. When a divine human returns to the earth they are in a different place than other humans.

Multiple perspectives allow increased vision needed to move forward in our spiritual evolutionary process. We need to locate our gratitude and ALLOW it to grow until it feels like *JOY bubbling up* from within. FEEL and hear your gratitude.

***

UNSEEN WORLD support

There are hundreds of entities around humans from the invisible realm who would never, ever judge them no matter who they are or what they have done. Open your senses and heart to feel them. Many humans refuse to do that much. Have CURIOSITY about what is going on in all the realms. Feel the surge of love and compassion from your soul. Receive the peace you feel about who and what you are. How you embrace your new awareness is individual and all actions are different and appropriate.

Jesus said, "I am the son of God. And so ARE YOU." There is no battle for the human soul and never has been except in the mind of some humans. We are responsible for the ratio of dark to light in ourselves. We must take responsibility for our reality, our creations and own them. We created what we have and by owning that we can also alter our reality.

Our spiritual path unites us with our soul.

FEELING **lonely** on your spiritual path is the way of things, own that. Our fears are a part of karma, duality and little human goals. Those things drop away as you meld with your soul. Synchronicity brought by your soul helps the human through the melding process.

Your entourage is your support group from the invisible realm.

Ascended humans emanate LIGHT to the rest of the world.

Even the "elements" respond to our energy. Pure light can not have any bias attached to it, pure light can only cast illumination that is LITERALLY what raises the vibration.

The energy has changed greatly since Biblical times and it is harder now to ascend. The new definition of ascension is a human who moves into the next lifetime without physical death and becomes multidimensional going beyond the third dimensional time and space. An ascended human leaves a trail of light wherever they walk. They are slow to anger and never judgmental. Humans who have gone through the shifts of ascension look ordinary and carry the legion of lights love and compassion.

SOME WAYS soul WORKS WITH you on the 5th level.

The human may not have anything to say or write or do but the soul, your 90%er does and it will urge you in that direction, even if it is the furthest thing from what the conscious little human wants or knows anything about. Then the synchronicities start to happen and the human is being moved along in a surprising direction. Your soul is not at all surprised because it was carefully orchestrated.

When you gracefully move with the synchronicity and go in the direction your soul is taking you, life is *smoother and easier* and so much more ENJOYABLE. There are many perks along the way when you follow your knowingness. You fall into interesting situations and people. The feeling of well being and peace is wonderful because you are in the great cosmic flow of well being and enjoyment. Working with your soul is a new very subtle experience. The soul drops thoughts or directions or behaviors generally NOT characteristic of the particular human.

There are specific things your soul wants you to share with others and that is why you get prompted in certain directions. When what you have been prompted to do is new and scary your soul will help you feel more comfortable and brave.

SOUL WANTS all our **ASPECTS HOME**

We create our life from the inside out and used many ASPECTS and PIECES to help us experience life. It is time to come back to their creator, TELL their STORY, **meld** into the "I AM" of the human and celebrate so the human can move to move the next level. THIS JOURNEY or quest is about the **acceptance of ALL of yourself** and about calling home EVERY part, piece and aspect of you that has been FRAGMENTED or **abandoned** or *wounded* or GIVEN away or **taken** from you in the past. The essence of the human is perfect.

Soul is always discovering itself by creating aspects and identities of itself, blessing them and giving them their freedom to do as they wish and then they in turn create aspects of the aspect, of the aspects. The aspects can move in and out of our consciousness depending when we want them or need them. Many layers and levels with negative intent can cause chaos, dissociative identity disorder or schizophrenia or human depression.

It is the crazy aspects that causing the confusion. If you have aloud an aspect or two to run your life it will be challenging to take things away from them, they love the power you gave away. Aspects are SPIRITUAL and **energetic**. Incorporating your aspects will help you return to your perfect center.

AFTER DEATH

When a human holds onto ISSUES even after death, they are unable to let themselves go with any grace or dignity at the time of their physical death.

FOE EXAMPLE

When at death you are blaming others for any injustice or slight you feel strongly about, you might well stay in the near realms to punish or torment them. Doing that PREVENTS your spiritual evolution and awareness of how this earth game works and you may create diseases and suffering.

When the human FIRST CREATES a complete aspect it mirrors the human and then adapts and adjusts in its own way. Humans create aspects, *as many as they need,* to get through TRAUMA or to **control others**. We create aspects to handle our **conflict, stress and pain**. The aspect created to handle the NEGATIVE emotions can cause *major imbalances* and can have control issues with the human. Sometimes we send them off or they go off into other realms and become WAY too WOUNDED to have anything to do with their creator, the human. Aspects can also be programed INTO the human. Many aspects are TAUNTING and **belittling** and enjoy sending you on wild goose chases.

We resist change. *Yet we get bored without change.*

Everything is the journey there IS NO DESTINATION, we are ETERNAL.

Generally speaking if you are enjoying your life the multitude of your aspects are enjoying life also. Reincarnation weaves the web of life with BILLIONS of life forms interacting throughout space and "now time." All these life forms make the universe and our life stream MORE complicated and complex. That means each being is not only itself it is also composed of the remnants of those which came before it.

All the remnants and bits of you that came before are **imparting "their knowingness"** which traditionally has been UNKNOWN to us. Our impulses or lack of impulse, our knowledge or lack of knowledge we didn't realize we have come from ALL our pieces and aspects. All the remnants of us and our energy excesses and depletion's are always trying to rebalance themselves and trying to create a unified whole.

RECEIVE abundance in the MANNER it is OFFERED. **DO** not claim more than you need.

***

CHAPTER 10
LEVEL SIX

LEVEL 6. **Balancing** your biology, your DNA and 80% of the time you are functioning in divine will and compassion. You are functioning as a lot more soul than little human.
90-95% **light**

Your thoughts, emotions and biology are balanced most of the time. There is continued fine tuning of your biology and your thoughts and feelings, you are in the cosmic flow and all your past lifetimes are being rewritten. The human sees the wisdom and need to care for and nurture THEIR biology. They take the time and awareness to do what is necessary to maintain the biology and keep the miracle functioning at peak efficiency.

There is deep compassion for the biology. There is ongoing communication and respect for the biology. Deep breathing and enough pure water is offered to the human aspect which helps keep the biology balanced. Issues and stuck areas are easier and faster to clear up that way. Your awareness has increased enough so you do not misdirect your energy in punishing or rejecting the biology for what the human considered a betrayal. The biology loved you enough to experience ALL your abuse WITH you. What a pal.

WHEN we are **at odds with our biology** it will be VERY HARD to achieve a sense of total self love and self worth. All these things are connected. If you know that you need to exercise or have more sleep but you don't do it **where is the love** for your biology?

Humans PROJECT their shortcomings onto their soul.

Look in your ethereal bodies to see if you built some sort of hideout or structure to keep your SOUL OUT when you went through horrible things and felt abandoned and betrayed by the unseen world. Soul didn't rescue you and you felt very rejected and unloved. When all soul was doing was honoring your free will.

If you want to meld more with your soul, you need to destroy those structures so your soul has access to you all the time. Our soul is our unique, individual, unified identity. Soul is the COLLECTION of everything we have ever done, been or thought. Our soul understands every PROBABILITY and **potential** and all the shadow potentials.

The soul is pure *positive energy*, TRUSTING, loving and adores the human. SOUL is in concert with the LEGION of LIGHT. The soul is androgynous, self contained and self sufficient. Our soul NEVER blames or JUDGES the human. Our divine self is the soul and cannot be defined or structured or controlled. Soul is multidimensional.

***

Balance PATHOLOGY

Family pathology has gone on a long, long time. The percentage of child abuse now is almost the same percentages as it was at the time of Christ. I bring this subject up over and OVER again BECAUSE if awakening, spiritual growth or ascension is your goal it will get *stopped cold* in its tracks if you do not deal with and heal ALL these OLD EMOTIONAL ISSUES and patterns that got started after we went through the wall of fire and have not changed much since that time.

Through the eons of time these issues have have changed VERY LITTLE if at all. These family traditions of ABUSE, **negativity**, HUMILIATION, **cruelty**, CONTROL and SOUL MURDER are little changed. Just where did we leave our awareness and sensitivity to the child? To yourself?

When you start moving into more light there is no turning back. Some try to get back to their old self and don't succeed in doing that. You cannot succeed at that ever again because the old self no longer exists.

The OLD earth and its ways are gone now.

The new earth seems strange and disorganized because we are not used to it yet. We are going in and out of different types of consciousness at this time because that is the way energy is working now.

Playing the victim is not wise or helpful to you.

Consciousness has gone to a whole new level and continues to move higher and faster as it goes. YOUR *dark family pathologies* that all family members are carrying around in their DNA need to be released and transmuted, CORDS need to be cut, DARK RELATIONSHIPS need to be severed, those that are more dark than light.

Commit to the side of light you WANT to be on. Now is the time to "Stand and deliver!" We have had two thousand years to decide the amount and measure of light we want to carry, now the time to "think about it" is over. Avoid just reacting and having others decide for you, DECIDE and CHOOSE what you want.

Multidimensional physics dictates that if the human wants to embrace their family members or loves or friends or jobs or churches that are more than 50% dark your soul CANNOT live in your aura. You must choose, *your soul* or the darker ones.

For YOUR spirituality to evolve on earth at this time you must accept that the legion of light is now and always has been embodied in all humans. And now that we are vibrating higher you need to CHOOSE to release the darkness, the density even when it is found in other people close to you that you love. They have made their choices, honor their path and MOSTLY honor yours.

Be patient and compassionate with yourself.

Nurture each other during this process of change and evolution. Confusion and difficulties are understandable and to be expected as we incorporate the higher vibrations into our lower vibrating biology and thoughts. Give yourself time to assimilate and embrace all of these changes. Avoid distracting yourself with third dimension busyness.

Compassion and understanding for all. 1987 was the start of the NEW ENERGY and the new options. Earth reached a vibratory rate of **SPIRITUAL NEUTRALITY** in 1987. Our future WAS pulled into a higher interdimensional level and we lost the Armageddon option.

Humans were invited to create **their own reality.**

The window of opportunity to become more spiritually aware is 1987—2012. Our DNA strands are becoming loops if we are more light than dark, which will help us see, feel and hear the invisible realm. Our DNA is getting encoded for multidimensionality and adjusting to the slow down of the magnetic grid and the firing up of the crystalline grid. The reversing of the earth's poles and and the earth passing through the photon belt . All are happening around 2012.

Remember our 90%er, the soul was never separated from reality as the human 10%er has been.

LEVELS OF COMPASSION

Our **honesty and integrity** with ourselves and others has been increasing and continues to increase. Have you noticed that when some one is not speaking the truth you notice they aren't and you sort of know what the truth is. Soon all will know what you think. There will not be deception. Souls might not like your thoughts but they will read and know them if they wish to.

Seeing THROUGH your soul's point of perception increases your SENSORY awareness and sensitivity to all the different energies.

80% of the time you are functioning in **divine will**. Free will is what you came from in the third dimension. On level 6 the human has committed more energy and awareness to melding with their soul and functioning in divine will. The human is gaining more control of their thoughts, feelings and is able to emanate more light. The soul is altering the human DNA and the human feels less and less attachment to the third dimension and its illusions. As our senses expand into nonphysical dimensions we feel our etheric aura more and more.

COMPASSION and self love for the human by the human is greatly increased. The little human has learned to **TRUST the soul** most of the time and released any blame toward the soul for not RESCUING the human in this and other lifetimes. The the soul acted with as much compassion and love that was possible for them while following the rules of this game of free choice we played at the earth school. Soul also has to follow universal laws of attraction or vibration.

Moving from duality into true freedom and balance is not sold at Wal-Mart. The bottom line is NOT financial profit. The mind and heart need to stay OPEN. True balance and freedom doesn't know **greed**, LACK, *selfishness*, **hate** or separation from the legion of light. It takes a great deal of INNER

WORK physically, mentally, **ESPECIALLY** emotionally and SPIRITUALLY to see through the illusion of duality and discover what is real. Balance of body, emotion, mind and soul is the light that is not only carrying you, but also is welcoming you home.

Sovereignty, your feeding cords to and from you have been cut. Now and then a real old cord might show up to get your attention so you can address what it is telling you about yourself and what you have allowed into your life. An issue that needs addressing or looking at. Stay consciously aware of when someone or thing attaches to you. The wisdom you carry will guide you to appropriate behavior. CHOOSE sovereignty as often as you need to over and over again.

You CANNOT allow feeding!

Feeding is too low a vibration to be in AND be in divine will at the same time. Feeding supports darkness just as carrying others darkness lowers YOUR vibration and raises their vibration. The law of entrainment gets triggered and down goes your vibration and your connection with your soul. You can share energy as a gift but no feeding cords.

***

HUMAN DNA by Kryon

Within our DNA is the core of everything spiritual. DNA contains your higher self, the akashic record of your existence on earth, healing, mastery, and consciousness of ascension. The building blocks of ascension are within our biology. The following are bits of information about our DNA from a much larger body of work from **Kryon** of Magnetic Service, channeled by **Lee Carroll** kryon.com

LEVELS OF COMPASSION

GROUNDING LAYERS of DNA
1. Biological record of this lifetime and instructions for the other eleven layers.

2. Life lessons. Layer 2 and 8 work together.

3. Ascension (a catalyst) works with layer 6, affiliated with the pineal gland.

DIVINE HUMAN GROUP
4.& 5. Angelic expression or essence of our most important spiritual attributes. Who we are in the universe and what we have done.

6. Communication with our invisible parts. Layer 6 and 3 work together.

LEMURIAN LAYER as a gift to us
7. Multi dimensions.

8. Wisdom and responsibility. Layer 8 works with layer 2.

9. Healing and expansion.

GOD LAYER call to action to understand your divinity.
10. **Call to understanding your divinity.**

11. **Compassion in its purest state.**

12. **You are God Also.**

Layers 10, -12. The last three are the ACTION layers, they facilitate the divine within and are different than 1- 9.

Layer Ten is also a 1, the energy of new beginnings and the first of the legion of light layers facilitating enlightenment and remembrance of who you are. Which is going on all over the planet.

Layer Eleven is wisdom of the divine feminine energy and **pure compassion** Compassion is MISSING in duality AND is the secret of peace on earth compassion, BALANCE and COMPROMISE. Humans with this layer enhanced are balanced with the masculine and feminine energy. Fear dissolves with the masculine energy of **knowledge and wisdom.** Knowledge is sorted and stored in the head. Feminine energy works with perfection together with masculine energy. Feminine energy, **receives, incubates and nurtures.** Working together these divine systems are amazing and do not have any "naughty bits."

Layer Twelve is the legion of light layer, the most divine and our "You Are God Also" layer. There are many divine layers, but this one is 12 the last and highest in vibration of all of them. This layer provides PEACE, shelter, and a sense of being home at last.

DNA RELEASE and balancing on level 6. As we work on raising our vibration by controlling our thoughts and emotions our soul starts releasing the little human PAINFUL emotions around issues planted in our DNA. On level 6 there is fine tuning for some reoccurring issues too.

***

Level 6 Awareness'

Awareness on level 6 is building upon what you personally have mastered in level 5. Our mastery is increased or stepped up just as connection with our soul and our self love is increased. Its starting to be some real fun now. The truth is we create continuously. It is wise to recognize ourselves as the creative genius we are. Acknowledge that we always create whether it is new and exciting or only REPLICATING a past creation in the form of habits. Both experiences REQUIRE that you

SHOW UP for the experience of creating something. Your ability to sustain your focus and *concentration is where your power lies.*

Sustained focus allows humans freedom from DEPRESSION, **anger,** GREED and **or drama.** When focus is keenly fixed upon a spiritual goal, the path is clear and the goal real. Anything we do on earth is spiritual. All creation starts in the MIND which is why it is **most important to pay critical attention to what goes on in your mind.** BE AWARE of what is going on in YOUR mind. Know just who and what is hanging out in your mind at all times.

When we came to earth we were WELL provided for.

We were prepared before leaving all that is to deal with ANY need or contingency that might arise. **We are well** *stocked with any* materials or supplies we might need. There is nothing fractured or broken within us other than our PERCEPTIONS of ourselves. We are the ambassadors of the legion of light experiencing being human on their behalf.

If you desire to save this world you MUST **start with YOU.**

WE cannot exist other than as light and love.

As you think so you are.

Positive energy draws positive energy and has CLARITY and **warmth**.

Some humans as children were NOT ALLOWED to have boundaries. The child was forced to learn that any bigger, nastier or stronger person could violate their SPACE, their **biology,** their **SENSE of control** over themselves and their SELF WORTH. The child was NOT honored. The child was forced to give into satisfying what the bully wanted at all times if they wanted to stay alive and keep their biology alive. That certainly was the child's perception and reality.

The coping method of these children generally, was one of HOPING the bully got distracted. Since they were powerless this was a doable strategy for a child just as dissociation is.

As an adult—hoping for the bullies in their life to get distracted is not such a good strategy. When you are an adult with NO boundaries, the bullies of the world pick up your vibration and consider you an easy mark. They take and take from you and you hope they get distracted—THEY never DO get distracted. There is little LIGHT and CONSCIOUSNESS left for you the human or your soul to work with when you allow bullies to bully you.

To continue having ascensions YOU MUST make boundaries, draw lines, say "NO I will not because I do not want to." This is not a fun game for me. That is the only way to raise your vibration high ENOUGH to get OUT of the bully / victim vibration. You must take a stand to prove YOU love yourself enough to protect yourself and raise your vibration.

FOR EXAMPLE

Actively creating boundaries is a new behavior and you feel fearful doing it because you might well get hurt. Be brave and set limits, you will find that can be most liberating. After you get more comfortable setting boundaries and you do it with some grace and get good results your soul releases that lesson from your DNA and energy tube and your vibration goes up a bit. A win-win- win.

A SIMILAR ISSUE

When you read the inside of a person and get a VASTLY different feel from what their mouth is saying you freeze up not knowing what to do with the discrepancy. The larger the gap the angrier and more betrayed you feel. You brace yourself for the fallout of the deception you KNOW is to come, as it always has come.

LIES are generally an **aspect of the truth** that doesn't want to **OWN ITSELF**. Just a frightened bit of **dark** energy in the liar trying to deny what it is. A dark bit of essence that has judged itself not worthy of love or compassion. It forgot that it was love having an experience on behalf of the legion of light.

Develop compassion for the dark that judged itself.

It doesn't matter when someone lies to you because you are NOT dependent on them any longer in now time, *you are sovereign*. That is their path NOT yours. When there is a gap between the words you hear and what you feel, you MUST go with what you feel and act accordingly.

PASSION READY

Soul will not be creating passion in the human UNTIL the human is loving themselves, is reasonably SOVEREIGN, and has considerable control of their thoughts and feelings. The ascension process is NOT a thing or event or another human, the ascension process is **NOTHING outside the biology.** Ascension is an **INWARD process** of the human connecting to their soul until they operate as one unit. When you operate together your soul KNOWS what it wants to CREATE and will convey that to you the human. BEFORE the human and soul create, the human needs to be in WORKING order *first*.

On level 6 you are balanced enough to be "passion ready" for your soul's DOWNLOADS. Even if your soul and you created together previously, more and more of the little human gets embraced and melded and your wisdom is increasing by leaps and bounds via the cosmic flow your soul gives you access to. Being passion ready mean's the soul and human are trial running your SOUL'S passions and desires to create.

You are loving you most of the time.

You feel peaceful most of the time.

You sing to yourself instead of running old tired loops of thought.

You are SOVEREIGN, no feeding and have control of your thoughts and feelings. You feel mellow most of the time having the cosmic flow present running through you. You have lots of shiveries and you TRUST your soul's wisdom and vantage point.

Old wounds and old aspects that were more deeply hidden are still coming up during this stage of ascension from all lifetimes. You need to **FEEL them** and own them before they meld, transmute or are released.

Your awareness that your soul has always been pure *positive energy*, TRUSTING, loving and adores the human is finely accepted and believed by the human. SOUL is in concert with the LEGION of LIGHT and always has been. The soul is androgynous, self contained and self sufficient. Our soul **NEVER** blamed or **JUDGED or ABANDONED** the human. Our divine self is the soul and cannot be defined or structured or controlled.

The little human projected its low vibrational behavior and thought onto the soul. So again if you have built walls or any barriers against the soul clear them away. You need to OWN your upset over what you DECIDED the soul did to you. DO IT NOW! You have upset *your own self*. Your soul honored your wishes to experience using your free will to upset yourself. ENLIGHTENMENT is when a human is in balance and has compassion for EVERYONE. They have found and possess the "divine attribute" humans find *inside* themselves. They radiate divine compassion. We are the sons and daughters of the creator, just as Jesus told us we were two thousand years ago.

Enlightenment historically, before 1987 had nothing to do with ascension. At times humans have experienced states of bliss. These are moments of COSMIC awareness and not ascension. Moments of bliss can become an addiction, but are really a belief system. We believed when enlightened we will know everything MENTALLY. The mind cannot even understand ascension, so that would really be sad to judge others with your mind. We are not linear, so there is no predictable sequence to base your spiritual reality on. There is no bias on your arrival at ascension no judgment of you. There is only love and compassion when you *VIBRATE high enough to feel it.*

***

ENERGY / LIGHT

We live and play in a sandbox of energy so I trust you are making friends with that energy and being nice. Talk to the energy and seek its companionship and cooperation in building your new creations. You know not to send an attitude or concept or visualization out to others because you would be forcing or creating for another. Pure light is LIGHT sent without **bias** or IDEA. Your soul will take your light and put it where it will do the most good for the greater good.

There is integrity in NOT casting your ideas on others. ONLY offer pure illumination.

Soul sets up your synchronicities.

WISDOM and better ways of thinking get illuminated.

PEACEFUL solutions and changed lives happen.

When you are allowed to create a reality for yourself, is there anyway to avoid affecting somebody else and their reality? When you do something grand like creating what **you need** in your life, it WILL impact those around you. How, with integrity do you create for yourself?

The little human doesn't have enough information to do that.

TO CREATE, the human uses the synchronicity the soul has lined up, the system and spiritual mechanics of creation is in round time and multidimensional. Your soul sees your need long before you have awareness of having a need and lines up the synchronicities of potentials and answers that will be a win-win-win for all involved.

A system where all things are known about the potentials of those affected by soul's creating. Third dimensional creations appearing to be a coincidence or accident are NOT. Your soul put that synchronicity together for you using invisible realm logic and senses. Synchronicity is prepared within the interdimensional soup long before you need it.

Synchronicities are energies that ALIGN with PURPOSE.

Synchronicity is you at the right time and place with the potentials aligned that *you asked for*. Certainly **NOT** *the way you asked for them*. You have to take some action like accept an invitation or make a phone call or an electronic communication. You might need to put your body someplace as part of the synchronicity piece.

Understand the way and balance of things. Synchronicity works **piecemeal** and we are **required to connect the pieces together** for the whole thing to happen in a way you NEVER anticipated. Yes co-creation. And this is all done with divine timing and NOT with third dimensional linear timing and that makes us JUST crazy and frustrated.

Our intuition is a product of synchronicity.

A very real way for the invisible realm to communicate with humans. When we hear the intuition said in our voice it appears as though the human thought of it. They probably did not.

Synchronicity is the system the creator uses to help us limited humans. The human IS very much a part of the system.

Some humans MISTAKENLY believe they will evolve to a heightened state where sex will no longer be a part of their experience. As long as we are in finite form we will have the VALUABLE tool of *sex available to us.* The energy you feel flowing in the biology, the feeling of bliss, JOY or almost any sensuous pleasure comes from the soul flowing cosmic energy through you when you are functioning as a unit, human and soul.

HEALING and converting the biology to crystalline form DOES lower your VIBRATION so do not think you are being abandoned or punished if your vibration drops some and are a bit cranky. ASK your biology or SOUL, "Am I healing?" Yes or no? When the human is in healing mode, ridding themselves of pockets of density their VIBRATION drops and it is a bit harder to feel their soul and it is a bit lonely too. There is an **energetic point of separation** that is ALL part of the process. Try to flow with it in grace, our whining gets tedious.

HEALING LOWERS your VIBRATION. That is just the way of it.

We move from who we THOUGHT we were to *NO identity*, by going through "spiritual depression" and voids to embrace an ever EXPANDING multidimensional identity. At times the process causes MUCH sadness and doubt because it is SO new and different. We grieve for the human we thought we were.

***

YOUR SIGNATURE
and the LAW OF ATTRACTION

In every moment our "resonant signature," the dominant energy of our aura matches frequencies to keep us on the path we are on. No thought is required and this match up will continue ad infinitum with great efficiency and thoughtless indifference to what the human may wish. Dramas of the third dimensional kind have played and replayed themselves AD NAUSEAM. Humans build their resonant signature with every **thought they think** and BELIEF we hold dear. Our emotions keep it all glued together. Our emotional reactions let everyone know our beliefs. Emotions always speak the truth. Even to those that lie to themselves. Your emotions, even the negative ones, do not judge or analyze they simply **REFLECT with clarity** and TRUTH what you are holding in your energy field. When you are easily angered, you are still probably angry about childhood events. Ask your soul or angel to show you what it is. Releasing that past rage releases the current angers.

BELIEF SYSTEMS

Beliefs are formed by the repeated thoughts that dwell in us WITHOUT our conscious awareness of them. Our thoughts feed our "resonant signature," with a constant flow of energy or vibration.

OUR THOUGHTS are

*Beliefs we have picked up and adopted telepathically since birth.

*Conflicting beliefs we get about the self from home and in school.

*The lies, secrets and deceptions of our homes and community.

CONFLICTING BELIEFS result in CONFUSION, *stress* and a lower vibrational resonant signature resulting in future lower frequency. The conflicting inappropriate beliefs vibrate as your reality because the **unconscious mind believes all**

it hears. *No sorting goes on* UNLESS you become consciously aware of your beliefs and choose to RETAIN or **release them**. The universe does not care if your thoughts and emotions are REAL or **imagined.**

Knowing YOUR personal belief's enables you to own them. That is why I go back to the childhood over and over again because, that is the origin of most of the belief's that trip up the adult. Knowing and feeling your childhood trauma cleans up the nutty belief's in a hurry. Your soul or angel, using synchronicity, will bring you awareness of what belief you need to address next so you can consciously live in truth. The truth of who you are and what frequencies you resonant. Our natural state is being creative and expansive. In the quiet practice of NOT resisting the seeds of wisdom our soul **plants within us.**

When we allow ourselves to feel unloved, unworthy, or guilty, negative energies come up from a deep core in us. These memories are surfacing to be released once and for all. This is our ancestral DNA. We chose our physical body and family to bring forth **misdirected thought forms** and energies needing change, embracing or release, bringing us into balance.

Our thoughts have a dramatic impact on our etheric bodies. The etheric body WAS to maintain a **higher-frequency** pattern than the biology. However, over time the etheric body became susceptible to **negative thought forms** from the mental and emotional bodies. Our etheric body is gradually being healed and returned to a harmonious state. Our etheric body stays with you until we transcend then gradually disintegrates and returns to the devic elemental kingdom it came from.

Our conscious mind is constantly being affected by our *unconscious mind*. The unconscious mind is a composite of all our past experiences in this lifetime, as well as a bit of the collective consciousness of humanity that we agreed to bring forth to rectify. Every soul comes into this lifetime pure and innocent. **BUT we also bring our unconscious mind and DNA** a bit of imbalanced vibrational patterns created by us in past lifetimes and our ancestral lineage, original sin or karma. To experience the lessons involved in healing those imbalances. Your conscious mind contains those things that you have accepted as valid and true, whether positive or negative. Those stuck in the illusion of the third and fourth dimension of density have rigid beliefs resistant to change.

Consciousness and melding with your soul and the harmonious collective consciousness of the higher realms *harmonizes* our levels of consciousness and the **unconscious mind** gets REPROGRAMMED as we clear out negative, restrictive concepts, and self-limiting thoughts that can be modified when brought to your awareness.

Law of attraction

The law of attraction is as active on earth as anywhere else in the universe. Everything that happens to you on any given day is based on the law of attraction. Many humans understanding of this law is that it is for the LITTLE HUMAN to amuse itself with. When you reduce the law of attraction to an EXTREMELY small limited thing or toys like a car or house or money. The human self is saying, **MY NEEDS** and my need for **grandiosity come first** and are more important than soul's creations. The soul gets pushed aside and you miss the entire SPIRITUAL POINT and YOUR ENLIGHTENMENT when the human is allowed priority.

You already have **ALL YOU NEED in the moment** and don't realize it.

If you have tried to WORK the law of attraction you know it generally doesn't work very well because all sorts of higher vibrational behavior needs to be in place for it to work. Generally the higher vibrational behaviors are not in place when you are not in alignment with your soul. Your soul never wants toys and status symbols to make you feel important and valued. Worrying about the right words to use or saying it just right, does not matter. You need to have control over your thoughts and emotions. You need to be in integrity and able to focus. You need to be compassionate and nonjudgmental.

In the true energy of the law of attraction you do not concern yourself with **superficial cravings** because they take *CARE OF THEMSELVES.* The Law of Attraction is really about the ATTRACTION of your SOUL. The attraction of the ***needs and desires of the expression of consciousness.*** Whatever you ask for look around and you will see it is ALREADY THERE.

Your *consciousness* takes precedence over everything.

The human is only TEMPORARY and was **never designed to rule.** Through expression **the soul celebrates life in a human body** or on the nonphysical realms. *Refresh your soul* by having gratitude for all *you are and have ever been* and will ever be. Live with a THANKFUL HEART. Even the darker spaces helped you grow. Earth is the toughest school in the universe. On the third dimensional level the law of attraction helps to open up the mind and body connection. Invisible realm uses the law of attraction to experience **changing our thoughts** and not to try to force something to happen. Forcing something to happen does not allow us to ACCEPT **ourselves as we are NOW.**

***

She woke to feeling a ring being slipped on her finger.
She married her soul.
On to level 7.

***

CHAPTER 11
LEVEL SEVEN

LEVEL 7. **Soaring,** little human emotions and concerns are almost gone. Let the joyful expansion and celebration continue.
95-100% light.

Our biology, thoughts and ideas, our feelings and realizations are all music played by our soul and the legion of light. Our contribution is to be present in our biology awake, alive and in present time. Not dissociated, absent or dwelling in opposition. VERY fine tuning is happening. We are ever ready and available for expansive experiences and awareness. *There is NO spiritual starvation*, we are FULLY AWAKE, fully CONSCIOUS, FEELING the expanded LOVE available and creating.

There is nothing routine about being a human.

Soul gives its light and love perpetually without conditions or boundaries. The love inside us is continual.

Unending compassion is our new TRUTH.

There are many **choices** to work with as you are multidimensional.

As a melded human and soul you cannot depend on another human for your love. You can only find the deep contented love within.

You want to enjoy another human?

Soul will bring you a human that SENSES and **sees** your inner love and wants to help you with the little human hurts and issues you have. While you wait for the synchronicity of that event, concentrate on loving your own self. Do things for you and watch another human appear before you. A human that **replicates and enjoys you to the fullest.**

Living as a human with your soul fully incorporated. Interacting with other humans as a fully balanced being. Residing comfortably within soul gives the human access to *divine timing*, UNIVERSAL LAW and unconditional love, what is not to love about all of that.

The learning and the need for the earth classroom is completed. Our larger experience on Gaia has been temporary AWARENESS building for the divine human. As we slip into oneness and higher vibration there is nothing more to learn or understand for the legion of light.

The tests, the big bad tests that humans feel they are given by the invisible realm on lower levels seem small and relatively easy when you are around 90% melded with your soul. We are talking only 10% little human that is very committed to their soul.

The human melded with soul is perfection.

***

Level 7 Awareness'

SAD and feeling **elated** at the same time.

Your cellular consciousness is having its LAYERS being *pulled apart* when human sadness and elation happen at the same time. The pure emotion of love MOVES through your biology looking for anything that IS NOT love and *pulls it free*. There is no way to *pull the energy free* without your awareness of the sadness being released. When you feel the ELATION of love and the *sadness* at times you feel the final stage of duality energy being released into oneness. When YOUR emotions *flow freely*, you are dragging the sadness through your cellular AWARENESS one layer after another layer of energy. Release of what is no longer needed is the greatest celebration in the world. The celebration is wrapped in your many, many, tears.

All emotion is EXCELLENT!

Crying is RELEASING LOVE out into the world.

When we cry, we cry from love.

After a deep full sob we feel a bit better. Holding the tears back makes us suffer. Tears *are the manifestation of love.* It is not possible to cry without emotion.

Emotion is love.

Remind yourself you are expressing your love, as you cry you cleanse your biology and the soul. The energy from your thoughts and strong emotion open and *EXPAND you*. Feeling deeply TRIGGERS your **cellular awareness** to new levels and possibilities for healing.

By our experiencing *love for the SELF,* we travel from cell to cell healing each cell in the process.

NEGATIVE THOUGHTS

The **misaligned cell is** not in alignment with LOVING *itself* resulting in the cell **giving OFF chaotic energy.** This chaotic energy sends out vibrations to match up with other chaotic energy. The same way unhappy people and children find each other. The chaotic energy finds your weakest points or other chaotic energy and THEY HOOK up in your biology. Negative thought patterns hold the chaotic energy all together in your biology.

When you allow yourself to feel YOUR emotions **without NEGATIVE thoughts,** as they are not helpful, you find PEACE and harmony in your cellular body. You celebrate your fear and hurt *without judgment*, CONCERN or **blame** because thought can BLOCK, twist or shut down your emotions.

FOR EXAMPLE

"My child went back to the legion of light." You know your child's safer than it ever would have been here in your care. You're crying because you *feel the vulnerability* of being light yourself.

Think from a different point of perception allowing no NEGATIVITY in your **thoughts.**

Our emotions positive or negative, are the energetic glue holding our pockets of dense matter, IN PLACE, in our aura. Releasing negative emotional thoughts tied to people and events allow you to move forward *in the now moment* with all of your pieces and parts fully present.

EMOTIONS belong to the LITTLE human and are *easily* manipulated or controlled going off into MISDIRECTED energy.

FEEL the sensory perceptions of your emotion, don't engage the brain. When you take a bit of negativity and turn it into a positive, that's maybe a twenty minute cry. Choose a positive reaction to your experiences to build the love in your emotional body. Hate, fear and anger are found in the *mental body* and that is why we go to the **mental body** to find and develop the POSITIVE way to EXPERIENCE our experiences. You can be so skilled at finding the positive point of perception in everything that it will become your **truth**.

Great relationships, health and money are the byproduct of being in love with the self. Our emotions want more love and more positive energy.

FOR EXAMPLE

Were you a fool and betrayed OR trusting and open?

Were you lonely OR feeling separate from soul?

Were you unfaithful OR looking for love in all the wrong places? A human that enjoys and creates drama all the time is not capable of loving them self or others very much. This is not a person to find peace and love with.

Celebrate the job loss because your options have increased.

When we CELEBRATE *transitioning*, **physical death** our spiritual body moves into our cellular AWARENESS to shut the systems all down. Then the mental body envelops the whole process. As the biology shuts down the emotional body absorbs the feelings and thoughts, TRANSMUTING them all into love so that is our memory. That is why so few turn around once the death process has started.

***

ONE SOUL, ELEVEN experiences

The collective vibration is reaching critical mass and we will ALL be seeing things we have not seen in awhile. Our one soul having eleven experiences. There are twelve dimensions each having **one point of perception** or *dimension*. Eleven different experiences of the soul that we will become aware of. Same soul, different realities playing out as a result of different choices. We can see our "negative experiences" or challenges in the other ten different points of perception giving us incredible gifts and awareness.

Self-confidence comes from taking chances and being positively reinforced learning more from FAILING than succeeding. The human **knowing and dreaming** coming from within, from the soul. As the individual becomes aware of their soul essence they find joy.

Accepting who and how you are is vital to your self-esteem.

Explore the simplicity and embrace the honesty.

Make love and grow through laughter and shared experiences.

Others will place their expectations on you KNOW that is **about THEIR needs** and not yours. You are a physical manifestation of *nonphysical reality*. You can relive your physical past and many lifetimes *not letting go of one of them*, or you can live in the present lifetime enjoying the time you have.

Focus ON THE TASK, not the fear of the task.

Speak out and be proud of your views.

All that is real is eternal and infinite in grace and light.

Know yourself, because that helps you avoid getting pulled into other people's perceptions of what they want you to be or their perception of what they consider themselves to be. Stay in your now moment being deeply involved in your passion and expressions.

ENERGY WAVES

In the invisible realm there are energy waves. Those without biology travel upon (not in or through) them. When you choose to use the energy waves you become one with them in an intimate way. And they choose oneness with you and share their energy beingness.

By living in the fifth dimension as some are doing now, CAUSE and EFFECT is no longer one of our truths. We ARE the cause and the effect. This can only be grasped by the divine human mind. The divine mind is unlimited and unfathomable and free flowing and independent of third dimension.

LIFE FORCE

All things have life force within them in varying degrees. Fruits, vegetables, nuts and seeds all contain life force energy.

The vegetable kingdom and certain selected animals, fish and fowl agreed to provide sustenance for the human kingdom for a certain span of time. As we evolve into a higher vibration we will draw more of our needed sustenance from a HIGHER SOURCE. An overlay of **love and gratitude** adds beneficial qualities to everything you EAT or DO.

SEX

In the past, priests, priestesses, and druids used the energy of orgasm for astral projection. They could energize themselves to such an extent they could fill out and balance their auric bodies. Done in absolute, unconditional love, they would astrally project out of their bodies and come back when they wanted to.

Now, when all seven chakras are integrated and you are working from your heart as the fulcrum, the orgasm, instead of running down your legs, will literally run up our spine because the heart brings it up, up, up, up and up, through the top of your head, the crown chakra, and it **comes back down like a shower,** feeding your aura in a beautiful rush of energy.

***

ROMANCE on LEVEL 6 and 7
NO DRAMA
The Multidimensional Romantic Relationship is here!

All relationships are CREATIONS.

Old energy romantic relationship started a while back can certainly be updated and brought into the new energy if both parties want that and would enjoy that. Many of our old energy relationships ended because the contract between the two or more, no longer served them. In the new energy the old contracts lost their meaning and usefulness.

When you have melded with your soul, finding a romantic relationship is a job left up to the soul and not the human. Soul does the creating, the synchronicities and hooks you up! The number of humans and sexual preference is ALSO the souls choice. I trust soul listens to and honors the little humans input and preferences as best it can. But soul knows lots more than the human does about what the human would enjoy the most. I PROMISE!

Higher vibrational love is based on **SOVEREIGN humans** coming together in **STRONG friendship** and **CONSTRUCTIVE purpose**. This couple or group regardless where they are at, be it work, home or Costco have *excellent COMMUNICATION*. They are **conscious** and AWARE of all their energies being put out and all the energies around them.

Higher vibrational love and romance understands WHAT is SAID or **needed** and they share SIMILAR values. EACH member feels free to speak their mind to the other human(s) and that makes the relationship thrive. I am talking deep heartfelt communication and understanding, not exchanging PLEASANTRIES like "yes dear," or TOLERATING another.

Often, all the other human wants is someone to listen to them. After listening with your HEART, you are able to talk to them about their feelings. Let them express themselves to you in all the ways they need to express themselves. When people are in love beautiful arcs of rose light connect their hearts and a beautiful rose color is added to the normal golden pulsation from them. The purpose of sex in the fifth dimension or higher vibrations is to express UNCONDITIONAL love which lets us know the highest benefit from sexual activity.

Heightened sexual experience comes with a ***deeper level of communication and understanding.***

LEVELS OF COMPASSION

ALL relationships, intimate or otherwise become DEEPER relationships of communication, understanding and compassion on the 5th, 6th, or 7th level or the *relationship ends.* That is the way of the divvine human.

When a relationship you had falls apart, you have learned all you could from it and it naturally ends. Possibly you decided the other chose to leave or abandon you. Be aware that, for a relationship to end, BOTH PARTIES must come to the awareness that **evolutionary growth has ceased for both parties**. There is generally pain because you GAVE YOUR HEART and they didn't share their heart or *took it back*. THEN your outside world breaks up or changes when a relationship ends.

You cry because you are FREE to find a new relationship.

Maybe finding or waiting for a new relationship isn't what you wanted to do.

The nature of creation is to change and grow into its next evolutionary stage. New earth energy mandates relationships be from the HEART and *in compassion.* There is a built-in freedom for each individual that comes with compassion and from the heart.

When you have a meaningful relationship a THIRD vibration gets started, the harmonic of the two, AND the relationship. In old energy many were attached to the idea or concept of HAVING a RELATIONSHIP and NOT the **love for each other**. As you evolve, you release attachment to the concept of conditional love and move to unconditional love.

Soul has started a hologram of love for you and with you. Your soul can choose a higher vibrational love for you based with another SOVEREIGN human coming together in STRONG friendship and CONSTRUCTIVE purpose by choosing on multidimensional levels.

Humans are multifaceted with different parts of them inside different dimensions of reality. When you fall in love with the different dimensions or aspects of another it creates a fuller, deeper connection that will get stronger as you move from one level to the next.

***

PAUL

A small bit of Paul's soul history.

Paul lived during the time of christ as did many of his shaumbra friends. He was and is a *Specialist in Universal Creation* as his friends were and are. They all left their "homes" eons ago on a mission. They volunteered to help each world they entered. They further agreed to adopt each world's lifestyle and ways as they demonstrated and taught THE WAY of the legion of light. These shaumbra had forgotten their homes and who they were in the process. Especially on this planet of free will it has been very hard to remember we are from love and all that it means, coming from love.

Paul got killed by the King that lifetime because the King was not too impressed with Paul's messages.

A pattern was set for Paul!

Between the time of christ and now Paul had twenty six lifetimes, and got killed by various leaders most of those lifetimes. Thirteen of those lifetimes he was tortured on the RACK and EVENTUALLY died and he wonders why his biology is in a great deal of pain and hurts during this lifetime.

If your biology has been abused, it might be nice to tell your body how sorry you are for putting it through so much pain and suffering. Go on and on about how grateful you are that it has stood by you and functioned beautifully until the end. Thank you, Thank you biology, what can I do to return the favor?

It seems Paul was a TRUTHFUL man and a bit outspoken, bucking the system for change, yes a trouble maker. And what has he done this lifetime? The same of course. A slow learner? Maybe. Stubborn? hum! A courageous legion of light worker who forgot who he was, probably.

To show his body how much he cares he came in THIS lifetime with a mom that enjoyed KICKING the infant and child. That was all the child's fault because mom was forced to marry the man, that offered the seed, that created the child and he was too poor to support her like she wanted to be supported. Paul's parents and grandparents and great, great grandparents, and all family members were "satanic cult members," so by definition Paul's body was in for all types of strange abuse, verbal, sexual, mental and lots of physical abuse. Maybe mom was ONLY doing him a favor by toughening him up for all the fun that lay ahead.

GAMES and DRAMA

Games we learn as very small children from those in our environment. When you are raised in an environment with humans that are more DARK then light, which means most of us humans, you learn many games that are **anti love** and *anti compassion* for the SELF.

TRIANGLE GAME mastered as a small child.

Two family members bond to EXCLUDE others. The others can't figure out what is wrong with themselves and their self esteem plummets. "The two" are frequently a parent and child leaving the spouse and other children out in the EMOTION cold, so to speak.

SECOND LEVEL of the TRIANGLE GAME

One of the original two bonded family members feels they are not being treated well enough or can get more from a different family member. And for a short bit they bond with one of the family members left out in the emotional cold making them their "special friend" for a bit and milking it for all it is worth.

Now all this nuttiness and codependency is a great opportunity for all manner of DRAMA which can be carried on all of your lifetime and many more lifetimes in fact. This is a fun game if you really love being in the third dimensional illusion as some people do.

Then there is judging each family member and their behavior as being good, bad or stupid, how fun is that game? Gossip and secrets go on into the next generations about each other.

Dark ones trade "services" and "care taking" as an *imitation of love* or cold prickles. Love and compassion is not an option for those that are more than 50% dark.

Back to Paul, he was born into this nice dark family and painfully learned all their dark lessons, once again. Paul had a lot of light for the family members to feed on and they did enjoy feeding off of him.

Isn't that what a "good son" does?

Then when Paul was old enough to feel his hormones and he suffered all the shame, guilt, confusion and anxiety about his value and worth as a human. The lack of self love and self disgust the family had passed down from one generation to the next. The messages and belief's about sexual things were also handed down. What Paul learned as a child was of no help to him as he looked for love and compassion from females raised in the same type of home as he was raised in.

Like most boys, they tend to be drawn and have relationships with girls that behave as their mom's did and do. So we know the girls were dysfunctional, not nice, judgmental, unfaithful and were unable to love themselves or others, especially their own children.

Paul had a small "god complex" meaning he desperately wanted to help others "do right." I think he picked his mom to rescue her from herself. Failing at that goal, he tried helping his sister and as he got older, Paul moved on to women with at least two sons. The oldest son which the woman vented on and humiliated and out and out abused.

In the birth order of Paul's family what was he? Good you paid attention, Paul was the eldest. Paul's mom and the women he interacted with or lived with, felt HOW about the second son? I know you know the answer!

The second son was the "special one." This son got what mom considered to be her love, dressed in CONTROL and manipulation and *sexual titillation.* Yes he got to be the surrogate spouse.

You are asking how did Paul behave? There was the "god complex" FEAR, dissociation, GUILT, blame and CONTROL that he had developed in childhood. He felt safest when the woman was more dysfunctional than he and he could help her "get a grip" and do right. Paul was trying to EARN love from women that had no idea what love was about.

Paul wanted to control the situation, restore order, parent the children as he had done for his siblings. None of the families he stepped into wanted to change their ways and when Paul got frustrated he dissociated, felt guilty and blamed himself.

Now I am not sure what was most important to Paul, to rescue the women from their "evil ways" or to help the children as much as he could.

The lesson hopefully learned by Paul was...

***

Taking *anyone off their spiritual path* takes you off your path and you are all miserable.

***

All along Paul was not getting what he hoped for, which was a little love and compassion. He always studied and took classes to learn how to be a better person and get what he wanted. He tried therapy, studied many spiritual works and ways. Paul learned all the ways the mind can control the biology. None of these EXTERNAL methods succeeded in getting Paul the love and compassion he craved and always looked for in others.

Paul studied the early channeled works from Kryon and Tobias about what was happening spiritually and in the new energy being delivered to earth. He learned how the vibrations on this planet are raising and people are becoming more spiritual. Paul started to value himself a bit more and decided to end relationships that were more painful than not. In the last year or so Paul gave up on personal relationships as being too painful to engage in. The sexual aspects were as frustrating as the intimate aspects were, just more guilt, shame and self loathing.

Paul was in his 5th decade and had invited his parents over for his birthday. All Paul had ever wanted for the past 50 years plus, was to get along with his parents and enjoy their company and hopefully they could enjoy their son. The parents started up the old games of blaming and shaming which historically made Paul feel little and guilty, confused and anxious.

LEVELS OF COMPASSION

This birthday was different he knew there was nothing wrong with him and he had done nothing wrong. Paul stood up for himself and refused to play the game of "two against the one, to make the one feel small and little." Paul said "no more, this is not a fun game for me."

Refusing drama and judgment is the only way to raise your vibration high ENOUGH to get OUT of the bully / victim vibration. You must take a stand to prove YOU love yourself enough to protect yourself from other people and their dark ways and negativity. If you continue to ALLOW being victimized you cannot increase your light and move out of that vibration.

Actively creating boundaries was a new behavior for Paul and he felt fearful doing it at first but he also felt FREEDOM and liberation standing up for himself and believing he had worth and value. The fear is about loosing the DARK people that have abused and put you down all your life—that would be how sad? Loss of the illusion of your parents being capable of loving themselves and you. After you get more comfortable setting boundaries and you do it with some grace and get good results your soul releases that lesson from your DNA and energy tube and your vibration goes up a bit. A win-win-win. Refuse to be controlled and increase your awareness about the games going on in your life. Your awareness *ends the GAMES of control* over you.

Awareness brings new information to light.

In reviewing his past relationships Paul realized he was loved and cared for but never owned it because he had bought into the nasty things his parents told him his entire life. Finally the awareness came to Paul that his family is dark, not objective, not nice and any opinion they have on anything is highly suspect.

THESE AWARENESS' resulted in much sadness and depression, physical discomfort and pain, grieving and releasing the life of being used and abused he never owned previously. Paul tried not to embrace that reality because it felt so painful and lonely. He is very tired and wanting to leave this illusion it has not had much enjoyment.

After standing up to his parents and actively releasing other dark feeding relationships in his life Paul's computer crashed with the support from the invisible realm so Paul could totally release his hold on the old past energy. At the same time his vehicle stopped working so he could rest and reflect and spend some time rebuilding in the void.

His sick belly, was from Paul processing all the betrayal he became aware of. He felt betrayed by himself mostly, how could he not notice the pathology all around him? Why hadn't his soul rescued him? Why hadn't he followed and believed in his own suspicions he had all his life that, "something was rotten in the state of Denmark," just as what was said by Shakespeare in Hamlet Act 1, scene 4, 87–91 meaning the fish is rotting from the head down and all is not well at the top of the political hierarchy or at the top of Paul's family. Paul was judging himself for not seeing how dark and dangerous the people were that raised him. He was raised in a cult town and did not realize a childhood could be pleasant and supportive.

Paul's eyes are now opened and he works in concert with his soul making life much easier and joyful.

THE MORAL of the story?

Listen to your feelings and honor them, they tell the truth.

BRAVELY *own what you see and feel,* ALWAYS seek the CLARITY or larger picture. Love ALL your aspects, you are experiencing for the legion of light and there is no judgment or blame.

RELEASE your old PATTERNS to EVOLVE.

***

CHAPTER 12
LEVEL EIGHT

Level 8. **Oneness**, is the human functioning as one with their soul. This is how TWO become ONE. The soul and human are fully melded. Know the loneliness is gone now.
100% **light**.

***

The **physical, HUMAN** and **spiritual, SOUL** need to keep up the *dialogue* between them. The human needs to stop trying to figure things out for itself, with its limited awareness and ask the soul questions ALOUD. That way the soul knows exactly what the human is thinking and planning to do. Ask about the smallest and largest concern you, the human has.

Ask, breath, pause and listen. Do not try to figure it out yourself, get the larger picture of what your soul wants to share with you.

At this level we know, "WE ARE ALL ONE," Soul is hooked up with all the omniverse and you are hooked up to your soul. Own the oneness, be responsible and easy with the oneness, flow in harmony. *Feel the LACK of resistance.* Feel the power and freedom of no resistance. These are the lessons that The Abraham Group, and others have been teaching and sharing with humans.

All humans are unique but no two humans are alike. No two plants, flowers and all in nature are alike.

There are a few thousand humans on this level at this time of July 2008.

Level 8 is infinity and oneness.

***

12 STEPS on each level of MELDING with soul
FALLING INTO HARMONY

On each level of 5 through 8 are 12 steps that need to be mastered a bit more on each level. These are the same 12 steps on each level and you go deeper and deeper in any order you care to work on them.

1. Humans need to master relating to other humans without **BLAME, judgment** or **DRAMA**. Take notice of and feel the energies and multidimensions for that is YOUR true reality. The third dimension is an illusion. Listen to and feel nature, commune with this intentional community. Follow its flow and example. Know the value of life and feel how we are all connected regardless of the biology we have on. Learn the order or way of things so you can **fall into HARMONY** with them.

2. Observe and **know the cosmic order** and flow of "All That Is," so you can stay present in the flow without blame, judgment or drama. Place yourself harmoniously into the global, cosmic community, always broadening your awareness. HAVE FAITH in your infinite ability to remake yourselves and your experiences, over and over again.

3. **Connect solidly with your soul** and the invisible realm, have awareness of their presence and communication, fall into harmony and awareness with them.

4. Connect to YOURSELF know who and what you are and are NOT. **Stand in your belief's LOUD and PROUD.** Have faith in your infinite ability and joy to recreate yourself.

5. **Side by side** you walk with the legion of light, know and honor that.

6. Humans are in community with the higher angelic realms and not the third dimension, **Know you come from LOVE and are LOVE.**

7. **ALLOWING** and **knowing** is the order and flow. This awareness happens slowly and naturally INSIDE US. It can be *your voice* you hear, a SMELL or taste or the shivery feeling we get when our soul or entourage is in agreement and wanting to reinforce our direction. We can know we are feeling the *energy of compassion,* a spiritual interdimensional allowing and knowing.

8. Knowing is first and then comes action. Link THOUGHT, *dimension* and then **purpose** and a clear path emerges for you to follow. Fall into the harmony of WHAT exists.

9. **TRUST** yourself and the awareness YOU live in.

10. SELF LOVE first, you can only give what you have.

11. Compassion and Love for SELF first and then ALL else.

12. Creating and manifesting is what we DO.

Now you are seeing through all the illusions and enjoying all the pleasures of having a fine operating biology. You are enjoying your biology and doing all the things the invisible realm cannot unless they take a biology.

The invisible realm needs humans to help awaken the humans NOT awake yet. It is your choice to leave or stay and help.

And So It Is.

***

CHAPTER 13
LEVEL NINE

Level 9. **Completion**, the completion of an ERA, cycle, or LEVEL.
Level nine is the SILENCE of completeness, the end of an era.
On level 9 there is new awareness of the self and soul.
There is silence of the mind, no more chatter just peace.

***

Normally completion would signal a biological death. This time it does not mean you are done. This time it does not mean you are to die. It has not made much sense to keep dying and forgetting, dying and forgetting, most of what you know. When you are willing to stay alive when the TWO, soul and human, are ONE that goes into your DNA.

When you reproduce, your off spring will have the same DNA and level of awareness' you have. You will pass on all the knowledge and awareness you have to your child. Without physical death we can excellerate things and have a much faster evolution.

248 humans have reached level nine as of July 2008.

***

CHAPTER 14
ATLANTIS on EARTH

Many call Earth "Gaia," the land, the water, the skies. Gaia is the soul of the earth while humans were unable to hold the earth's energy. Gaia has attended to and nurtured all the elements, all of the animals and all the forests, ever since the beginning of the earth.

HUMANS are made from Gaia and Gaia loves us dearly. Gaia is slowly, slowly leaving in a balanced way and the only ones going to take over the responsibility of this planet are the humans and their human consciousness. Gaia is leaving so the humans can take responsibility for the water, the lands, and sky and for all of the plants and the animal life. Have gratitude for all Gaia has done on our behalf.

The continents and lands of the earth are designed to move in WHOLE or in part, ABOVE or **beneath the seas**. Humans have lived ABOVE, **beneath** and within different worlds. We forget things. We remember things and forget them and recreate them in a new way. The more flawed the world APPEARS the more perfect the human will make it and perfect the human in the process of remaking.

Greater tremors will becoming to rearrange the land, some over and some under the water. The cycles are well experienced and never REPEATED exactly the same way. We are clever, original and inventive.

Deep under the great ocean floor are fissures and cracks that reveal the earth within. Not wounds and do not require healing. The openings are to facilitate powerful surges of energy being release from deep within the earth. Elemental intelligence is monitoring them.

The earth is restoring itself in new ways as humans are raising their vibration and spirituality. Deciding to participate and not become the victim might be enjoyable for a change. This is a time of recreating yourself and our earth in a new way. We are the "MATTER masters". If humans do not take responsibility for earth in the dimension they live in the planet will simply go away. We are one.

***

PEACE

Peace is the ability to allow everything and everyone to be exactly as they are. Within real peace there is *no need to be right* or have a **right way** to be peaceful. The seeds of peace are a potential creation waiting to match the human vibration of peace. Little humans envision peace as everyone satisfied with no hunger or pain. On a planet of *free choice* that is NOT POSSIBLE. There is **one Earth,** as there is one you. We remake ourselves continuously in creative and endless expressions. All of our expressions are still us. TRUST in your infinite ability to remake you and your experiences.

We can be free of **MAJOR wars**.

A one world government won't work.

Humans need **different LEADERS** and governments to maintain profoundly *different ways of life*. Governments and communities will intertwine in very unique ways. Peace needs to be made of agreements to respect each others choice of HOW they want to live and exist.

No more *forcing others* from family members to countries.

There will always be disputes, hunger and situations where many need what others have. Neighbors will trade with neighbors.

Neighbors will need and depend on each other.

That will be the way of peace. Below is a review of how atlantis worked with different ways of being. I present this NOT TO COPY OR EMULATE but to see another point of perception. Increase your wisdom by seeing the patterns then and now.

The earth is crowded and full of people and places. Not a simple time.

Earth needs nourishing so that it can nourish humans. ALL need to give to receive the abundance of the earth and its humans in the **WAY it is offered.**

RECEIVE abundance in the MANNER it is OFFERED. DO not claim more than you need. Earth can house the cold, feed the hungry and drive away thirst, but it will not be controlled by the petty tyrants. Arm yourselves against danger and protect the home of the soul or all will be lost. Earth and her resources are on loan. The wealth of Gaia will redistribute itself fairly as humanity needs to do.

We left our "homes" eons ago on a mission, we volunteer to help each world we entered. Agreeing to adopt their lifestyle and ways. We teach the ways of the legion of light.

***

The information about Atlantis is taken from, Archangel Metatron through **James Tyberonn**, www.earth-keeper.com, tyberonn@earth-keeper.com, Atlantan crystals.

AT THIS TIME seventy percent of all those living on earth NOW were Atlantians. We can visit healing and old and new lessons if we choose.

Atlantis existed for over 200,000 years and they were mostly light filled. From 17,500 B.C.E. to 10,500 B.C.E. were dark with a **WEALTH of lessons.** Atlantis had a high vibrational awareness but it was not higher than NOW.

After the second deluge, Atlantis split into five islands. The three major islands were Poseida, Og and Aryan with two smaller islands under Aryan rule, were Atalya and Eyre. There were two opposing philosophies and lifestyles.

"The Sons of Belial" on the Isle of Aryan and exerted influence and political control over Og, Atalya and Eyre.

"Law of One," mostly on the Isle of which was earth's strongest vortex portal complex and housed the temple of healing, sound, regeneration, knowledge and major centers for higher learning. These were placed on Poseida because of its location in the geodesic power grids, called posers and the nucleus of the **crystalline power grid** and **INTERDIMENSIONAL tunnel system** and electromagnetic energies spiraling up from the earth's core. Crystal Energy was used all throughout Atlantis. A great crystalline satellite, the second moon of Atlantis, floated above received, amplified and reflected refined energy back to the crystals for various beneficial purposes including exerting control over weather patterns and TIDES.

A gentle race of giants, ten to twelve feet, involved in cultural, artistic and educational pursuits were the seed of Pleadean and were centered in Poseida.

Specialized energy fields were projected into agricultural and crystal growing areas to amplify and accelerate growth. Specialized energy fields created a sense of well being and invigoration for workers and students.

The temples were astonishing works of sacred geometry and stunning architecture. Many of the great temples were covered in a dome of projected **crystalline amplified light somewhat like a glowing force field**. These were various colors that glowed day and night according to the purpose of the temple complex. Some temples projected domes and fields of vibratory light and resonate sound frequencies that amplified the SENSES and **chakras**. Others amplified the receptive LEARNING abilities of the mind others facilitated multidimensional awareness, COMMUNICATION and **transport**.

The Atlantan pyramids In the golden age of Atlantis were three and four-sided depending on what they were used for. Three sided pyramids were used as antennas to draw and amplify energies and fed them into the poser grid to power homes, factories and create energy fields for various utilities. They were generally made of marble, granite and complex crystals.

TRIANGULATED PYRAMID GRID complexes were concentric. Meaning they are circles or triangles or any shapes that share the SAME center, the larger shape often surrounding the smaller ones. There were over a hundred triangulated pyramid grid complexes set up in concentric triangular patterns all over earth, establishing a grid network of **crystalline and electromagnetic energy** around earth and divided the areas of Atlantis into America, Africa, Mediterranean Europe and South America to create demographic centers. The areas of Mongolia and Tibet were also part of this complex, connected by *interdimensional LEY tunnels.*

The capital city of Poseida was called the Emerald City because of the glowing green light dome projected over it. Using Arcturian technology Atlantians rapidly grew *crystals of every structure and essence* in **underground crystal beds** of

Arkansas, Tibet and Brazil, which were Atlantan colonies, accessed through the interdimensional tunnel system.

The four-sided pyramids were TEMPLE complexes generally set on hilltops or along the coastlines to receive both *telluric and celestial energies.* The land below the hilltop was excavated to allow for the downward pyramid of the octahedron design. A diamond shape to connect energetically above and below. The crystals were a living amalgam of many crystalline forms filled with an alloy of platinum and gold and housed in temples of marble, crystalline sheets of beryl, corundum and diamond.

A highly disciplined and evolved sect of **SCIENTIST PRIESTS** called Atla-Ra, had the technical wisdom and expertise to maintain the crystal power grids. They maintained a high, pure consciousness resonant with the twelfth dimension of light and energy. They sustained higher telepathic contact with the advanced space brethren from Pleades, Arcturius, Andromeda and Sirius. They were exempt from governmental control keeping the knowledge of crystal technology largely a secret.

The vast majority of Atla-Ra were of the tall golden race, but there were also members from the bronze, white, Lemurian brown and Cetean races. At that time there were Cetean dolphin beings that walked on two legs and communicated verbally and had lungs. Both sexes were present with life spans of six to twelve thousand years. Reproduction was through regeneration of the mind and through technology of the temple of rejuvenation. Ones as Galileo, Isaac Newton, Einstein, Tesla, Edison, Marcel Vogel, Ronna Herman, Tyberonn, Oneronn and DaVinci were among the Atla-Ra, scientist priest.

ARYAN was the largest and most populated of the islands. Aryan was the **commercial center** having the largest influence on the **ECONOMY, agriculture and military**. After the second deluge the infrastructure required considerable rebuilding and in this process, the state became controlled by an elitist, affluent "white" race that gained control. The majority of the populace were from the bronze or red race. Aryan grew corrupt and power hungry interested in getting rid of the Law of One and using Atlantis's technology to control the world using crystalline energy for weapons of mass destruction.

Before the take over, genetic engineering work developed on Aryan was used to remove appendages, claws, feathers, reptilian skins and scales in the temple of purification, a specialized medical center. Tremendous genetic advances including cloning and physical limitations for betterment were used wisely.

The corrupt power structure used genetic engineering to create soldiers and a race of worker-slaves and hybrid human-animals. Some of us still carry the guilt of the things they did to others.

Literally hundreds of thousands of hybrid mutations and monstrosities were created by robotically controlling their minds with the silver head bands or "crowns" to work the fields or do the bidding of their "masters." Others had genetic lobotomies rendering them useless sexually and emotionally. Many trapped in monstrous or subintelligent androgynous human bodies still carry that horrendous pain of being imprisoned in physical embodiments, which allowed for no advanced learning or **spiritual growth** or *emotional expression*. The society of Aryan became quite dependent on them.

The creation and use of the genetically engineered servant classes led to a great rift between the Law of One and the Sons of Belial. The Sons of Belial became materialistic and ambitions loosing sight of spiritual ETHICS.

For several millennia the two ideologies never agreed.

The Poseidans were wise and gentle enough to not fight the Aryans, who outnumbered the Poseidans 3:1. Things change to a military-fascist state controlled by Aryans. The colonies, particularly in Greece and Turkey sought to break away and regional colonial wars raged on with neither side able to dominate. The Aryan wanted to use crystal energy to take control. The Poseidans retaliated by shutting down the power. The Aryans responded by stopping the food supply and manufactured goods.

Representatives from the Law of One and the Sons of Belial came together and a federation was sanctified and for several decades. The genetic slavery and crystal energy management, remained unresolved.

From within the Sons of Belial rose a charismatic leader and large militaristic legions were formed. The hybrid mutants were used to terrorize and the Aryan group were master manipulators of the media. Within a few years the wars in the Mediterranean escalated and the rebelling colonies were gaining the advantage.

Pressure mounted to use crystal beams for "national security."

The second moon of Atlantis, a massive crystalline satellite, and fire crystals came under GOVERNMENTAL control and their use altered. The crystalline satellite was an enormous unmanned sphere of brilliant engineering, approximately five miles in diameter. It amplified and controlled the various crystal beams sent from the fire, healing and energy crystals. It was a computerized macro chip that refracted and amplified refined beams of energy. A rainbow kaleidoscopic energy band of antigravity plasma swirled around the sphere, and often appeared as what you now term the aurora or northern lights.

The satellite crystal moon did not orbit the earth: it moved as programmed, self-directed, constantly shifting locations in order to perform its myriad tasks over Atlantis, Africa and the eastern seaboard of Brazil.

After the crystalline grid complex legally came under federalized Aryan control, the Belial group integrated their own technologists into the engineering group and quickly replaced key department heads with their own. The Atla-Ra attempted to block attempt to reprogram the satellite for war usage, explaining that overloading the satellite would dissipate the antigravity field that maneuvered it, and a catastrophic crash could occur. Some of the Atla-Ra were threatened and removed while others started to disappear. The satellite become a strategic defense weapon, certain it would function as programmed, and bring a quick end to the rebellion wars.

They sent destructive thermal light beams to initiate volcanic eruptions and massive earthquakes against colonies and nations refusing to cooperate (Greece and Turkey) causing great devastation. The Crystal Moon began to overload, weakening the antigravity field that kept it afloat. After several months of prolonged war use, the satellite began to erratically swerve and shift, power blackouts began to occur. Tireless attempts to correct it were unsuccessful. Most of the Atla-Ra were asked to lend support and most refused. Tyberonn and Oberonn gathered an inner group of loyalists within the Atla-Ra and Law of One to plan a circuitry disconnection and imminent relocation of the fire and energy crystals to various safe locations before the impending crash of the master satellite. This was done with the technology and assistance of those from Sirius B. The relocation of the precious crystals was very risky, and required careful planning and great secrecy. It had to be done before it crashed and without knowledge of the governing council.

The Atla-Ra knew that once the modulated motherboard of the crystal moon satellite lost its antigravity field, it would crash in a huge explosion. Its crashing would subsequently reek havoc on the major and poser energy crystals, creating catastrophic secondary explosions of a nuclear-class within hours, or days, of the crash.

The Atla-Ra and Sirians wanted to save the master crystals from destruction or further negative purpose. They understood the power required to transport them would be lost after the crash. Seven of the enormous primary crystals and two slightly smaller but incredible Arcturian crystals were relocated within the bulk transport systems of the underground tunnel system with help from Sirius B. Three huge primary crystals were relocated to the Atlantan crystal fields of Arkansas; two were relocated to the underground crystal farms of Brazil in the areas of Bahia and Mineas Gerais; one was relocated to underground chasm below Mount Shasta; and the great fire crystal was placed underground in a chasm below the Bimini Bank in the Sargasso Sea. The two sacred Acturian crystals were relocated in the chasms below the area of Tiajuanaco, Bolivia, near Lake Titicaca. All nine were put in dimensional locks, essentially powered down into energetic dormancy through the technology of the Sirians. Dozens of other master crystals were lost.

After a few months of being utilized for the thermal death ray technology, the great crystal satellite overloaded. Its antigravity cushion weakened and it crashed with the accelerated velocity of a massive comet in a horrific explosion that devastated most of Og and critically weakened the tectonic stability of the Atlantan plate, vaporizing massive sections of substrata. The great crystal satellite shattered into billions of fragmented crystalline shards, which now fill the deep trenches of the Atlantic. Massive clouds of dust and smoke erupted, hiding the sun. Waves of earthquakes and tsunamis devastated the island and sent great waves over two-thirds of Aryan. Within minutes, the remaining power stations exploded with the strength of nuclear bombs. Atlantis, the eastern coast of Brazil and the western coast of Africa were devastated with subsequent earthquakes. Panic and havoc ensued for three weeks as the remaining dry areas shook and land masses collapsed into the sea. And then in one shattering gasp, the remaining lands collapsed downward into the sea. In what became known as the great flood, the displaced seas sent dozens of enormous tsunamis that spilled over South America, Africa and Europe. It is a scene that has for many, many lifetimes plagued and darkened the memories of many of you who were indeed a part of it. Dear ones, it is time to let it go.

Events happen in the highest good **WHEN you create the highest good**. In the dramatic school of hologram reality, you cycle and recycle until you gain the wisdom. **TIME and probability** is a beautiful illusionary paradox. The golden age of Atlantis is actually our future we think is our past.

MOVE ahead 12,500 years to the Atlantan colony we call Arkansas. Arkansas chosen to house three major mega crystals because it was already a crystal mining and harvest area. One of the primary interdimensional tunnels from Poseida is already established and transport complexes are available to transport the crystals to the area. The Atlantians had developed techniques that allowed for highly accelerated growth of crystals and pre existing deep caverns existed that would be quite out of the reach of mining concerns. It was understood that the vortex in place in the area of Arkansas would play a major role in the 2012 planetary ascension.

Arkansas's unique geology of quartz, diamonds, magnetic lodestone, iron, limestone and massive caverns made it the perfect incubator for the crystalline plantations. Crystals had been planted and grown in Arkansas for thousand of years before the deluge. A very benevolent colony of the blue-skinned Lemurians exist underground in Arkansas, as well as an underground base of Sirians. The two were in agreement to be caretakers for the sleeping crystals. Now, the three crystals placed in Arkansas are preprogrammed to a network-grid that axialtonally connects to the remaining five enormous master crystals placed in Brazil, Shasta and Bimini, and the two exquisite wisdom crystals placed under Lake Titicaca. These are specialized healing, wisdom, energy and transport crystals, used in the temple of healing, the temple of sound and light, the temple of knowledge, the temple of one, the temple of Thoth, the ruby temple of fire and the temple of regeneration. The crystals were specifically placed in areas of supreme importance for the new earth emerging in the 2012 Ascension. Areas that were easily accessed through the **Atlantan interdimensional tunnel system**, that would emerge as mega vortex infinity points in your current times. These are defined, located and placed with activation dates as follows:

Arkansas: Blue Crystal of Knowledge (Interface), August 8, 2008; Emerald Crystal of Healing, September 9 2009; Platinum Crystal of Communication (Bio Plasmic

Interface), November 11, 2011

Bimini Bank: The Ruby Fire Crystal of Energy, December 12, 2012

Brazil: Gold Crystal of Healing Regeneration, September 9, 2009; Violet Crystal of Sound, October 10, 2010

Mount Shasta: The Crystal of Multidimensional Interface, September 9, 2009

Tiajuanaco-Lake Titicaca, Bolivia: Sun-Moon Crystal of Light, September 9, 2009; Crystal of Thoth, December 12, 2012

Each opens on the triple date portals. Each will be tied to the activation of the four. None moves into full strength before 2012. Only the **BLUE knowledge crystal**, the **EMERALD healing crystal** and the *Sun-Moon crystal* will be at full power by 2012. They will awaken, reboot with new downloads and reprogramming. They will network with the quantum crystalline frequency of ascension. These are the new patterns or blueprints for our DNA. The effects will be subtle and a greater sense of well being.

You MUST have **enough light to ABSORB this frequency**. Arkansas, will open our ability to perceive our star brethren that have always been present. The Atlantan crystals will open the dimensional portals that will allow us to interface with the invisible realm. We are the Sirians, the Pleadeans, the Arcturians and much more. We are the multidimensional sparks of the legion of light.

The gate opens in 2008 to the crystalline vortex of Arkansas. Those who connect to the blue crystal will be able to experience their multidimensionality, joyously and easily in time. As your vibration increases their is a greater facility than we have known for eons.

***

CHAPTER 15
FEELING and HEALING

Review of dates for ALL HUMANS on earth.
1987—2012 oneness and higher vibration for earth.

1987—1993 we received **NEW** *spiritual guidance.*

1994—1999 ASSIMILATED the spiritual concepts mentally.

2000—2006 clearing the emotional level or body.
Including the heart as of 2004.

2007- 2012 the last five-six years of the shift our bodies are *clearing on the **physical** level.* We are feeling pressure on the lower chakras. The *legs are heavy* and the energetic connections are not as quick or easily accessible as they once were. The biology feels the need to release pressure. We are feeling poorly, are tired, and our focus wanders. Chronic aches and pains are flaring up. Our reality seems to be getting heavier and denser, we are clearing the patterns of illness from our ***electromagnetic fields.***

***

BIOLOGY and DNA by KRYON

The human biology is not designed to communicate with the human, except through pain. Our biology is a one-dimensional aspect we were given early in this game so we could survive, keep it alive. So we would know if it got frost bit or injured or had a physical wound. Pain is one of our greatest gifts to keep the biology alive. But it is a one way communication. You can't ask questions.

Cancer is something your body develops through **irritation and unbalance**. A runaway growth you are unaware of until the body decides to give you pain and often then it's too late at that point to do much.

We have always been able to go to certain levels of our biology to see what is happening inside but few do it. Kinesiology has bridged that gap of communication, but few use it. Something that has been proven over time to allow the body to speak to you directly, bypassing the brain.

Every piece of DNA has a field around it and is next to another piece of DNA, and a field surrounds a field surrounds a field creating a oneness of consciousness. It is all grouped, not strung out as humans draw it. A oneness of trillions of pieces and a quantumness of reality. An interlocking, overlapping interdimensional field.

It is a whole body experience when you speak to your biology. You are addressing it all at once because it listens all at once. By the time you get trillions of overlapping fields together with focus you get light. You can speak to your cells and they are listening. Complete communications in an interdimensional way with our massive DNA field. Every piece of the body is enlightened and waits for you to speak to it through your own consciousness, address your cellular structure all at once to start changing it.

In this new energy we can begin to do interdimensional healing. Perhaps a total healing would be for you to do both 3D and interdimensional healing. The divinity within our cells are waiting for commitment by the human to keep their biology.

One way to heal is to rewind time to before you had an illness. That way your cells never had a problem.

Part of our spiritual karma has to do with genealogy. There are predispositions built into our genes, created by our DNA that are weaknesses having a propensity for a disease. A man who has the disease often had a father who had the same disease, knowing his children may get the same disease, and their children. A predisposed genetic flaw creating a lineage of early death, challenge and sorrow.

When we heal our self of a major disease, the genetic flaw that created the issue with all your relatives will disappear within you and within your existing children and go away. Your DNA will change, and spiritually the cycle will end with you. The action of the one can change the karmic attributes of the many. It's about how light can be created by one, yet light up an entire room of people. It's not about healing the children. It's about changing their karmic disposition and what you do with your own DNA sends a signal to their DNA.

We are all connected.

There is no such thing as a past life. We have PARALLEL lives with our existing life. We are able to stop the karmic progression of the next generation and the next by what you do NOW. Within our DNA are interdimensional aspects. Soul doesn't see you being born and then dying, and then being born and then dying. Soul sees you all the time as an angelic piece of the legion of light. Soul sees the magnificent one who can change the very fabric of an entire karmic group.

***

Our SENSORY AWARENESS is basically the way the human allows the biology to heal itself. The mind CAN NOT do it.

Our BIOLOGY is an aspect of our larger self and wants to serve you. Every energy wants to serve us, but when the little human gets too distracted with the third dimensional energy it can't heal or serve.

HEALING is not linear or time dependent.

Find the synchronicity that works the system for you.

Everyone sees change as scary. But to arrive at a NEW solution MEANS change MUST happen.

IMMUNE SYSTEM TO THYMUS

Our immune system of opposition and fighting will be changing to the **thymus** which will absorb and transmuter invaders, embrace and meld with them. In human anatomy, the thymus is an organ located in the upper anterior portion of the chest cavity just behind the sternum. Hormones produced by this organ stimulate the production of certain infection-fighting cells. It is of central importance in the maturation of our T cells.

CRYSTALLINE bones and muscles.

Our carbon based biology of muscles and bones are being slowly replaced into crystalline muscles and bones which are lighter and more durable and a bit more invisible.

CHAKRAS

All seven chakras are melding into one large chakra at the heart surrounding the body because the light body or crystalline biology can hold all the energy now. Orgasm is the highest level of divine energy that the human biology can contain without damage. Now we are expanding our awareness into our true size. We will see that the only way to truly function is with ALL OF OUR LAYERS doing everything in balance, all the time.

GENETIC ENGINEERING OF FOOD

Manipulating the genetics of our food is a cheap substitute for encouraging the energy of the seed in the ground. There is plenty of food to feed the world. So don't buy into that manipulation.

Many are being affected by biological and chemical pollutants they are not even aware of. Man-made toxins clog up our bodies and speed up the aging process. These toxins can damage our lungs and suppress our immune system. All the preservatives, flavor enhancers, colorants and other chemicals are toxic. Add to that all the artificial scents, cleaning solvents and beauty products filling our environment and water supply. Some countries feed their unsuspecting population genetically altered grains, causing a sharp rise in allergies to many common foods that never caused problems before.

Our body eventually gets overloaded with toxins the biology does not **recognize**, PROCESS or release. Add air and water pollution from toxic dumps leaching into our water tables and our bodies are being exposed to more toxins than at any other time in history. Be more aware of what you put INTO, on and *around your body*.

Listen better to what your biology says to you.

Remember, only your mental layer speaks English.

Our other layers give HUMANS sensory awareness. Our "intuition", is really our auric layers communicating with us. As we grow into our auras we expand into communion with our entire electromagnetic structure. And there is much housecleaning to do. There is a lot of "gunk" build up.

Many have found great relief in natural detoxifying processes, especially if you have suddenly developed allergies or asthma, also an allergic reaction whether to an outside agent or from **YOUR internal stress**. Start keeping track of where you were and what you ate each time you get sick. You may find the culprit to be easily remedied by honoring your body's signals and changing your diet.

Faulty belief systems is a big barrier to healing because our biology follows our beliefs. Feel joy and gratitude for all you DO HAVE to clear your mind of looping negative thoughts that DEPRESS your BIOLOGY. We create what we focus on and our TOTAL BEING vibrates on the level we THINK and FEEL at.

AT ALL times it is our creation and choice.

GAS and OIL

We will get off of gasoline and oil in this lifetime. There are so many new fuel energy concepts just waiting to come in. One more change to adjust to and it is a good thing.

***

There are those that enjoy a good wallow in the darkness loving their drama, persecution and victimhood. THEY chose that and are not available for healing at this time. You can't heal those that don't want to be healed. All you can do is shine your light as they walk their path and experience their experience. Allow their lesson to go down as they wish their lesson to proceed.

Humanity in general is starting to SENSE the shift happening.

Healers do not HEAL, they BALANCE. True healing is facilitation for self-balance and self-empowerment.

We cannot give and teach what we don't truly know.

Being real is being wide-open and honest. Speaking our truth, walking our talk and living our love. We just live there all the time.

***

CHAPTER 16
LAWS of the UNIVERSE
a few of them

The Universal Laws are all interrelated and multidimensional. There is no first or last. Everything in the universe is energy. Understanding the universals laws help us to create our realities as we learn to control our *thoughts and emotions.*

LAW OF ENTRAINMENT

The law of entrainment requires two resonance's existing in the same location MUST adjust and combine. On a scale of 1-10 if one individual or object is at a 3 the other is at a 7 the law of entrainment requires they are both at the level 5. Unless one is an overpowering resonance and pulls the other to their level.

You carrying someone else's dark energy can postponed your ascension by holding you in a negative range. Return any darkness you carry for another so they can transmute it to another useful energy. Learn what you can from that experience, forgive both of you and grieve the loss of the entrainment. *It will alter you.*

We are a gigantic energetic creature. Every thought we have creates energetic ripples. The rising energies on Gaia are forcing us to clear and purify all of our four bodies. The toxins or any illness patterns and our emotional and mental blockages are all low density imbalances rising up at this time to be cleared. Drink plenty of water to flush out cellular debris. We are clearing out low density energy damage normal for us to be carrying in third dimension energy.

Our body anchors our energetic layers that fan out in ever-widening circles of vibrating frequency. Our auras touch each other at six feet from the biology. That is why it makes us feel uncomfortable when a stranger stands too close. They are standing in our dense etheric bodies of emotion, mental and spiritual energies. As our auras become more sensitive it can become downright painful to have a disgruntled or unpleasant energy in your spiritual, mental or emotional space. Our energetic bodies grow more dense and real to humans as they connect to higher frequencies.

LAW OF ACTION

The law of action says you must **ACT** in order for something you want to start moving in the direction you want it to move. Others join you after you make the first move.

LAW OF ALLOWING

The law of allowing is the state of the human aligning with their soul and the soul's feeling of well being so their vibration is high enough to receive what they asked for. When you are in a state of allowing you always feel good just as your soul always feels good because it is in the universal flow.

Allowing means dropping ALL judgments and ALL EMOTIONAL attachments to what others are, have or do. This is quite different from being tolerant which is not liking what someone else is or does and you *holding negative thoughts* about it but let them be or do it anyway. Practicing The Universal Law of Allowing requires granting others the right to be, have and do whatever THEY choose.

LAW OF ATTRACTION
YOUR SIGNATURE

In every moment our "resonant signature," the dominant energy of our aura matches frequencies to keep us on the path we are on. No thought is required and this match up will continue ad infinitum with thoughtless indifference to what the human may wish, with great efficiency. Dramas of the third dimensional kind have played and replayed themselves AD NAUSEAM. We build our resonant signature with every thought we think and every belief we hold. Our emotions keep it all glued together. Our emotional reactions let everyone know our beliefs. Emotions always speak the truth. Even to those that lie to themselves.

EMOTIONS

Your emotions, even the negative ones, do not judge or analyze they simply reflect with clarity and truth what you are holding in your energy field. When you are easily angered, you are still probably angry about a childhood event. Ask your soul or angel to show you what it is. Releasing that past rage releases the current angers.

BELIEF SYSTEMS

Beliefs are formed by the repeated thoughts that dwell in us WITHOUT our conscious awareness of them, most of the time, feeding your resonance with a constant flow of energy or vibration.

-Beliefs we have adopted and picked up telepathically since birth.

-Conflicting beliefs we get about the self at home and in school.

-The lies, secrets and deceptions of our homes and community.

Conflicting beliefs result in CONFUSION, stress and a lower vibrational resonant signature resulting in future lower frequency. The conflicting inappropriate beliefs vibrate as your reality because the unconscious mind believes all that it hears. *No sorting goes on* UNLESS you become consciously aware of your beliefs and choose to RETAIN or **release them**.

Knowing YOUR personal belief's enables you to own them. That is why I go back to the childhood over and over again because, that is the origin of most of the belief's that trip up the adult. Knowing and feeling your childhood trauma cleans up the nutty belief's in a hurry. Your soul or angel, using synchronicity, will bring you awareness of what belief you need to address next so you can consciously live in truth. The truth of who you are and what frequencies your resonant. Our natural state is being creative and expansive.

In the quiet practice of nonresistance the seeds of wisdom from our soul are planted within us.

The universe does not care if your thoughts and emotions are REAL or **imagined.** The law of attraction is as active on earth as anywhere else in the Universe. Everything that happens to you in any given day is based on this law of attraction.

Many humans understanding of this law is that it is for the LITTLE HUMAN to amuse itself with. When you reduce the law of attraction to an EXTREMELY small limited thing or toys like a car or house or money. The human self is saying, **MY NEEDS** and my need for **grandiosity come first** and are more important than soul. Soul gets pushed aside and you miss the entire SPIRITUAL POINT and YOUR ENLIGHTENMENT when the human is allowed priority.

LEVELS OF COMPASSION

You already have **ALL YOU NEED in the moment** and don't realize it.

If you have tried to WORK the law of attraction you know it generally doesn't work very well because all sorts of higher vibrational behavior needs to be in place for it to work. Generally the higher vibrational behaviors are not in place when you are not in alignment with your soul. Your soul never wants toys and status symbols to make you feel important and valued. Worrying about the right words to use or saying it just right does not matter. You need to have control over your thought and emotions. You need to be in integrity and able to focus. You need to be compassionate and nonjudgmental.

In the true energy of the law of attraction you do not concern yourself with **superficial cravings** because they take *CARE OF THEMSELVES.* The Law of Attraction is really about the ATTRACTION of your SOUL. The attraction of the *needs and desires of the expression of consciousness.* Whatever you ask for look around and you will see it is ALREADY THERE.

Your *consciousness* takes precedence over everything. The human is only TEMPORARY and **never designed to rule**. Consciousness needs are rather simple only to EXPAND and EXPRESS over and over again. Through expression **the soul celebrates life in a human body** or on the nonphysical realms. *Refresh your soul* by having gratitude for all *you are and have ever been* and will ever be. Live with a THANKFUL HEART. Even the darker spaces helped you grow. Earth is the toughest school in the universe.

The law of attraction is not a law on this level **it is a law on the level of our soul self**. Your soul self can manifest whatever. On the third dimensional level the law of attraction helps to open up the mind and body connection. As many have noticed they have focused their intention on piles of money and it does not come. The difficulty with little humans is wanting something more than you have in the present. Invisible realm uses the law of attraction to experience **changing our thoughts** and not to try to force something to happen. Forcing something to happen does not allow us to ACCEPT **ourselves as we are NOW**. The truth is we are infinite beings and are infinitely abundant in every way. Infinite in love. What prevents our manifesting is our limiting beliefs and inability to appreciate what we have in the now moment.

There will be some people who follow the rules of the law of attraction and attract to them what they want. Not really attract that was what had already been planned.

LAW OF BALANCE

The Law of Balance means maintaining order within the divine universe. Each entity makes the choice to exist. When those choices are made in synchronicity with the flow of other entities and events, balance is maintained. Humans are part human and part spiritual being. We need to ACCEPT those traits we see in ourselves as not spiritual. That is who we are. How do you ignore part of yourself. Address the part you don't care for and change it. Accept the human traits you have within your being. They are as important as the spiritual gifts you are trying to attain. We are balancing spiritual energy to physical matter. The ultimate goal of all life is to maintain a harmonious balance.

LAW OF LOVE or DIVINE ONENESS

The law of love all things exist within this law and are created out of it. Love is total and complete acceptance of what is. Love allows. Without the law of love free will could not exist. Free will does not come in portions you either have it or you do not have it. The Universe is a place of creation and experience.

The law of divine oneness we live in a world where everything is connected to everything else. Everything we think and feel affects the whole universe around us.

LAW OF CAUSE AND EFFECT

The Law of Cause and Effect says nothing happens by chance or outside the universal laws. Every action has a reaction or consequence.

LAW OF PERPETUAL TRANSMUTATION OF ENERGY

The law of perpetual transmutation of energy all humans have the power to change the conditions in their lives.

LAW OF COMPENSATION

The law of COMPENSATION We do NOT RECEIVE in the exact manner and time we choose but the invisible realm works in its own way and time. There is no service lovingly and willingly rendered that ever goes without reward. The reward seldom comes from the source to which the service was given. Be a gracious receiver of what ever you get.

We demonstrate the exact EQUIVALENT of our ability to RECEIVE. There is no limit to compensation. The only limitation is THE ONE WE CREATE through refusal to use what we have or an inability to accept what we are lovingly given.

The law is that—AS WE THINK, SPEAK AND ACT, WE RECEIVE.

***

CHAPTER 17
MASTER NUMBERS

Master Numbers are **TRIGGERS** that appear in our reality.
One is the singular **I AM** that I am vibration.
OM vibration is the unity consciousness as expressed in the third dimension. Oneness is what we are returning to. One is infinite and contains all things and the beginning.

11:11 is the *trigger to our DNA to start reconnecting.* ACTIVATING the shift from duality into oneness. The **portal** or bridge to ascension and our doorway home has opened once again on this planet. Humanity has twenty years to pass through the eleven gates to oneness.

11:11 the activation runs from January 11,1992 to 2012. The two sets of two ones signify the first reality traveling THROUGH to the second reality.

Polarity has allowed the infinite to study itself as finite. Polarity has enabled us to experience individuality and aloneness and receive energy imprints which have been necessary to play out our illusion or conduct our research to increase our spiritual awareness.

12:12 is a trigger to our biology that we are emerging from the second dimension into the third dimension "two sets of threes." The date 12/12/12, we are not ALL going to ascend for it is happening now.

02-02-02 humans noticed the first shift of the NEW energy.

03-03-03 the magnetic grids were fully in place and ready to move to the next level.

333 in the third dimension moving into the second part where all are three's and has not finished playing out just yet. We played so long in the third dimension that it is entering a third stage or the third millennium. Steps have been taken that never had been taken before. Different choices have **opened** us into the UNKNOWN.

Our entire existence can be explained by dividing by threes, the triangular shape defining the third dimension. Three is the base number for CREATION as all things are based on the **TRIAD**. The trinity will have a deeper meaning as we move into our next phase of evolution.

444 mastery and empowerment of the **SELF** a representation of the *fourth dimension seen from the third dimension*. Our relationship to everything is changing and this is representative of this movement.

04-04-04 all the portals were firmly in place on earth. The crystal energy has been filtering in through the sun to be stored in the tectonic plates of earth. Our biology and the atmosphere itself has been adjusting to the new energy. But there is much more energy stored in the tectonic plates of earth that we have not been able to adjust yet.

555 triple five is a trigger that our biology is ready to receive our divinity.

"555" being noticed on our clock faces to symbolize the fifth dimension and the threes are not yet finished. 05-05-05 was Cinco de Mayo.

LEVELS OF COMPASSION

555 is the beginning of the fifth dimension. The fifth dimension was being created in the land of Atlantis and during that time humans chose to see LACK, limitation and CONTROL. The not so subtle expression of **slavery** and GREED came to our greatly "advanced" planet of free choice. That misdirection of energy has showed up many other times including now. We felt the need to decide who could use the technology and who COULD NOT.

There was enough for all if we acknowledged everyone was playing important parts and contributing to the whole. The effects of our misdirection's in Atlantis are here now unrelenting warning and challenging our movement forward into the fifth dimension. That is why the word was handed down that WE ALL move forward or no one does.

All are playing important parts on the ladder of human advancement. And all will not advance until all rungs of the ladder are filled. "Spiritual competition" is one of the most destructive ways to misdirect energy. For example do you believe seeing the numbers 555 means that you are more advanced that those seeing 11:11?

Our biology needs different signals at different times so the number triggers will NOT appear in **LINEAR fashion** there are many *circles on circles* and then you will repeat cycles more than once. There is no order of importance so please do not attempt to apply human attributes and linear time to the workings of our sweet invisible realm.

Make life choices without spiritual competition and judgment, DISCERNMENT is the only way to go. Find one small success that impresses YOU and build on it. Find one thing that you absolutely adore about yourself and build on that it will serve you well.

666 or six, six, six, the human sign for the devil is humorous to the invisible realm because we doubled threes. And humans are a manifestation of God in finite form.

6-6-6 is the perfect alignment of COMPLETION.

Each 6 represents an important aspect of our body, mind and spirit. When these come into full alignment it signifies the end of an old cycle and the beginning of a new cycle.

666 could be evil if you try to control others OR you FEAR YOURSELF and your evolvement. Do you fear your awareness? You will go into fear because you are fearing the beast that is within you.

6-6-6 the alignment of these three numbers and you in balance means you are being real and true with yourself. You are in perfect alignment to move to the next level. Much as when you see the triple seven or any of these very interesting different numerological alignments.

Which 666 do you choose?

07-07-07 ring your chimes seven times and take a breath with each ring of the chime. It is your reminder to your wonderful self and acknowledgment of the now moment. This time of our own alignment, balance and completion of a cycle and the start of a new one.

When numbers align like 9-9, 4-4, the alignments are also a type of wink or nod from your soul to you. Saying it is nice that you are recognizing alignments and the synchronicities in your life. You see you are in alignment with yourself following the path of your highest potentials.

The 9:11 combo. the numerological message? It is: The end of the old, into the illumination of the new. That's what it's about.

(9) and a one (1) together. Indeed this combination happens every decade, but this is the first occurrence. It is the first one within the generation of the 2012 transition! All of this should have been flagged for you. You should have looked at it very carefully and said: "What might happen when you're going from 2007, which is a *nine* (9), to 2008, which is a *one* (1)?" Nine represents "completion" and one represents "New beginnings." Wouldn't you think it means something?

Five is change! What is the numerological value of 2012? It's also five (5). Just think: change/change. fresh and clean. It is not an upgrade. It does not take an old energy and add to it. That is linear.

Humans expect linear change. Soul does not work that way. The energy is interdimensional and spiritual in nature. The transition between 2007 and 2008 is a transition that is numerological from nine to one. The nine and the one together, back to back, create a situation that only happens each decade. But this is the first time it has happened in this millennium and it is the last time before 2012.

2008 is new beginnings things being replaced and enhanced. There are new tools. The earth is shifting. **The few have decided** for everyone on this planet that the vibration of planet earth, will rise from the third dimension to the fifth dimension. The point of **NO RETURN** has already been passed.

2012 with mark the time of "zero point energy" and the movement from magnetic energy to crystalline energy. The magnetic energy pull is weakening and will stop for three days around 2012 and then the magnetic poles of north and south will shift directions as they have shifted five times before.

The planet is on the path to a simpler, more spiritual way of life. Your choices need to be made in that framework or you will be most frustrated.

Five is change! What is the numerological value of 2012? It's also five (5). Just think: change/change. Prepare for shift. There will be no significant spiritual happening in 2012, only the celebration that tells us, we have arrived. The slow development of peace on earth, a consciousness of compromise. Don't pay attention to the news. They are going to bring you the worst of the worst. They won't tell you about those trying to build peace outside of the government. They won't tell you that there are hundreds of thousands of them on both sides of the issue who are coming together right now.

The integrity of the legion of light always shouts its love for humanity, is noncompetitive, acceptance for every single human who listens, without judgment. The energy of the legion of light is not compartmentalized or structured into a doctrine other than only give and receive love.

***

CHAPTER 18
A through D words and concepts

Many of the definitions in my books are multidimensional. In the third single dimension words like **VIBRATION**, frequency, **tone**, EMOTION and **FEELING** all have a different definition based on the single dimension scientific theories.

In multidimensions and the laws of the universe the words *tone, emotion, vibration, frequency and feeling* all mean roughly, the same thing. Because when you have one of those the others will be present along with a COLOR and a LIGHT.

FOR EXAMPLE

If you are depressed you feel low which makes a deeper DULL sound and a muddy blue color, you are vibrating slowly and your light is very low making you feel like do do.

***

<u>ABUNDANCE</u> is sustenance.

Poverty and abundance are the same thing. Abundance comes when you are alone with yourself and acknowledge your divinity. When you open your heart and realize that **everything is COMPLETE in the** now **MOMENT**.

The NOW moment is filled with HEALING and WISDOM and compassion. Abundance is all about your *soul's desire* to have its love energy in motion doing something. Live life for what it is in the moment.

Avoid dwelling on anything you do not have as you can create whatever you want. It is easier to create something new than it is to fix something that already exists.

Abundance is rather secondary to everything else. Abundance is a by product of living in the moment with your soul *MOVING ENERGY* having fun and feeling good.

Wealth is not the accumulation of money. It is the gathering of RESOURCES and WISDOM. Where your soul and matter are well balanced, there is no difference between spiritual wealth and monetary wealth.

ACKNOWLEDGMENT Something said or done to inform another that their statement or action has been noted understood and received. This does not necessarily imply an approval or disapproval or any other thing beyond the knowledge that an action or statement is observed and received.

ACTION, Law of you must ACT in order for something you want to start moving.

ACTIVE PATIENCE To achieve **active patience** stop trying to see what you can see. SEE nothing in the UNDEFINABLE places of "no definition" keep relaxed and let go remain holographic. You cannot use your WILL to see the future. Trust that the answers will be there as the need arises. They are so subtle even the most enlightened could miss them. As you are in that undefinable stillness your ears become attuned and you can hear the truth maybe not in words. The truth might be a song or tone. Not a word at first. The energy to accomplishment is there too.

ADDICTION In sacred geometry, addiction is a square of you taking in a substance or behavior, something YOU might decide is addictive. That square is sitting inside a larger square of belief. YOU *believe* you are trapped and can't get out because "it" controls you. "IT" is YOU not taking responsibility for yourself.

During Atlantis, we built electrical grids of pleasure in the body, mind and emotions to get us to stay in our biology. Our bodies are very much a part of us now. It is very stressful to be in biology and as things go faster and keep changing we get more stressed and seek more pleasure. Addictions are in reality an extreme sensitivity to those grids of pleasure and not a sign of weakness. Addiction is a BELIEF SYSTEM many people are addicted to things like suffering or depression.

Chocolate and breathing has a soft effect on our pleasure system, sex has the most profound effect. Our pleasure centers can be shut down by not using them along with turning on our joy in life. The breath is very helpful in making the switch from pleasure to joy.

AFFINITY the feeling of love or liking for something or someone or something. The phenomena of space and the willingness to occupy the same space as the thing which is loved or liked. A good feeling a type on energy that can be produced at will.

AKASHIC RECORD is the record of all the angelic souls who would come and go within the human body. The records are kept in crystals in the cave of creation. Each time an angel came into biology to be a Lemurian the essence of their energy would then be placed into a crystal with their name on it. The crystal would go into the cave of creation implanted with the energy of 350 million souls.

ALLOWING is the state of alignment with the feeling of well being emanating from the legion of light. When you are in a state of allowing you always feel good.

ALLOWING, law of means dropping ALL judgments and ALL EMOTIONAL attachments to what others are, have or do. This is quite different from being tolerant which is not liking what someone else is or does and you *holding negative thoughts* about it but let them be or do it anyway. Practicing The Universal Law of Allowing requires granting others the right to be, have and do whatever THEY choose.

ALZHEIMER'S has to do with the process of interdimensionality and walking between the worlds. A certain desire to expand and explore some of the other realms. Sometimes that causes grief for those in the third dimension. When they are in the Alzheimer's mode they appear to be forgetful but are actually traveling inter-dimensionally having a wonderful time testing the other dimensions. Sometimes they go back into the near Earth realms to explore what it's going to be like when they do cross over. It is a type of consciousness affliction that's happening right now. They are also some of the pioneers who are venturing out Multidimensionally while still in the body. Don't look at this as a negative thing.

When you go visit you could join in the interdimensional or the expanded consciousness mode with them. Now they have a friend to go on the journey with. Visit when you feel it in your heart. Don't talk to them like they're idiots or stupid. Join them in the multidimensional experience but do it a little different. Stay very present in your body and breathe be in the now moment and expand your energy to meet theirs. Go on a trip with them. Generally they're going out of their body leaving the Now moment taking little side trips. That's will let them know you can expand and be multidimensional and still be totally in the now.

ANGELS work with us through grace and help us stay alive. Generally they have not been human and are not blessed with emotions as we are. They are objective and paint pictures in a positive light. Angels certainly see the positive side of all situations and are kind and gracious and exceedingly patient. The bottom line is you must go within yourself and discern what is true for you and rely on no one else's judgment but your own, not even the angels.

ANGER is natural and at the deepest part of us. Anger covers hurt, frustration, and fear and helps one avoid feeling pain. Anger helps to move energy and release old stuck energy. True anger is HOLDING hate in one intense spot. When you move the hate a little above or below the emotion dissipate.

ANTAGONISM a feeling of irritation and annoyance caused by the advances of others. Antagonism can be used to suppress and intimidate another.

ANUNNAKI are playing their part in Gaia's ascension process. They are playing the darkest of the dark energy of separation and we have agreed to assist them on their journey back to the legion of light. They cannot access information as we can when we open to love and light. They only have low level truths.

LEVELS OF INFORMATION are **restricted by the vibration** of our emotional body.

When you know the game anunnaki play and understand the rules you can have a some fun. A fine line is being walked by the anunnaki. They push agendas that will prevent reconnection with the earth energetically. They use fear and a **FALSE sense of action**. They want expansion of nuclear programs. In third dimension this is not healthy or in harmony with humans. They have not learned to live in balance with a celestial body. A lesson humans will teach them.

APATHY is withdrawal and no real attempt to contact the self or others. They are docile and obedient. A null point of dissonance on the threshold of death, it imitates death.

ARMAGEDDON was scheduled for 1999 to 2001 and it came and went. Against all odds and all prophesy, countries who were powerful players of the end time scenario changed greatly.

ASCENDEE Imagine all the lifetimes you have lived are in a circle around you and they have designated you in this lifetime to be the "ascendee" for all of them the "healee" for all of them. As you heal and ascend you rewrite your perception of the history of every past life you have ever had. We are clearing across the lines of time, seven generations back and seven generations forward. All time is now and all of your ancestors across all time, thank you for your efforts. Once you clear enough fear out of your bodies, this will indeed ripple through the tapestry of time. At the DNA level we are clearing away all old, inherited limiting beliefs, plus clearing the trauma pattern to your body blueprint that records all of your physical lives and deaths.

LEVELS OF COMPASSION

Is an individual that is fulfilled at the soul level and no longer seeking to complete the self with someone or something else. You 10%er and your soul 90%er ARE complete. You have gone through a period of letting go, releasing, getting sick, losing jobs and homes so you can stand firmly in the new energy as a fulfilled BEING.

You can and might ALSO be the designated ascendee for all your ancestors on both sides of your family to heal and ascend them.

<u>ASCENSION</u> is the human, **with FREE choice** moving into the next lifetime without biologic death. Moving to the NEXT LEVEL of spiritual awareness and wisdom in the same biology. This can and does happen to humans choosing this path over and over again. With each ascension the human releases MORE of the little human FEAR, **agenda**, BLAME, doubt, **judgment** and 3D. We release the contracts, karma and vows of the human living in duality. Ascension is the ENERGY of the masters in an **interdimensional state** who told you that you could be just like them, seeing things through the awareness of their soul. Giving your energy (power) away to NO ONE else and we becoming sovereign. Ascended leave a trail of light wherever they walk. They look into the eyes of fear and it goes away. They carry the calmness and the peace of the legion of light in every situation and are slow to anger, and quick to act on wisdom.

We move from who we THOUGHT we were to *NO identity*, by going through "spiritual depression" and voids to embrace an ever EXPANDING multidimensional identity. At times the process causes MUCH sadness and doubt because it is SO new and different. We grieve for the human we thought we were. Literally it is an ascension of the Akashic Record, going beyond 3D, time and reason.

A state of GRACE, ascension is, and reached through clearing and balancing all of our bodies the physical, emotional, mental and spiritual. When we choose to ascend our free will is released for divine will and we become a divine human working with our soul. Some let go of their soul and grab the little human back frequently and the soul waits. Waffling can put you back in duality and 3D.

The **entire solar system** is ascending along with the planetary ascension. The entire quadrant is ascending and catapulting its effect on all that is. Which is the legion of light's plan of expansion and growth. The legion of light is creation and all of its creation is ever expanding and growing.

ASPECTOLOGY is understanding and being aware of the huge number of aspects a souled being has. As a creator we make aspects of ourselves to go out and experience things on our behalf. Soul is always discovering itself by creating aspects and identities of itself, blessing them and giving them their freedom to do as they wish and then they in turn create aspects of the aspect, of the aspects. When we release theses aspect they do as they wish generally or you can control them to do your bidding which is a dark game. **THE CALL HAS GONE OUT** for our **ASPECTS** and **PIECES**.

We also have aspects in this life or what we call roles, like child, worker or parent. Aspects from past lives, multidimensional realities and dreams. The aspects can move in and out of our consciousness depending when we want them or need them. Many layers and levels along with negative intent can also cause chaos, dissociative identity disorder or schizophrenia or depression. Aspects are SPIRITUAL and **energetic**.

ATLANTIS or ALT existed for thousands of years. Shaumbra worked in the temples of Tien (present day Cuba). They were scientists doing energy and healing work. They lived in two dimensions one of which was invisible.

During the end of the time of Atlantis a mean spirited ruler took over, Azure Tamu (blue hues to his skin) "all mighty" (many times worse than Hitler) took over and tortured people physically. Tamu also used mental abuse, a metal band placed around the head to control people and implants were used as a form of government programming. He tore apart families and eventually unbalanced the planet to the point of destruction. Very approximately 15,000 to 11,000 B.C.

ATTENTION is when an interest becomes fixed. A motion that must stay at an optimum effort.

ATTRACTION, Law of says our feelings or emotions and thoughts produce a vibrational energy which attracts THE SAME vibrational energies to us that we put out. We get back more of the same energy that we project consciously or unconsciously. The universe does not care if your thoughts and emotions are real or imagined.

AWAKEN is awareness of our spirituality that we are soul pretending to be human. Those that are unawakened think they are victims instead of creators.

BALANCE of the PRACTICAL with the SPIRITUAL gives us far more understanding of how things can turn around and eventually work. Our DNA is now able to go beyond the RESTRICTIONS placed there by **ages of dark energy** and INACTIVITY. Our DNA is now able to revert to the Lemurian "time-stamp."

With EMOTIONAL and RATIONAL stability and calm or discernment is accurate.

Unbalanced sexual energy in humans gets TWISTED, dark and **depressed.** Then we go feeding because we have been fed on. This inappropriately used sexual energy is a method of stealing energy from others and ENTRAPPING, **manipulating** and CONTROLLING them. When we **repress or deny** this UNBALANCED energy it builds a force this energy would NOT normally have. Let unbalanced sexual energy FLOW through you and release your belief systems around it.

<u>**BEING**</u> one is as they are able to assume viewpoints or an energy production source. The emotion of shame comes into play when a being feels ashamed to be oneself so while in one body they function in another body.

<u>**BEINGNESS**</u> the identification of self with an object or choosing an identity. The person one should be in order to survive. A soul interacting with matter.

<u>**BELIEF**</u> is an **electromagnetic** wave form. Our beliefs evoke our emotions which in turn drive our creations. It is not WHAT we have, it is what we THINK about what we have. When you think you do not have ENOUGH that becomes a judgment. You have created a belief of lack. When we THINK we lack we get SCARED or fearful.

BETRAYAL a help turned to destruction.

BLAME renders you POWERLESS. When YOU assign *cause to another* person or thing you deliver ENERGY or power to the other. Blame cancels **your responsibility** in the situation and you have become the victim. Blame is a very low vibrating energy that will keep you stuck and powerless.

BLESSINGS are energies in a potential state waiting to be activated. Awareness opportunities or synchronicities that your soul orchestrates for you to increase your consciousness or awareness.

BODY is a carbon, oxygen engine that runs at 98.6 degrees Fahrenheit. The soul is the engineer running this engine. A carbon-oxygen engine that runs on low combustion fuel generally derived from other life forms.

BOREDOM is a state of idle action with some fear of penalties, but feels powerless to affect a change. This is a high state of apathy.

BRIDGE of FLOWERS is the point of separation from the near realms and the lower negative vibration INTO a positive range of emotions and the angelic realms. When a soul leaves their biology to get help and guidance they can go to the bridge of flowers where **the angels** meet and greet the soul to help it adjust to the transition and a higher vibrational level. They also help the soul process the new energy. Of those trying to get to the bridge after death only twenty percent arrive and the other eighty percent get lost in the near realms and take another body without increasing their wisdom or vibration generally.

Humans can take souls directly to the bridge of flowers so they do not get side tracked or lost in the near realms. I agreed to to that before taking a biology. I was asked to educated the souls that might want to cross over. I gave them enough knowledge to let them release their blaming and rage. After that they wanted to cross over. I have crossed over many large groups; victims, predators, women furious about their abuse, mentally imbalanced, our angelic relatives, souls from other stars and planets and lately the gray aliens.

Doors can be a representation of the Bridge of Flowers, of your angelic family back home, and it is very attractive because they are ones who love you dearly.

They are in a different dimension waiting for us. They are waiting to see what happens with you as the one who came to Earth and has taken on many lifetimes and has learned to deal with yourself as a creator. They are willing to accept you back in the purest, deepest love at any point. Two doors in the scenario because it is about choices, and the choices are about staying on Earth right now.

CAVE of CREATION is a real cave in the third dimension with physical crystalline energy in the form of many crystals in the cave. The cave is shielded from detection those not spiritually awakened would think it a beautiful cave of crystals but not be able to sense what was present. The Akashic Records are the master storage of everything that happened on earth. Our DNA is the storage of current events happening. The current happenings we can take out to reevaluate or enhance our spiritual wisdom.

LEVELS OF COMPASSION

CELLULAR MEMORIES are our soul's imprint on the physical body.

CHAIN of MEMORIES is a recording of similar experiences strung out in time. A whole activity related by the same subject, people or location from a few days apart to billions of years.

CHANGE is a redirection of energy. When it happens to fast or slow the being and their ability to have it suffers.

CHANNELING When a nonphysical entity or angel speaks through a human. The human translates the entity's "thought packets" into words for others to hear or read.

CHARGE is harmful energy or forced stored resulting from conflicts and unpleasant experiences the human has had. The electrical impulse stored in a recreate able potential of energy. An emotional charge of energy like anger, fear, grief or apathy. These misemotions can be restimulated and affect the person in now time.

CHILDREN *are angels in disguise.* LITERALLY They are mature angels even if they are little children in biology. With ALL of US **being MATURE ANGELS** we can all develop freely the way we want to. **The parent NEVER OWNS the child,** NEVER, never. They're disguised as your children but they are souled beings. The parent ACCEPTS THE **RESPONSIBILITY** of bringing them into the world and for a SHORT time and then grants them their freedom. A parent is to give them food and shelter and to help educate them in the early stages and then LET GO of that responsibility. They are NOT your life long personal friend to jerk around forever.

CHRIST CONSCIOUSNESS or Christ Seed comes from the root energy of crystal or Christos meaning **CLEAR** or **NEW**. It is about the *clearness or newness*. Around two thousand years ago shaumbra were here on Gaia to plant the seeds of the new consciousness that has come to fruition. Shaumbra came back at this time to be the ones to harvest and share the new consciousness with others in the world.

COLLECTIVE CONSCIOUSNESS all thoughts that have ever been thought continue to exist and we have access to it through our perceptions.

COMPASSION s feeling whole and complete honoring and accepting without condition. Compassion is strong and thick for any experience we are having and creates an INTERDIMENSIONAL ACTION and increases our light. Compassion is the *catalyst for change* and is the one connection that each one of us has for each other. With compassion we participate by living and teaching *by example*. We LISTEN well and *help when asked.* Serve without taking over. Compassion is easily observed in the aura of an enlightened human.

Respect is incomplete compassion.

Empathy tends to take on and carry other's dark energy.

Compassion is such a deep form of love it shows in your aura. The compassionate FEEL and GIVE GRATITUDE frequently. When you live in the cosmic flow of energy you DO feel grateful all the time. When you move into pastime, fear, negative emotions or controlling another you move out

COMPETITION tethers you to your fear. When competing with the self how can one win or lose? You are always dearly loved by your soul no matter what experience you chose. So what are you thinking by competing with another human?

COMPROMISE is a settlement in which two or more sides agree to accept less than they originally hoped for or thought possible. We can compromise our **energy and mind** so much that we lose touch with WHO we are. A human that has compromised too much might appear stubborn. When you are not true to yourself you fragment and split yourself. **Compromise IS OVER** in the fifth dimension.

Searching outside the self for answers is compromise and makes your *energy drop putting you back* into old energy and duality. In compromise you DENY your divinity. Our core beliefs and essence are compromise when we appease other humans or are fearful of being our own I AM. Compromise of the self is when you know something and then doubt yourself and hold back.

COMPUTERS everywhere are failing particularly data storage as hard drives are most sensitive and least likely to adapt to higher energy. You will continue to experience unexplained failures especially in large systems. The crystals are rewiring themselves to accommodate higher energy just as our biology is.

CONFLICTING MONOTHEISM is the time we are in now will. The age of conflicting monotheism. All agrees there is one God. But no one agrees which one.

CONSCIOUSNESS means something has been defined and structured in a certain way. It is an awareness from every part of us including our stomach, shoulders and ALL of our SENSES and mind, our dreams and imagination. **Pure consciousness** has *passion and clarity* and does not have an AGENDA or need **direction and control**. Pure consciousness (**experiences**) evolving and growing is the opposite of conflict. Awareness of your external environment, other people and your pure self. It is awareness and *not an energy*. It goes beyond ENERGY, beyond consciousness and into NO CONSCIOUSNESS. We are moving beyond the world of experience into the world of the INDEFINABLE.

We chose to be in biology during the greatest change of consciousness in the history of humanity. We came to be the **first to experience** the new expanding energy and melding with our soul. Through our soul connection we have access to universal energy and knowledge. Breathe deeply and let your brain rest while you allow yourself to expand into the new energy ways. Feel **YOUR I AM** presence within you. Answers and tools for you SHOW UP **as you need them**. The tools and answers are DIFFERENT each time you go back to work with them, they work in harmony with you adjusting constantly to your changes and evolution. Allow yourself to **FEEL your ANSWER**. The soul does not address the mind. Soul communicates and connects through the senses.

CONSPIRACY is a joining together of ideals, goals and thoughts.

CORDS *are strings of energy* or a vibration of electromagnetic energy. These strands of energy are found EVERYWHERE humans have a low or negative emotional vibration they are feeding from. The cords are **visible** to the invisible realm and some humans. Cords are grown and developed by humans connecting to everything we have an attachment to or are feeding from. Others have cords to us that we allow to feed on us. There are cords from us to our BELIEFS, events and other humans we have known in this life time or past life times.

Maybe there is a cord to the waitress you verbally assaulted or the child you were cruel to. You create the DRAMA energy strands you FEED from.

The **size** of the cord shows you the depth of YOUR attachment or the amount of energy that flows through the cord.

The **location** of the cord on the body speaks volumes about your relationships with that person, event or place you are in relationship with.

Cords connect you and and what you feed from. Cords contain the *energy* that goes *back and forth*. Energy of all kinds, black, white and all the shades of gray energy going back and forth from you and to you from what or who is at the other end of YOUR CORD. It could be the energy of fear or control and sexual addiction or love and compassion. Strong and often reoccurring beliefs or concepts can have a thick or thin cord coming out of our physical body or ANYONE of our etheric bodies, the emotional, mental or spiritual body.

Cords help you stay *connected* or keep you *STUCK* in an emotion or thought pattern of energy. Like I hate her or I love him. Sometimes you will see or feel a **ball and chain,** or a **package,** or dark **cloud,** or a **syphon.** These things can represent: FEAR, anger, BETRAYAL, regret, GUILT, a *shared negative belief* or low vibrating energy. This is a way to hold one's negative beliefs all together into a bundle. Hanging on to your belief's and emotions, ties up some pretty intense energy.

HOLDING that energy triggers the law of entrainment which in turn creates a pattern of being stuck.

As the photon energy comes in and the vibration on the planet gets higher, little by little the energy **feeding cords are DRYING up** or disappearing from humans. Those doing the largest amount of feeding are in the greatest amount of ANXIETY and CONFUSION at this time because they have to master feeding themselves in a spiritual manner, in a rather short period of time.

<u>COSMIC INTELLIGENCE</u> or universal energy comes through our soul to the human. This energy knows where it's going and what it's going to do and who it will affect. Cosmic intelligence shines on humans as a light for them to see clearer. Allowing free choice of the person it shins on including when healing.

<u>CREATING</u> *is what the **human** does.* When you think thoughts that bring **strong emotion** you access the magnetic power of the universe. Decide what you want and focus on that with clear thought and emotion. Your power is in staying focused long enough to create, manufacture, construct, postulate, bring into beingness. The time is getting shorter and shorter. The creator views life as perfect. You can create by deciding what energy is **to be removed**. Sometimes it's with the MIND or **real action**. The creator walks in a perfect place, even with a dying child, crime or suffering. Another human's anger, suffering, drama or imbalance never changes the reality that all is in a state of perfection. The closer you get to perfection the more you remove what is inappropriate in your life. When you start resonating with the perfection within your creation, you get manifestation. The process begins by claiming and

acting on your integrity in all areas of your life. We are in charge of our reality. When you can take responsibility for the illusion you created for yourself that cancels out any possibility of you being the victim. If you were the victim that is what you wanted. You absolutely created ALL of what you have.

CRIMSON CIRCLE is the group of humans and the angelic realm involved in facilitating this spiritual journey of the new energy and all are preparing to become teachers to others on their spiritual journey. A a global affiliation of teachers. It is a meeting place, both in a physical form and in a consciousness form.

CRIMSON COUNCIL is made up of educators giving themselves in service. They have studied the SPIRITUAL aspects of entities on both sides of the veil. They go to unexplored physical and none physical dimensions or places of consciousness and asses them and how they operate. Then they report back to the Angels to teach that information to others and how to deal with the new energies.

CRYSTAL ENERGY describes the vibration of "All That Is" in crystalline form. Humans have been imprinted with the crystal energy which has been coming in from the sun in THE FORM of solar flares. This energy has been storing in the earth for several years. It has been building and will now provide us with the material to manifest the new hologram for the intentional creation of the new earth.

At this time we are slowly moving from carbon based bodies to forming silicon or crystalline bodies. We are moving from an immune system based in opposition to the thymus that will absorb and transmute any pathogen. As we fully integrate our seven core chakras into one chakra creating a unified field we move beyond passing everything through our heart and MOVE THROUGH our SOUL and the COSMIC flow. At that time we will be walking harmlessly because we will fully feel the legion of lights vibration within our expanded body.

The crystals in our computers are what make up the heart of the computer. Silicone (crystal) diodes or semiconductors are the foundation of all computers. The semiconductors are no different than the crystals we keep around the home or carry with us. Crystal has the highest vibration of the mineral kingdom and is as alive as we are. Crystals are living breathing entities that hold vibration and since they make up the very heart of your computers it could easily be said the computers are alive. They too are going through an evolutionary process as a result of our evolution.

Crystals store frequencies and frequencies ARE a language. Frequencies arranged in the proper manner, numbers and cycles are the language our souls use.

CRYSTALLINE GRID has always been present in parallel and probability it is a geodesic sphere of pentagons and triangles. It sparkles like a brilliantly faceted diamond. We are past the half way mark of raising our frequency into the crystalline frequency which will resonate harmonically **individually** and as a PLANET so we have access to the crystalline grid. When we tap into the crystalline grid it activates the *human and the grid* in the process. When you are not in sync with this frequency you will not sense it.

The crystalline grid of Gaia is the **MEMORY of earth** and is now the ACTIVE grid and the slate we write energy on as we move forward into higher vibrations. Any human that is spiritually awakening is known by Gaia. Light emanates from their intent and **voids our** third dimensional aspects of reality.

Every SOUL ENERGY on Gaia leaves an enduring **MARK imprinted** on the crystalline grid of earth FOREVER. It needs to be like that because the **vibration of earth is an accumulation of all of the entities upon it.** When the biology leaves that does not diminish the energy in the crystalline grid. The energy you have today is imprinted and stays here. The crystalline grid is rewiring our software.

Whales are living portions of the crystalline grid. They contain the "history of earth", within them, they coordinate and cooperate with the grid. Dolphins are their cousins and support group. Whales dolphins, amphibians, birds, and insects all navigate to breeding ground or migration every year via the magnetic grid/ ley lines. Since it changed so much, so quickly the animals haven't adjusted and are confused that is why some have beached themselves. The energy around us is called the cosmic lattice.

We have the history of our planet stored in the Crystalline structure of the planet. The Crystalline Grid and Akashic Records on the planet are being rewritten currently and the result will be that human consciousness will be changed also. The facts will not change all our wars, conquerors, and the many civilizations and what you had for breakfast today will stay the same. But we can change ALL of the DNA history AROUND the past that is alive today, like your spiritual awareness. You still have time to decide you hated or loved what you ate for breakfast today, if you wish.

When we come up with a new perspective of the events in our lives THAT CAN alter our DNA information. You could realize it was not breakfast you hated it was the person you were eating with that turned your stomach. Then you and your DNA will stop reacting emotionally and dramatically to eating breakfast and any other layers of history you have with breakfast.

We are rewriting the history of the living grid of human consciousness at this time. The rewrite changes our views on the meaning and definition of what has happened inside of us, our many thoughts and emotional reactions to what has happened. Looking at events in a new way can increase our spiritual wisdom.

<u>DNA</u> has ALWAYS been interdimensional all twelve loops. Two loops are visible to humans and ten are invisible. The invisible ones are our karmic residue, life lessons, a print of what we used to be, the energy of our spiritual vows and spiritual contracts which haven't been written since 1997 they are obsolete in the new energy.

DNA is not a strand but a loop within loops. With the loops overlapping other loops there is the potential for an ELECTRIC CURRENT. The human is a BIOELECTRIC device and the synapse of our brain and muscles all work with our neurons firing trillions of impulses. The current flowing through a loop creates a magnetic field. Our ***DNA conducts electricity*** similar to a superconductor.

DNA has a small magnetic field all its own. You take those trillions of magnetic fields in the body and the entire human becomes magnetic. When one magnetic field overlaps another you get *inductance*. Inductance is when two magnetic fields overlap and intertwine that allows communication and a transfer of energy.

Inductance is the engine of DNA change.

Our astrological magnetic attributes and energy of our birth, day, hour, time and solar system are wrapped around gravity and time. Our DNA is twisted in the third dimension because of the magnetics here. The ladder shape is unique and a result of chemical reactions and atomic structure attributes. Our DNA has a very small magnetic charge and physical light in the DNA.

The ends of our strands of DNA are telomeres. These long strands seem to do nothing but shorten as we age—a copy of a copy of a copy. Telomeres are actually supposed to be connected together. The DNA loop was cut to give humans the illusion of being finite. The magnetic grid around earth is the hardware and our DNA is our software. The crystalline grid is rewiring our software.

DARK is the absence of light. Darkness can do nothing to affect light, but light can destroy darkness. All of the demons you have seen and felt or heard about in your life have been generated by human consciousness.

DARK ASCENSION When you are **CARRYING darkness** for a spouse, family members (generally starting in YOUR childhood) other PEOPLE, events or **organizations** that DEFINITELY changes your ratio of dark to LIGHT. When you allow others to syphon your light, it brings down the amount of LIGHT YOU carry.

Carrying others dark and taking care of them keeps you TRAPPED in the third dimension. Most are unaware of JUST how much they cripple their own growth and development SPIRITUALLY by supporting and carrying others dark energy for them. Generally people are unaware of the dark held for others. Ask your entourage what dark you carry for others, they will help YOU give it back to them.

We carry OUR FAMILY *darkness and secrets*. If something needs to be a SECRET it must be DARK. Family, including your parents will give the very small child their darkness to carry. The child also reads the dark telepathically. Sometimes one spouse will force the other to carry ALL THEIR darkness so they look clean and pure to other HUMANS. The spouse carrying all the darkness is so codependent they carry both people's dark plus their biological family dark.

Work places and religious organizations can give you dark to carry when they are UNETHICAL and SECRETIVE as most are. Friends do the same. When they are more than half dark, people, video games and organizations will keep you anchored in the third dimension if you keep them close to you. *It is just multidimensional physics.* KNOW that and choose again.

When you have a lot of light and you are giving or allowing dark to syphon your light AND you want to ascend you will have dark ascensions until you have severed your ties with them and returned the dark you carry on their behalf.

Would you go to a sex offender list to find a baby sitter? Your soul knows you still "don't get it" when you carry others dark. You do not **LOVE YOURSELF enough** to allow them to travel their path WITHOUT you trying to FIX them. Ignorance of the universal laws is no defense! That is why we say *we are awakening and becoming aware.* Aware of what is spiritual (light) and what is NOT.

ASCENSION is to stay in your current biology but move to the NEXT LEVEL of spiritual awareness in this lifetime. This moving to higher and higher levels of spiritual wisdom and awareness can and does happen to many over and over again. Once you get the hang of how the universe operates, you just want more and more of it because it feels so much better than duality.

LEVELS OF COMPASSION

Ascension levels are discerned by the amounts of; **agenda,** lesson, **BLAME, judgment,** doubt, gossip, **DRAMA, COMPROMISE, lack,** karma and **spiritual competition** the little human *has released.* **WHEN** you decide to pull ANY of these back into YOUR life you will drop back to the third dimension.

It is **YOUR JOB to notice** the differences and CHOOSE AGAIN.

<u>DEATH</u> is leaving your physical body behind and transitioning to a different level of consciousness. Death is a cessation of your biology. Life and personality go on. 80% of those that die get lost in the forth dimension frequently and start the cycle of taking a body and going back to the forth dimension and ultimately staying earth bound. Of those that keep cycling from a body to forth dimension only ten percent are able to evolve out of that and get to the bridge of flowers on there own.

At death humans have a type of conditioning that reminds us instantly of the many, many times we have crossed over before. We have done it a thousand or more times so we know the drill. The consciousness that comes back shortly before death actually helps us release our biology easier

<u>DENIAL</u> is a CHOICE to hide other choices to avoid feeling, seeing or touching something you do not want to experience and want to keep away from your awareness. *Judgment* is a form of **DENIAL.** When you narrow your focus small enough to judge only an aspect of someone or something you avoid knowing about what you do not want to know or feel about the SELF or others. You focus on a small aspect of the OTHER individual or situation to avoid focus on your

inability to be *COMPASSIONATE* and loving to YOURSELF and others. In the MIND denial is in thought forms like fear, overwhelm, comparison, confusion and lack.

In the MIND denial and dissociation is in THOUGHT FORMS about fear or being overwhelmed. Negative and judgmental thoughts about comparisons or confusion and lack.

In the EMOTIONS denial and dissociation is all about blame, guilt, shame and contradiction.

In the BIOLOGY denial and dissociation is all about delay, lack and disease. The greater your need to deny or dissociation the more distorted and twisted things get for the human and their creations.

DEPRESSION Human depression not related to the ascension process is about this lifetime. It is getting into a very low energy wave a very slow vibration. Usually the person is absorbed in HATING of themselves it is an addiction to hanging onto and wallowing in the pain of their story. They get energized by talking about themselves and their suffering in THEIR STORY. A story about what they should be… What they should of accomplished…and their SUPPRESSED anger at the self. Releasing your *expectations* can release the depression. A sadness about something in your life can move into a depression. Depression can last three months to all lifetime or something in between. Depression CAN BE used as a fuel to ascension.

DIMENSIONS are *only consciousness* and **DO NOT occupy** any time or ANY space. You can create as many dimensions as would please you there is "no limit" and they are exceedingly flexible. Dimensions swirl, move, shift and intersect each other all the time. There are positive and negative dimensions, unpredictable dimensions and there are ABSOLUTELY *no words* to **describe them**. Sometimes they are identical to each other but different dimensions before they split off and go on their own, not on a mental level but on a KNOWINGNESS level.

Dimensions are all related and contain elements of each other and relative to the thing they are describing. All the thoughts that have ever been thought about a given subject, for example "eating ice cream" will all be in one dimension. If you commune with the invisible realm you can go to that dimension and collect the information BUT discern what will serve your needs.

What we call the universe exists in **many DIMENSIONAL realities** all at once. Dimensions are defined by **WAVELENGTH** or FREQUENCY.

A human has several concurrent dimensional realities. There are many versions of us existing side by side in slightly different dimensional realities. When we solve problems or do certain spiritual things we GO interdimensional in the process. The most interdimensional thing we have is our own DNA. Working with your past lives in any form is interdimensional energy. Creator thoughts and ideas can shoot from this dimension into another type of dimension not defined, out of obvious recognition and return to the creator that shot them out. Expansional energy always finds its way back to you the zero point, the Now.

Dimension is the distance from the point of view to the anchor point in space. Rising through the dimensions is a melding into higher frequencies that can only be achieved IF YOU RELEASE the low-frequency **imbalances** in you.

We travel in space by going into one dimension and out into another. Traveling in SPACE is a matter of changing dimensions. Energy with our imagination moves and flows in and out of dimensions. We solve challenges by going through the dimensions to collect information. One of the best uses of crystalline energy is to shift and travel between dimensions. At times it is just a matter of closing your eyes and using and expressing the energy anyway that pleases you.

Dimensions are **pockets of energy movement** and not levels like many humans have been led to believe they are. Scientists say there are at least eleven dimensions in the heart of atomic structure but they forgot to count the dimension zero. A point of perception is also a dimension.

DISCERNMENT is the art of making choices without judgment or heavily invested emotionally, a fifth dimensional tool. With discernment you decide and flow with what unfolds. As we center or balance our energy we become more cognizant of the effects people have on us and we have on them. Purposely choosing what is in our life is needed to alter our life in a constructive way. Our reality is a direct result of our choices. We do not have control over the thoughts entering our consciousness. We DO have full control over the thoughts we dwell on.

Before we can ascend we use ONLY discernment. We discern which of our beliefs will serve us in the future on our soul path. Discernment is an integral part of your intuition.

DISSOCIATION is a state in which some integrated part of a person's life becomes separated from the rest of their personality and functions independently from the core personality. A lack of connection between things, like you are living physically on earth but constantly distract yourself from being conscious of being here.

Dissociated experiences are not integrated into the usual sense of self. Disconnection occurs in the usually integrated functions of consciousness, memory, identity, or perception. For example, you think about an event that was very upsetting yet have no FEELINGS about it, there is emotional numbing. A hallmark of post-traumatic stress disorder.

Dissociation may affect one subjectively, like when you have a thought, feeling, or action coming out of nowhere. As if it were controlled by a force other than you. This can be described as feeling like a "passenger" in one's body and not the driver.

Dissociation is when certain thoughts, emotions, sensations, and or memories are compartmentalized because they are too overwhelming for the conscious mind to integrate. This is a coping mechanism to handle powerful NEGATIVE emotions. These thoughts, emotions, sensations, and or memories are "split off" from the integrated personality.

DIVINE INTUITION Is a guidance system helping you to know how fast to go and which way to turn. It is our personal collected knowledge that directs you to what is best for the conglomerate of entities you are. You will not get this information in advance you get it in the now moment just as you need it. This is also the entire collection of your lives and experiences in kind of a soup so you can pull out and use any spiritual wisdom or skills or training you gained in the past.

DIVINE HUMAN commits to be there when they are called. The divine human avoids being evangelical and reaches out to touch another that ASKED (not always verbally) to be touched. Touch those who are ready to accept. No need to fix something that is not broken or the ones not ready, honor their path.

When the human holds the hand of its soul and works together with it. That is when we feel joy and universal love we are holding the hand of our soul and being a divine human. A divine human no longer **lets itself be ruled by potentials**. It knows how to CREATE POTENTIAL. There is no need to have an infinite set of potentials to follow. The creator only needs **the ONE** being manifested. Choice is replaced by multiple potentials.

<u>DIVINE WILL</u> is loving acceptance of ALL THINGS. Humans have the FREE WILL to choose to connect with their soul. BUT when they decide to meld with their soul the human moves into **DIVINE WILL**. Leaving their free will behind them in the third dimension. Understand the true essence of freedom, which is not the ability to follow every impulse that is generated by the little human. Real freedom comes from within through the soul, harmony and universal energy.

<u>DIVINITY</u> is the purest essence and innocent energy there is. Divinity is being one with all things. Divinity EQUALS oneness. The energy of the solution is always present in our divinity. Experiencing oneness ABOLISHES the veil and ends our illusion.

DIVINE PURPOSE is the larger picture reflecting your place in oneness. The human rarely sees how they fit in this big picture. DIVINE INTENT with **divine purpose** helps the human see **their own next step** as an individual. Do not be concerned if you do not know your highest good or what divine service is. DIVINE SERVICE is what your SOUL came here to do through the human

LEVELS OF COMPASSION

<u>DOUBT</u> When the mind cannot rescue you, **depression**, loss of passion and joy come in. You question and DOUBT yourself, it is very different than being negative. One can be *highly negative and **never doubt** themselves.* **Doubt** is looking at a very distorted and smoky, cloudy mirror. When you allow yourself to doubt **WHO you are** and **WHY you are here** and don't follow **the TRUTH within**, you DO NOT see yourself as you are.

When doubt is brought in the flow of energy is restricted.

YOU compress yourself energetically and doubt becomes a type of virus that starts eating away at you, segmenting you. The best way out of your doubt is to go back into what you truly feel and know about yourself is true and express it.

DOUBT is a GAME all humans play and can be additive. How often everyday do you doubt your decisions, actions or thoughts rather than **take ownership** and responsibility for your journey into new awareness? Using doubt makes it very difficult to have triumphant discoveries and go off into new realms of consciousness. Truly experiencing adventures in the fullest way without running away. With doubt you can continue to be a VICTIM and **hide**. Doubt was NOT known in the angelic realms. Angel's just had experiences. Sometimes the experience was intense or didn't have the expected outcome. Doubt came in when the angelic beings chose to forget who they were when they came to Earth. Doubt is very, very strong on earth. So strong that when humans die and cross over to the near earth realms, they bring doubt with them and in a way doubt gets transferred even to the angelic realms. Now there are a lot of doubting angels because the humans brought that virus back with them.

Doubt tells you that you can make a bad choice BUT YOU CANNOT. You can *only experience*. Doubt causes you to stay little.

DRAMATIZATION is repeating an action that one has experienced in the past. A replay of what happened then. The degree of dramatization is in direct relation to the stuck energy in an experienced trauma. To go through the cycle over and over demanded by the trauma. This can happen over and over again and definitely is NOT in NOW time.

DRAMA prevents the human from feeling *their OWN feelings*. Our **true feelings** are in service to us. Owning the truth of your thoughts and feelings keeps them in useful service to you by not letting you ignore what you feel. Staying in the present moment, facing your **feelings of fear** and moving into SOLUTIONS and *resolutions* help the individual and the collective.

Our **DREAM STATE** is now filled with confusion because we have become aware of our *multidimensional dreaming*. Dreaming and memory act the same in that they are on a chain or pile of the same type memories. All the memories or dreams with the same theme or common thread are grouped or linked together. The events in dreams or memory appear confusing because they are ARRANGED and present themselves in their order of **IMPORTANCE** to YOU. These memory chains or piles or slide shows are NOT in chronological order. The past, future and present are are all put together by theme and importance to you. This is closer to the "way of reality." Our DNA is reacting to the new alignment of the magnetic grid creating dreams out of time and space, heartwarming and fearful and more real than ever.

FOR EXAMPLE

All the times we *baked bread* in the **past, FUTURE and currently will come forward into your awareness** as a group, or on a chain, or in a slide show. The images will be out of time sequence. They will be arranged and present themselves in their order of **IMPORTANCE** to you.

<u>DUALITY</u> Everything we have experienced on Earth until now has been seen through the illusion of duality or opposition. All our perceptions have been clouded by our personal veil of forgetfulness. This includes what we see with our physical eyes to our highest spiritual truths. We have been living our lives and making our decisions or creating our relationships and following our goals under a VERY diminished reality system and using far lesser truths. Duality gains its energy from separation and opposing poles like male or female, good or bad, dark or light. Up and down are relative to where you are. Right and wrong are judgments. There is no black or white, only shades of gray. Fear and love are sides of the same circle.

We become a being surrounded by other physical beings that we are isolated from. Being in biology and separate is the game duality requires. Duality and separation are inextricably intertwined. Once you release the consciousness of duality you become an ENERGETIC BEING with a physical core **linked** to the energy of "all that is."

***

CHAPTER 19
E through H words and concepts

EGO literally means "I go" or "move forward" or "express." Ego ultimately is about the creation of aspects that are there to SERVE you. Ego means your ability to express yourself in a variety of **different manners**, or through aspects, while remaining **absolutely integrated YOURSELF** and understanding that you are the *CREATOR of aspects.*

An out-of-balance EGO is one where the **aspect believes** it is the Master.

The aspect believes they become more important than the human. So the aspect takes control IF the human allows that to happen. This could of got started in a past life. The aspect takes over because it thinks everyone else abandoned ship and IT CAN take over.

Underneath it all, the aspect on some level KNOWS it's **just an aspect** and can be easily gotten rid of. So the aspect lives in great FEAR and hides from that fear by *inflating its importance*. The aspect doesn't have a true base of LOVE or HONOR. It feeds by stealing energy from other humans through THEIR worship of the aspect and that is the negative definition of ego.

ELEVEN stands for illumination. Look into the illumination for the new.

11:11 is the *trigger to our DNA to start reconnecting.* ACTIVATING the shift from duality into oneness. Opening the **portal** or bridge to ascension and our doorway home has opened once again on this planet. Humanity has twenty years to pass through the eleven gates to oneness. The 11:11 activation runs from January 11,1992 to 2012. The two sets of two ones signify the first reality traveling THROUGH to the second reality. Polarity was allowed so the **INFINITE COULD** study itself as a **finite human**. Polarity has enabled us to experience individuality and aloneness and receive energy imprints which have been necessary to play out our illusion or conduct our research to increase our spiritual awareness.

1987 was the start of the NEW ENERGY and the harmonic convergence and later called the "11:11." The earth had reached a vibratory rate of **SPIRITUAL NEUTRALITY** the future could go either way. Pulled into a high interdimensional level or wallow in the old prophesies of doom.

ELECTROMAGNETIC GRID (the human grid) is at the level of the crust of the earth and extends upward in places as high as thirty thousand feet above sea level adjusting itself according to the elevation of the planet. This is the primary grid human consciousness has been connected to for the past 6,000 years. It regulates the electromagnetic systems like the ley lines and vortex systems of the planet. It is in the sacred geometric form of the icosahedron, a sphere with 20 facets.

EMBRACE is to hold tenderly. When you choose opposition your divinity will wait for your embrace. The embrace is the way your divinity will join you. If you do not embrace life you will not have potentials. Embrace but do not strangle your experience or get bogged down with the details.

The amount we embrace of our divine self will be the amount we lose of our **human self**. Ask for balance not answers.

EMBODYING is coming to terms with and a fearless acceptance of all that is without walls, barriers or judgment. Being brave enough to feel all the different energies while understanding that you will NEVER lose your identity or **integrity** while feeling other energies. The Kingdom of God literally lies within your torso and heart. It is your divine spark and connection to your soul and the cosmic flow.

EMOTIONAL BODY is the **layer next to the physical body** and it roughly follows the outline of the physical body and appears to be COLORED clouds of a fine substance in *continual fluid motion* that extends ONE to THREE inches from the body. The COLORS and sometimes the SHAPES change to reflect the **predominant emotional state** of the human. An angry or aggressive person might have a great deal of dirty red in their aura. An intellectual person might have a lot of yellow, intellectually in a negative direction a dirty yellow like mucus. A spiritual person would have blue or violet in the aura. The emotional body holds EVERYTHING and has the *largest influence* on third dimensional reality. The emotional body can **WITHHOLD energy and awareness** from our biology, keep secrets from our biology. When the mental body sends energy to the emotional body the emotional body filters what it **feeds the biology**. The emotional body *mixes or merges* together with the physical body it surrounds. Its colors vary from brilliant clear hues to dark muddy colors. Which reflect the clarity or *CONFUSION the human is experiencing.* Clear and highly energized feelings like love, excitement and joy or anger are bright and clear. When feeling confused or negative **the color is dark and muddy.**

Chronic emotional stress is caused by unresolved and generally suppressed negative emotional issues. Although forgotten by the physical human they *continually drain energy* from the three other body systems to sustain themselves.

The emotional body holds EVERYTHING and has the *largest influence* on third dimensional reality. The emotional body can **WITHHOLD energy and awareness** from our biology. The emotional body can keep secrets from our biology.

EMOTION FORMS are feelings and emotions that MANY humans have had and these emotions floating in the ethers will COALESCE together creating an ENORMOUSLY powerful **BLOCK** of feeling. This block of feeling will **float around almost everywhere.** When the individual human comes in contact with these blocks of emotion they can be easily influenced by them. Even overwhelmed by them.

At this time on earth there are MANY in an emotional state of fear and worry. Their fears and worries have coalesced together making and enormous emotional block of fear. Multiple times this emotional form of fear and worry has gone out away from the earth, turned around and all that coalesced energy came back hitting the earth in powerful waves. Upsetting many and they had no rational reason to be upset to their way of thinking. Remember it is only energy and you can take that energy and convert it to something constructive and compassionate.

EMOTIONS move from lower vibrations to higher vibrations and go the other direction also. The words **emotion**

or **VIBRATION** have the same meaning to the invisible realm and are interchangeable. To move your emotions from negative to positive is like walking up stairs, you take one step at a time. When you are at death or hopelessness emotionally you can move up emotionally to > depression. Spending some time at the vibration of depression you can move up to > the feeling of relief from depression. Then you might progress to > revenge, hopefully only in your thoughts and then on to > anger because you are feeling less powerless. After anger you can slide into or out of > frustration. Getting past frustration can lead you to > hope and on and on and on. You can also move down the emotional scale in reverse order.

Our emotions positive or negative, are the energetic glue that holds our pockets of dense matter in our aura. Releasing negative emotions tied to people and events allow you to move forward in the now with all of your pieces and parts fully present.

Emotions are the fuel that propels our behavior and creations for good or bad. EMOTIONS belong to the LITTLE human and are easily manipulated or controlled and go off into misdirected energy.

Accept and embrace ALL of your emotions. Think of your emotions as your PARTNER in awareness and consciousness raising moving you into total compassion. The more you partner with your emotions as the loving instructor and friend they are, the more you value your human self. The more self love you have the more you are brought back to your perfection.

EMPATHY tends to *take on and carry* other people's dark energy, whereas compassionate beings help the same people without taking over their work, lessons or karma for them.

ENDGAME is as important as the opening and middle game in chess and life.

In chess and life the **endgame** refers to the stage of the game when there are few pieces or options left on the board or in life. The line between middle game and endgame is often not clear and may occur gradually or with the quick exchange of a few pairs of pieces. Like the human and the soul.

The endgame tends to have different characteristics from the middle game and the players have correspondingly different STRATEGIC concerns. THE RULES AND GUIDELINES CHANGE. In particular, pawns (THE LITTLE PEOPLE) become more important; endgames often revolve around attempting to promote a pawn by advancing it to the eighth (big jump) rank. The king or SOUL which had to be protected in the middle game owing to the threat of checkmate or being OVERWHELMED by the boring human, becomes a **strong piece** in the endgame. It can be brought to the center of the board and be a useful **attacking** piece.

When does the endgame begin when there are only a few pieces or OPTIONS left. An endgame is a position in which the king (SOUL) can be used actively, but there are some famous exceptions to the Endgame favors an aggressive king or SOUL through the human.

ENERGETICALLY means in a nonphysical way.

ENERGY essentially is in a neutral state of being and is a potential waiting to be expressed through our imagination. Energy is just a TOOL and FUEL having many layers. Energy is created from nothingness. The nature of energy is to move in and out of definition. Energy in universal physics, goes back into itself and into a neutral state. Nonphysical energy is the electrical current at the basis of everything that exists.

ENERGY STAMP (experiences) or our DNA is a record of all our experiences. When the soul decides to keep an energy stamp it gets stored in the cells of our DNA that is ready to be triggered the next time it may be used to master a life lesson. Most of our energy stamps are never brought into play because they do not get triggered during the course of our life.

Normally during the final stage of our life the soul **resets** its own energy stamps in preparation for the next life. The soul keeps energy stamps (experiences) that may be useful in future lifetimes and releases those that no longer need to be experienced. The awareness of an experience never leaves you. Only **your strong emotional reaction** leaves you when the soul takes that out of your DNA. If you, the human wish to release the stamp it can be done at the time it comes into play in your life and you get THE WISDOM and no longer need that experience to help you master a life lesson.

When your soul and you choose ascension your soul removes the energy stamps which had put an emotional charge on your experiences.

FOR EXAMPLE

If you had 40 energy stamps and you were working on avoiding judgment of yourself and others successfully for a bit your soul would support you by taking that energy stamp out of your DNA. That STRONG emotional charge you might have around judgment in the third dimension. which makes it much easier to curb that misdirected energy This makes it much easier to slip on up to the higher vibration of discernment in the fifth dimension. Then you have only 39 other energy stamps to work on mastering with your soul.

When you have an energy stamp on the outside of your energy tube it restricts your ENERGY FLOW. Just as stepping on a garden hose restricts the flow of water. So when you push the energy through a blocked hose, it hurts some and is FELT in the emotional body.

Tragically many humans **DENY the pain** they experience. Others avoid the pain by choosing NOT to run energy through their tube or choose NOT to feel, and hold all the energy. Some humans create little magical tubes on the outside of them to run energy through to reroute it.

SOME HUMANS bravely step up and do WHATEVER it takes to heal the wound and gain the spiritual wisdom.

<u>**ENERGY TUBE**</u> is affected by vibrational changes, especially the shifts going on now. The vibrations in our biology and OUR SOUL can and will trigger emotional releases in the human. The tube needs to *stretch* with the large amount of energy coming in now and when it does the scar tissue (old trauma) does not stretch at the same rate causing PAIN and AWARENESS. Old issues start coming up when you least expect them. The energy tube is the **seat of human** EMOTIONS and runs from the finite biology to the infinite soul simultaneously.

HUMANS MOVE ENERGY through their energy tube *every second of every day.* Our biology is the *bridge between soul and matter* and the bridge between the EARTH and DIVINE ENERGIES. For the *first time ever* we do have the opportunity to integrate our awareness and CHANGE the *energy tube itself.* We can make it larger and less painful.

Many are beginning to channel and that will continue to happen because of the stretching of the energy tube. So when we rework and embrace our scar tissue we create an opportunity to move to the next level. New experiences trigger whole sets of new or OLD emotions and they are NOT **SETBACKS**. Perceive them as **opportunities to advance**. Embrace them and run with them.

When you can LAUGH or count *your painful experience as a BLESSING* after getting devastating information you are doing well. Celebrate, celebrate dance to the music.

Everything humans have made started first as a **thought form** IN THE ETHEREAL realms or mental body and had NO substance. When HUMANS bring it through the tube that runs from the ethers through our biology in front of the spine down our legs into the earth we create something that has substance and mass. We ground it which is actually a miracle. We take things having no substance and give them substance. Our biology is beautiful beyond description.

<u>**ENLIGHTENMENT**</u> is when a human is in balance and has compassion for EVERYONE. They have found and possess the "divine attribute" humans find *inside* themselves. They radiate divine compassion. We are the sons and daughters of the creator, just as Jesus told us we were two thousand years ago.

Enlightenment historically has had nothing to do with ascension.

At times humans have experienced states of bliss. These are moments of cosmic awareness not ascension. Moments of bliss can become an addiction, but are a belief system. We believe when enlightened we will know everything MENTALLY. The mind cannot understand ascension.

<u>**ENTOURAGE**</u> is a group of entities, not always invisible, attending or surrounding the important human. Your entourage has entities coming and going all the time depending on the

human's current need. Your 90%er or entourage members are always leaving you clues to find your spiritual wisdom and gifts in your life experiences. Some humans are most skilled at ignoring and denying their clues. They fear they are being tricked or teased. We need to discern when we are being tricked and when we are getting solid helpful information.

Our entourage are an infinite numbers of changeable energies that function in a goruplike fashion. The group is part of you forever. We feel the groups presence they are not numbered. They are energies not entities. The guides exist on both sides of the veil. They change when the human changes. Duality works overtime to keep the human isolated so they can make independent choices and not be swayed by the group we belong to. All part of the earth test. Each of us is surrounded by our own group of ourselves. They know exactly what you have been through. They stand ready to lead you in one direction or another, if you would allow it. Recognize you have the choice to ask for their guidance if you would like it.

ENTRAINMENT, law of The **law of entrainment requires** THAT two resonance's existing in the same location **MUST adjust and combine**. On a scale of 1-10 if one individual is at a 3 and the other is at a 7 the law of entrainment requires they will both be at 5 ish. Unless one is an overpowering resonance and pulls the other to their level. You carrying someone else's DARK ENERGY can postponed your ascension. Return the dark you carry for another. Learn what you can from that experience, forgive both of you and grieve the loss of the entrainment. *It will alter you.*

Humans are gigantic energetic creatures. Every thought we have creates energetic ripples. The rising energies on Gaia are forcing us to clear and purify all our bodies. The toxins or any illness patterns and our emotional and mental blockages are all low density imbalances rising up at this time to be cleared. Drink plenty of water to flush out cellular debris. We are clearing out low density energy damage normal for us to be carrying in third dimension. In the fifth dimension it is energy too heavy to carry.

Our body anchors our energetic layers, which fan out in every direction in ever-widening circles of vibrating frequency. Our auras touch each other at six feet from the body. Why do you suppose it makes you uncomfortable when a stranger stands too close. They are standing in our dense etheric bodies of emotion, mental and spiritual energies. As our auras become more sensitive it can become downright painful to have a disgruntled or unpleasant energy in your spiritual, mental or emotional space. Our energetic bodies grow more dense and real to humans as they connect to the higher frequencies.

ESSENCE is a type of dream or imagination state on the same level as our knowingness functions. When we go to other realms or dimensions we take our **essence** to those places *NOT the brain.* When we try to remember what we saw or did or experienced the brain has stayed on earth so it will be of no help when you want information from those trips. The challenging part is you need to go back into your essence for the information at your knowingness level. First you need to ground it in the third dimension, and after grounding it here the information starts transforming itself into an energy that eventually will be understood by the mind. That is where the breakthroughs and the "ahas" come from. We can even bring knowingness, breakthroughs in and "ahas" into the third dimension on behalf of other humans that want or need the information and are sadly trying to squeeze it out of their brain. POOR brain.

The ESSENCE of our soul is the accumulation of all the experiences our soul has incorporated up to this point that would include the good, bad, and ugly. When you carry negative experiences as energy stamps they color every thought and every relationship we have. We view the world from that bias.

EXPANSIONAL ENERGY The energy of the old consciousness was SPIRAL. New consciousness is expansional inwards and outwards and every direction going and coming from all different dimensions at one time. Expansional energy always finds its way back to you the zero point in the Now. Anything, desire or creative thought can be shot out of the now into these other dimensions, wandering, zooming off to collect energies, support, and information to come right back for you. When it comes back, it will look and feel different. Expansional energy will tie into the energy of your knowingness or gnost, for solutions. The trick is making sure that you comprehend all of the energies and answers that have come back to you. Then YOU activate it.

EXPANDED MOMENT allows you to be fully present right now AND allows you to expand into other realms and dimensions to feel and be aware of many other things around you all in the same moment. You can also move to past and future in the expanded moment. That is NOW time and not linear.

EXTERIOR PORTAL WORKER after the shift in consciousness happens on earth some humans will be *exterior portal workers*. One of the main functions of an exterior portal worker is to collect those who don't **make it into the awakened state.** They will go out and get souls that are lost, fearful and confused and get them through the portal. They will gather the highest vibrating individuals first because they won't fight with them. Most of the exterior workers are of the warrior class. The disoriented souls along with those functioning in denial will be ushered through the portals where they will be healed and cleansed of their blockages. Then they will be turned over to the *interior portal workers*.

FEARS as we walk through our personal fears we transmute them to LOVE energy. When we say we are ready for any change FEAR comes into challenge our resolve. All things have an energy consciousness. When you talk to it you are owning and embracing it because you let it express itself. You listened to your fear and converted the energy to something useful for you. When questioning the unseen world demand your answers come from truth and love.

Fear starts in the gut as a lower energy attribute of humans. Fear has nothing to do with enlightenment. Fear in the gut can be controlled BEFORE it moves quickly into the mind taking you over. Contain darkness or fear below your heart so you can keep it powerless. Fear is only a LACK of LOVE. Fear is not the opposite of love. We create our own fears so it should be easy for us to come up with a resolution for what we created. Fear is only a lack of information.

FEELINGS true feeling or SENSORY PERCEPTIONS go away when you try to *control or structure them*. Feeling deep, real, genuine feelings humans do not like TO DO so much. Feelings are awareness and sensitivities. They fight and get confused with true consciousness that might feel like a tidal wave of energy taking you over. Feelings can be overwhelming and throw old systems out of whack. In that swirl or vortex of energy of feeling you can feel exhilarated, fearful and ALWAYS FEEL very alive. Feelings are the method humans USE to **arrive at INTUITIVE knowledge** or divine wisdom. You can't go from third dimensional human knowledge, the brain to divine knowledge in one step. The multidimensional language process of sensing divine wisdom starts with you feeling it. Knowledge of YOUR larger SELF, your 90%er and ALL you are, come through your senses.

When you AVOID, **deny** or *suppress* your SENSORY AWARENESS there is a price to pay. Fun things like *mental disease*, HUMAN DEPRESSION, **anxiety**, issues of overweight or any of the ADDICTIONS.

When humans deliberately try to stop feeling they CRAVE excitement and sugar because they feel so dead. So feeling less humans will create a crisis of some sort or spend money for a temporary thrill and then crash. Feelings or senses are pulses of life and they are MEANT to be experienced.

FIFTH DIMENSION we are there if we think we are. It is a spiritual shift not a physical move what you see is what you EXPECT to see in the fifth dimension. Our point of perception determines our reality. Every morning we wake up in the fifth dimension and a heightened state of creation then we force ourselves back to third dimension with our beliefs and behaviors.

FIFTH DIMENSION ATTRIBUTES the creative powers of ALL HUMANS have been raised. Energy is being reshuffled inside and outside our bodies. We are fully in charge of OUR own PERSONAL REALITY and point of perception **in every** moment.

When you do not like what you created it is your RESPONSIBILITY to change it. By getting in the cosmic flow with your soul you create the highest and the best for the self. This is what helps creates the new energy and more of the higher vibrations.

Create the **highest and best** for YOUR heart and then radiate it outward into your environment. That is the highest use to your divinity. Find things that feed your passion and joy every day. There is integrity and no judgment or agendas. The divine human commits to BE THERE when they are called. Avoids being evangelical and reaches out to touch another that ASKS (not always verbally) to be touched. Touch those READY to accept. Go WITHIN for answers and reassurance. Take the time and energy to educate yourselves as to the beliefs and customs of those you oppose or fear. FIND the points of CONNECTION drop the focus on areas of disagreement. That is emulating the universal flow and oneness. There is NO right or wrong in oneness and when we are INSIDE ourselves. Become fully aware of the *vibrational pattern you send* out so you can understand what you get back and why. The Universe has only one answer to all requests: "**And so it is.**" Consider reworking YOUR question.

FIRST CIRCLE is Home the original creation of God or is referred to as the First Creation. This is where we came from before embarking on this journey for soul. When we went through the wall of fire and into the void and started the illusion of duality the first split of our oneness was into male and female.

FORGIVING is simply a letting go or a releasing. To be able to change you need to forgive YOURSELF for things that went on historically. Go through the process of saying yes it happened and cannot be changed. I acknowledge it and own I created it so now I can release it. I have assimilated the lesson and now I can let it go. When we forgive, we free ourselves of the sadness, burden and any lingering anger or hatred we have been dragging around. It is a simple process if you make it so.

Many people get stuck unable to release issues, people or events that have wounded them. Look at it in the detached broader view to see it does not need to harm you ANY LONGER. There is no need to carry it. Assimilate it and leave it behind. The person or event hurting you was something you created to learn from.

The **earth realm** is a creation of light and dark which WAS needed for lessons to be learned. Were it not for the darkness there would be no correlation or contrast to the light. When light is all-pervasive it is blinding and no learning and growth could take place. It is the **right of every living thing on Gaia to live as they see fit**. Be it man, animal or plant have that right EXCEPT when you take it AWAY from ANOTHER. To heal our body and emotions our mind and soul we need to forgive or release what still causes us pain. The PAIN is a signal to us what needs to be changed. That is our STRENGTH in this free will zone. We are free to make a different decision.

FOURTH DIMENSION is more of a transitory space for humans and Gaia to adjust to the new higher frequencies.

FREE WILL the ability to make your own personal choices. You have FREE WILL to choose to connect with soul or behave as you like. There are consequences that result from your choice.

GAIA is the **SOUL** of earth. Angels from the Order of the Arc WITH the House of Goddesses that Gaia came from shared their life force and *MELDED WITH THE ROCK* to get this earth rock "flowing with energy." These **angelic beings took 10% of their energy** and put it into biology to live in their creation. They agreed to share this experience and experiment and to wear a veil also. All were to maintain their ignorance of their origin. Gaia is very much a part of us and is a LIVING, **sentient**, THINKING, *breathing being* just as we are. The earth and everything humans perceive as the omniverse began as a hologram.

Gaia has MADE the CHOICE to ascend and started the process September 27, 2007. Her departure should take a few hundred years. Gaia has decided to relocate to the NEW EARTH so she can share all her wisdom.

Earth has been growing and evolving for approximately five billion years with Gaia. Angels joined Gaia approximately 4.7 billion years ago and Gaia has been their support system EMOTIONALLY, *physically* and **spiritually** for all that time and before.

GIFT A hidden gift of spiritual awareness is present in all we do. Our entourage is always leaving clues to be sure we find our wisdom and gifts. Finding and accepting the gift gracefully allows assimilation of the highest energy for our experience and enables us to move to the next lesson. Sometimes the experience is real yukkie. To RELEASE an experience you are NOT loving find the wisdom and gift, be grateful. Move to a new experience.

GOD at the core is LOVE and COMPASSION for all things, the "is-ness," unconditional love. God is and always has been **a legion of light,** a reflection of the human consciousness. As ANY leader is a reflection of its followers. God has a presence in us and all around us. **You are God also** in a different way than the God of Home. God is ALWAYS creating as an expression of love. God has always been multidimensional and humans made her a single dimension with exaggerated human male qualities.

We were all here when the earth was created because you are a piece of god. We sat together and watched as the earth was formed. God is a PARTNERSHIP and not a singular entity. The core of the puzzle or game we just finished WAS can humans discover who they are while not know their grandness or that we are all one. We were born with duality and brought to earth within a ***dark energy biased against us***.

The legion of light is not in a place since the concept of "place" cannot exist in a quantum state. Interdimensional energy is TIMELESS there is **no PLACE**. There is no time on the other side of the veil. So there is no past .

God is creation and all of his creation is ever expanding and growing. Once it is set into motion in perfect sacred geometry and spiritual science it is not a necessity that it grows. It is an absolutely balanced ongoing miracle that it grows.

<u>**GRATITUDE**</u> is recognizing, FEELING and **owning** what has been done for you. It is the wonderful feeling of emotion we get in the now moment and in the cosmic flow.

Gratitude, appreciation, or **thankfulness** is a positive emotion or attitude in acknowledgment of a benefit that one has received or will receive. Just existing IN BIOLOGY and BEING ABLE to experiencing DENSITY and FREE WILL is considered something to be **very** grateful for. he feeling of indebtedness has a negative connotation. The feelings of gratitude are beneficial to **our subjective emotional well-being** and increases experiences of *positive emotion*. Having a generalized grateful personality greatly diminishes the ups and downs that humans tend to have in life. People who tend to experience gratitude more frequently than others do, tend to be happier, more helpful and forgiving. Grateful humans are less depressed than their less grateful counterparts.

GRAVITY GRID is both within and on the surface of the planet and anchored to the spinning crystalline core of the earth. It is in the form of a dodecahedron which is a sphere with twelve facets. The gravity grid is primarily rooted in the first three dimensions. The dodecahedron was the primary consciousness and geometric shape of the planet from the time of the deluge of Atlantis until the emergence of the icosahedron about 4,000 BC.

GRIDS at this time **ALL GRIDS**, the internal grids and external overlaying grids are all in transition. The grids do not change OUR consciousness. *Our consciousness* **CHANGES THE GRIDS**. Grids are used to STORE and MOVE energy. The grids are very detailed webs of *interdimensional* **energies**. Energy that is always in motion. The way we RECEIVE ENERGY from outside of us or inside us is also changing. All grids have moved their location disorienting some animals.

The **magnetics** of this planet are linked to the changing consciousness of the human. In the human there is FOCUSED ENERGY, a *creator* energy when we ALLOW our *essence or soul to flow* through us. When our 90%er and 10%er are vibrating in sync we are at our very best.

While listening to our FEELINGS and our **senses** we ALLOW creation to flow freely through us. Our unconscious and conscious power is greatest in the now moment when we are feeling and sensing.

GROUNDING or anchoring a CONCEPT or **thought** or anything *that already exists* in the third dimensions is done by telling a few or many about what you're doing and trying to accomplish. Just being physically present grounds new businesses, homes and events or any place.

Sometimes potentials are put in the air and linger waiting for a human to connect with that potential and ground it or make it real. So the potential and a human picking it work together. The choice or creating potentials exists in other realms and it is very important.

Humans may want answers but are afraid to actually look for answers or expand there ideas. Sooner or later they do because they see the energies are very compatible. Humans need to put the potential out there for others to choose or choose a potential already present.

Our highest potential and collective goal as a group was to SPIRITUALIZE matter.

GUIDE is generally a person you have known in former lives whom you have asked to help you when you took a body this time around. So they are generally like-minded with you. They can have a lot or not so much information or wisdom just as they did in physical life. Guides have access to the unseen world's "web", or bulletin board. They read our aura which has all our information and traumas stuck in it. All the things you have done, think, or feel are read by anyone who cares to on the other side.

LEVELS OF COMPASSION

GUILT the most useless human emotion there is.

HATE is an intense emotion and focused vibration. Hate is love with no compassion, wisdom or understanding. The hate is a very deep wish to be loved and accepted by the one you hate. Just as hate love can become all consuming. You can be so FULL of hate there is no room for "other" personal relationships in your life. When we maintain a perception of anger or hate and die with that belief we will carry it with us into our next life. Since that becomes a life focus the law of attraction will support that and bring more until the real or IMAGINED focus changes.

These two individuals will look out in the world and see **only people that hate and torment each other for that is the vibration THEY LIVE in.** They hate and withhold love to punish others. They never see the price they pay for maintaining their focus on hate and withholding their love.

HARMONICS The untrained human ear typically does not perceive harmonics as the separate notes they are. We perceive an overall tone. Bells have clearer perceptible tones than most instruments. Antique singing bowls are known for their unique quality of producing multiple harmonics. The tight relationship between overtones and harmonics in music often leads to their being used synonymously, but they are counted separately. Practice the art of harmonics on earth by educating yourself and understanding the beliefs, habits and needs of those that seem to oppose you. Find the resonant harmonic strands of light connecting you to them and our oneness is remembered.

Harmonic Convergence August 16-17, 1987 marked the first time since the deluge of Atlantis that this planet carried more light energy than dark energy. The call to oneness was sounded by releasing duality. That's what we, our higher self and our soul decided at the harmonic convergence that this planet will have compassion for one another and understanding from country to country for Gaia and our environment.

1987 was ALSO the start of the NEW ENERGY and the harmonic convergence and later called the "11:11." The earth had reached a vibratory rate of **SPIRITUAL NEUTRALITY** the future could be pulled into a high interdimensional level or wallow in the old prophesies of doom.

Harmonic convergence and harmonic concordance are bookends to the changing, shifting energy humans have created. We are invited to create our own reality and reject our karmic set up. We are in a totally different energy.

Energy and numbers: 1987 was the year of the Harmonic Convergence. Adding these numbers in that year gives you a seven (7). Seven is the energy of sacredness. We made a sacred decision about changing our future.

It was in 1945 that the overall vibration of humanity made a course correction. This was a shift of human consciousness from a desire to follow the leader to trusting and following your own hearts. This was the very beginning of the Second Wave of Empowerment and opened the door for the ascension of humanity into higher vibrational levels. This was the event that set the stage for the higher vibrational measurement of the Harmonic Convergence.

Harmonic Concordance November 6-8, 2003 was one of a series of alignments of vibrational status that reached throughout all the cosmos, it was a checkpoint of our movement into oneness and into the universal energy flow. This was a quantum, interdimensional event signaled permission to rewrite our Akashic records and the crystalline sheath of our DNA. We were to change our vows to the vow of MASTER HOOD activate our creatorship and our divinity.

HARMONY is an **agreement** of FEELING, *approach* and INTERACTION between what you think, **feel,** SAY and DO. Working in harmony with everything around you is a form of grace or synergy.

HEALING is only *wisdom*. The future is a healed and balanced energy of the past. In new energy you need to want to heal the self no one can do it for you. They can hold a space for you but you heal yourself. HEALING and GUIDANCE can be the **same thing**. Channeled guidance can relieve and release CONFLICTS within you *that block the flow of your wisdom*. Practice the guidance you get **WHEN you get** it or the guidance fades and diminishes.

HIGHER SELF is part of our soul and vibrates higher than the human and lower than our 90%er. The invisible "**higher self**" is the **bridge** to our 90%er and is a multidimensional piece and an interdimensional piece of the human. The same higher self was and is present in every single past or concurrent life we have ever had. Our higher self knows every single human we have been. And it's all mixed into a soup together so we can take the best part of anyone of those lives and apply it to our current life! That is part of the system of the STRINGS OF VIBRATION.

The higher self is also our connection to all other human hearts and Gaia. The higher self was created when we squeezed

10% of our soul into a tiny bit of biology. We needed a connection to our 90%er and the universal flow to the human.

I frequently refer to the higher self as the soul in my books.

HOLOGRAM is a place where two or more sources of light cross each other and *create a third dimensional image in space*. Through holographic imaging we have placed the fifth dimension OVER the third dimension and by using the light source of our own THOUGHTS, *passion*, ideas and concepts a new hologram of light is being created in the same spot replacing the old. Humans with their 90%er will and have defined and created the fifth dimension. By mass consciousness reinforcing the hologram eventually it gets so strong and solid it overlays the original hologram we created on earth as angelic beings. The moment the legion of light or a divine human *entertains a thought,* two or more beams of light begin to create a hologram. When you are divine and have thoughts similar to your vibration that thought begins to create a hologram.

Holographic means any portion of the field contains everything in the field.

You can place a new childhood over your old childhood and mend what you would like to mend and change the outcome.

HUMAN the 10% of us which is temporarily wired into a carbon-based physical life form slowly turning crystalline. Humans are here to transmute matter from a lower vibratory level to a higher vibration of existence. This necessitates a physical body of lower vibration to pass as a gateway through which only the higher energy can rise. In order for this transmutation of matter to be accomplished it needed to be done by a consciousness that had forgotten who it was. That would be the human. We had forgotten our eternal Beingness and our vast presence as angels within the body of God and all over many universes. Humans have the "**street smarts of the Universe.**"

Human are the engines that generate the light and universal energy facilitates what it does after leaving us.

Humans **ARE the physical extension** of THEIR soul.

***

CHAPTER 20
"I" through R words and concepts

"I" <u>ENERGY</u> is the center of awareness and the part that is at cause. I is in the NOW moment and YOU are the focus. The era of care taking and enabling has PASSED. Be an inspirer of consciousness. We need to be CLEAR and to do it the EASY way. We need to release confusion, disease, doubt and hypnosis. They are not ours. Holding onto it will hurt you. "I" Put your pure divine self in consciousness right now to change the world.

<u>ICE AGE</u> is a part of a <u>WATER CYCLE</u> Our "global warming" is part of one of Gaia's cycles. Because her cycles take longer than a human lifetime to develop humans are not seeing the entire cycle. The global warming is part of a water cycle happening naturally and normally. It is the way Gaia balances herself.

She has large and small water cycles. There are many small ones between the large ones. The last small ice age was in the 1200s to 1400s. Around 200 years long. Right now we have the *beginning of another ice age*. A cold time starts with the warming. Water cycles vary in length. The little ones last as short as 150 years or as long as 400 years. Gaia is now at the beginning of a MEDIUM WATER CYCLE.

The *WATER* cycle is one of the most important contributors to changes of weather on earth. Humans are not responsible for the water cycles but this one is a little earlier than planned. The TEMPERATURE of the planet is dependent on how much water is on it. The water cycle of the planet is what controls the *temperature and the wind*. Part of the cycle is that it gets warm like it is now. We are at the beginning of a water cycle that will turn to a lower temperature eventually and that is typical, cyclical, and normal.

ILLUMINATION not a linear concept it is multidimensional. Pure light is sent without bias or idea. Your soul will take your light and put it where it will do the most good. Some things that may get illuminated are WISDOM, better ways of thinking, peaceful solutions or changed lives. There is integrity in NOT casting your ideas on others you are only offering illumination.

IMAGINATION is the intelligence of the new energy and is used by the creator to create with. There is no right or wrong. Your imagination can MOVE into and through all the DIMENSIONS and can solve challenges. Imagination is how we explore all our available probabilities so we can pick which ones we want to expand and develop. Integrate compassion into your being and your imagination goes off to see what is going on everywhere, it senses the many layers that surround you. Imagination is in a NEW TYPE of FLOW and when you send out for people or supplies they come to you.

Let yourself know you are in a safe place and now is the right time to ALLOW your imagination to come forward and be embraced and integrated with the rest of yourself. Imagination has largely been ignored and put down but it is one of the good guys. The new imagination realm is running parallel to the old fourth dimension realm. Allow the new fourth dimension to come into your life. All answers in the new energy are here and it is a safe place. If you want to be sure you are in the right place FEEL it. Is there freedom and no rules or laws? The new energy imagination realm is full, expressive, expansive and open.

INFORMATION is building and being downloaded into us until we can understand it or want to access it. Sometimes that is the noise you hear in your ear.

INNER SPACE is the humans TRUE reality and not the illusion of our thought forms. Our inner space is an orderly and harmonious system that *EXPANDS constantly* in terms of ENERGY and AWARENESS. Metatron is NOT *going forward* as our voice in spirit. As of 9-18-2007 **Yo-ham** is the transformation of Metatron into the physical more melded state and new vibration. Yo-ham or **"You are."** You are All That Is. You are that you are. Before becoming divine humans, converting inner space takes a great deal of cooperative congealed energy to be put into our physical dimensional realities.

The geometric, energetic grid that is being fired into brilliance, the 144 Crystalline Grid is bringing many changes to our physical reality through the laws of PHYSICS and laws of CONSCIOUSNESS that are currently beyond the scope of most of humanity and well above the conceptions of mainstream academia at this time.

INTEGRITY soundness of moral principle, uncorrupted, virtue, truthfulness, honesty and sincerity within the reality of ones own moral code and that of the group. **Integrity** is basing one's actions on an internally consistent framework of principles. One is said to have integrity to the extent that everything one does and believes is based on the same core set of values. While those values may change, it is their consistency with each other and with the person's actions that determine the person's integrity. The concept of integrity is directly linked to **responsibility** in that implementation spawning from principles is designed with a specific outcome in mind. When the action fails to achieve the desired effect, a change of principles is indicated. Accountability is achieved when a faulty principle is identified and changed to produce a more useful action.

INTENTION is a combination of Your DESIRE and EXPECTATION. When you intend something to happen it does. Verbalization is NOT the intention.

INTERDIMENSIONAL VOID In the interdimensional state is the future and past of the planet represented by every possible potential that exists. The future potentials created by the decisions of EVERY human on the planet. Everything we might do represented in one area. It is not a place but lovely strands of order for the multidimensional entities. In a interdimensional state nothing the human observes makes sense to the way we have been trained to see. Our decisions made in third dimension based on our life experience are NOT accurate for multidimensions. There is no third dimensional logic or clear perception there.

INTERDIMENSIONALITY or the **other side of the veil** isn't a place at all. It is an interdimensional state of ENERGY we can put ourselves into anytime we choose. Interdimensional energy is always around the human. We want it to be a place but it is not. The other side can look chaotic and confusing.

When we listen to the greatest music or see great art on earth we can know it came flowing through the veil. The always available energy in interdimensional space lays out all our potentials of what we can do, who we will meet, and our purpose in life. When you go to that place on purpose and engage that interdimensional energy you are drawing lines of energy "looking for and finding" the potentials you ask about. Where these lines meet is synchronicity. This is in an interdimensional language. There is actually great logic and purpose within it.

INTERIOR PORTAL WORKER will school the lost, fearful and confused souls after the shift in consciousness happens on earth to bring them into the higher vibration. Those inside portals are of the teacher class and they will use thought not language.

INTERNET GRID The internet is a human made grid and a form of communication never dreamt of in the beginning. It will continue to evolve as humanity does. At a certain vibrational level the physical wires *making up that grid will turn to* LIGHT and it will become a LIGHT GRID. Over a period of time the actual light itself will be integrated into our thought patterns that will connect all of you and emulate the universal energy on the physical realm of the fifth dimension. Our heart energy shared over this man-made grid has more of an effect than we can possibly understand. Spam even then might be a problem.

INVISIBLE REALM The invisible realm is everything humans have trained themselves NOT to see like all the other entities without bodies and the different dimensions. What is invisible is actually more permanent than our illusionary not real third dimension. Our leap of faith is to BELIEVE in ourselves above all to become eternal while wearing biology.

Realizing that there is a gap in our information is more productive than being stuck thinking that if you can't see it that it does not exist. Can you see radio waves or air or gravity. These are all invisible forces of energy we use every day and take for granted. Expand this understanding of things invisible to include the higher realms. Do invisible realms exist whether or not you believe they do. We must take the time and make the effort to reach from within us to know the invisible realm is there.

The invisible realm cannot do anything beyond what the human asks for. That would be overriding our free will. They hope you ask and ask. Our "intuition", is really our auric layers communicating with us. As we grow into our auras we expand into communion with our entire electromagnetic structure. And there is much house-cleaning to do.

JESUS wanted us to realize that each one of us can do exactly what he did! Our divinity has NO VOICE or WORDS. Our divinity is a feeling and a **knowingness** a warmth and depth. Jesus was / is **a collective of our energy** he does not have a soul but the energy is very real. The energy of Jesus is changing because we are different and changing. There is NO NEED for us to be **saved from anything**. FEELING from the heart is a natural gift from our soul. Childhood abuse does close the heart down pretty nicely. If that was your experience it is your job to be brave enough to **feel again and open up your heart** so you and soul can open up communication. That might not be easy and you might need some help with that. TO OPEN UP THE HEART allow yourself TO FEEL and breathe. Light and dark are the same energy embrace them both. Know that in every part of darkness there is light. There is no sin only the rules and laws that were created by humans to torment other humans. It is HUMANS that call certain behaviors SINFUL, not God. You will not find your soul through pain all you find that way is more pain. Suffering goes when YOU CHOOSE to release it.

JUDGMENT If you are still judging use it as a tool to point out **YOUR weak spots to you.** Acknowledge what you are doing with YOUR perception and understanding. Know what you find to judge others with is REALLY about how you **judge yourself.** Embrace the teaching your judgment brought you and move on. Honor rather than judge. Moving into appreciation helps you discontinue judgment.

KARMA is an energetic type of influence or balance. Karma is no longer ACTIVE in the new energy. Only in the third dimension are there past lives demanding a present one to "resolve" the energy. The new energy balance has the human creating a "past life support group" all surrounding them with tools and love they need to create mastery within themselves.

KRYON represent a very large group. She represent the trillions of pieces of God who know you. she is in many places and a multiple entity outside the third dimensionality. Kryon does not give rules or a place to report or ask you to join anything. You already have all of that as a piece of the legion of light. Our love is passive, it only waits for you to feel it. I am Kryon of Magnetic Service. I am in love with humanity.

KNOWINGNESS or gnost is NOT known to the brain. It is being certain, capability for truth, self determined knowledge. Knowingness comes from other dimensions or realms as our essence does, it is a type of dream or imagination state. Going to that state will allow you to bring information or essence into the third dimension, ground it here and it starts transforming itself into an energy eventually understood by the mind. That is where breakthroughs and "ahas" come from.

LEGION OF LIGHT is a term used for god or the creator or the source...What ever name you use, at the core is LOVE and COMPASSION for all things, UNCONDITIONAL love. The legion of light is **not in a place** since the concept of "place" cannot exist in a quantum state. INTERDIMENSIONAL energy is TIMELESS and there is no PLACE. There is no time on the other side of the veil. So there is no past. The legion of light is a *reflection* of the human consciousness. As ANY leader is a reflection of its followers. The legion of light is *ALWAYS creating* as an expression of LOVE. The legion of light is a being that animates matter.

God has always been multidimensional and humans have tried ever so hard to squeeze her into a single dimension. Humans in a single dimension make the legion of light with exaggerated human MALE qualities and not the nicest qualities.

The source is a PARTNERSHIP and not a singular entity. The core of the puzzle or game we just finished WAS, can humans discover who they are while not knowing their grandness or that we are all one. We were born into duality and brought to earth within a *dark energy biased against us*.

The legion of light is creation and all of this creation is ever expanding and growing. Once it is set into motion in perfect sacred **geometry** and SPIRITUAL SCIENCE it is not a necessity that it grows. It is an absolutely balanced ongoing miracle that DOES grow.

LIES are generally an **aspect of the truth** that doesn't want to **OWN ITSELF**. Just a frightened bit of **dark** energy in the liar trying to deny what it is. A dark bit of essence that has judged itself not worthy of love or compassion. It forgot that it was love having an experience on behalf of the legion of light.

LIGHT is a powerful energy and *spans* all DIMENSIONAL LEVELS *simultaneously*. The true vibration of light will rejuvenate your biology and soul. The higher meaning of Light is enlightenment or spiritual wisdom. Light can be reflected and that is easier for us to do instead of being the Light. GRACE mimics the natural FLOW of Light. Humans have earned the right to walk fully in the grace of the divine. When the word light hits your ears a resonance starts up creating an *interdimensional* vibration that weaves dimensions together to ACT AS ONE. Darkness can do nothing to affect light, but light can destroy darkness.

LIGHT BODY means making yourself energetically lighter by releasing your INTERNAL pressure. The energetic baggage and negativity humans carry keep them heavy and dense. All of the medical symptoms now will be about pressure related issues. Common diagnoses will be: high blood pressure as a result of the nervous system having too much pressure, fibromyalgia or skin tenderness from internal pressure, depression is an inability to release emotional mental density and phobias generally in the chest. Migraines, sinus, ear and allergy flare ups are the nervous system backing up. Arthritis is crystallized anger in the joints, creating joint blockages in the nervous system meridian flows, heart issues, palpitations are the body's rhythmic adjustments to the increasing frequencies. Gastritis-colitis is pressure blockages affecting gastrointestinal tract, sugar imbalances is too much unhappiness in life leading to an inability to process the sweet, lower back foundation and money issues, also reflected in shoulders, water retention fluctuating pressures affecting osmotic fluid balance in tissues.

LIMITING BELIEF is a belief that contradicts your desire. A limiting belief keeps you small and stuck. Recognizing and acknowledging our negative emotions will help point out our limited belief. Which we can release or choose to keep.

LITTLE HUMAN the or ego, is a **mist** just outside our body and is a beautiful, PERFECT veil of *light energy*. It is around us in anyway we choose to see it. This veil of energy is NOT PREDICTABLE but knows what it's going to do. The little human is so crisp and clear and ready to be in service to you.

Humans live in the third dimension to **honor our source** or the legion of light with an EXPERIENCE of being human. The little human has been very helpful to us to accomplish that goal. Without the little human we would not HAVE stayed in our biology. If we were to pop out of our biology and go back home we would **need** (as in having no choice) to come back again to finish this journey. We promised the legion of light that we would come here and accomplish certain tasks the best way we could. When we are finished we will know it because we will be in the universal flow with our soul. That is when we will go and stay gone.

The little human is the one presence we need to **learn to love** because it sets up our journey to bring forth our perfection by keeping us a little bit short of our goal. Allowing us to do our journey in full. The little human is what we really are. The LITTLE HUMANS have created this magnificent form of a physical body that holds the essence of *All That Is.*

Yet our little human keeps us on the journey here.

We ARE the I AM presence.

I AM that I AM the **DIVINE HUMAN** when I unite with my soul.

LOVE is a catalyst, an energy that provides the PUSH for transformation of one energy into another energy and into another energy NEVER changing the original energy. Love energy manifests WISDOM where there was ignorance and COMPASSION where there was judgment. Humans have total compassion, strong and thick from the unseen world for any experience we had and are having.

MAGNETICS is an *interdimensional FORCE* and the **largest force** in the universe. At our birth it was MAGNETICS that imprinted us with our astrological aspects and our DNA which is interdimensional and part of our cellular structure. Magnetics is even STRONGER than chemistry is in our universe.

The **magnetics** of this planet are linked to the changing consciousness of the human. In the human there is FOCUSED ENERGY, a *creator* energy when we ALLOW our *essence or soul to flow* through us. When our 90%er and 10%er are vibrating in sync we are at our very best. While feeling our FEELINGS and **senses** we ALLOW creation to flow freely through us. Our unconscious and conscious power is greatest in the now moment when we are feeling and sensing the magnetic grid around earth. The grid is the hardware and our DNA is our software.

Magnetics and universal love that goes way beyond human love are the same thing. A magnetic field that comes in contact with another magnetic field has the option of transmitting its frequencies and patterning onto it. The solar sun talks to our DNA by transmitting its energy and patterning into the magnetic field of earth. Our sun is communicating to you by sending its light in the **form of a magnetic field. We** can connect to others by following the example of the sun and use the magnetics we experience as universal love to radiate a light to beam of love from one magnetic field onto another.

MANIFESTING *is what the **soul** does.* When we have given up our free will to be in "divine will" we manifest our heart's desire or you manifest what your soul feels is best for your spiritual development or humanity.

MASTER NUMBERS are TRIGGERS in our reality to alert us to different events. **INTENT and WILL are far stronger** than astrological or numerical influences. Trinity dates are important but NOT more important than moments of free will which can accelerate the geometric activation of crystalline frequency speeding up the synergy.

MASTERY is taking something that has become negative in your life and finding a positive uses for it. Mastery is when you are not fearful and you are peaceful when others are not. A human's first reaction is to fight when provoked. A master's first reaction is to check herself to see if her integrity is in place and working.

MATTER is dense energy at a slow vibration. Energy is real. Matter and money is *mostly illusion.* OUR ENERGY is what supports and aligns the matter. Matter cannot create energy. Energy is our true form. Biology is matter and a light created form of energy that we can live in and experience in. We have been using light created forms of energy to EXPRESS our INTELLECT. Physical matter is simply a trick of the light. It is not real as light **OUR essence** is real.

MELCHIZEDEK or the **Order Of Melchizedek**, or the **White Brotherhood** and the **Brotherhood Of Light**. Are legions of ancient Brothers, Ascended Masters, angels, and light-bearing ascended species from different dimensions.

This diverse group **are the SCRIBES** for the legion of light. They gather information, knowledge and truth. They are in charge of the Akashic Records. They are the ones who remember it ALL. They teach others the concepts they have collected for all that is. They STAND WITNESS to others' progress and help WHENEVER they can. They are material mechanics and spiritual surgeons that minister to the humans. They are dedicated in this quadrant of the universe to the evolution of humanity through the transmission of wisdom and knowledge that becomes our truth and our power. They are here to help us CLEAR OUR FOUR BODIES and help balance us. They ask humans to believe in the invisible realm. That is the perceptual shift we are making now and it is not an easy one.

Humans are performing a vital service to humanity by transmitting and transmuting our physical reality into a higher expression. The **White Brotherhood** will gladly drop in and visit with you. That is what they dearly love to do. Just call them. They will come with as many cool special effects as your awareness can handle. The **Melchizedek Brotherhood** or the **Brotherhood of Light** resides in the fifth and sixth dimensions to be near the humans they work with. Many of them are from the seventh octave of consciousness and beyond in many different areas of existence and many different species. They have a conscious awareness up to the fourteenth dimension. Beyond the fourteenth dimension they could not communicate with humans at all. At the fourteenth dimension or level bodies are much larger and transitory. **MELDING** is when your energy field overlaps another's field so you can read each other telepathically. Like putting one circle over another circle. Remember NO SECRETS in higher vibrations.

MENTAL BODY is the third layer and extends beyond the emotional body and is composed of still finer substances which are associated with thoughts and our mental processes. This body usually appears as a **bright yellow light radiating about the head and shoulders** and extending around the whole body. This expands and becomes brighter when its owner is concentrating on mental processes. The mental body extends from three to eight inches from the body and contains the STRUCTURE of our ideas. The thought forms appear to be blobs of varying brightness and shape. These thought forms have additional colors superimposed on them *coming from the emotional body*. The color represents the person's emotion attachment to the particular thought form. The strength of the thought and emotion determines the size of a thought form and its duration as a separate entity. Duration depends on how much nurturing is generate by the repetition of the thought by its originator or others. A thought form is an **energy or consciousness** manifested either consciously or unconsciously by an individual or a group. A thought form may be benevolent or malevolent.

The type of thought determines its shape and a **clear thought has a well defined outline**. A glowing rose color is a wish to heal. Silver white would be a mental effort to strengthen and focus the mind. A yellow gold indicates intellect and has a darker dull tint if attached to lower negative goals.

Abstract ideas are represented by various geometrical forms. The merest abstraction in third dimension becomes a definite fact on the mental plane. When a human thinks of a concrete object like a pool or shed they build a tiny image of the object in matter in the mental body. These are so real they can be **moved about** and **rearranged by someone other than their creator**. The form can be seen by another that sees the invisible realm. The image floats in the upper part of that body generally in front of the face. When we think of another person a tiny portrait shows up.

When the thinkers became incarnate in biology the senseless animal, physical matter, becomes a thinking being by virtue of the angel present in it. Humans are the link between the divine and the animal. The mental body is of peculiar interest because after the mind is fairly developed the human spends nearly all its time in the mental body. Functioning in the physical world for brief snatches of mortal life.

Lack of ATTENTION or focus is the MAIN reason humans produce imperfect and sloppy images. Which is not very angel like. When the HUMAN mind is occupied with five different subjects simultaneously like household chores or business concerns, fatigue or the anticipation of pleasure that can all take up to 90% of the mental body. The remaining 10% or less results in fragmentary and unconnected thought forms. No orderly edifice is built there.

MERIDIAN SYSTEM is composed of our physical NERVOUS SYSTEM within our biology and the ENERGETIC MERIDIANS within our auric field. Together they form the energetic framework of our multilayered bodies.

To rise from the denser third dimension to the lighter fifth dimension requires shedding third dimensional density by releasing *faulty belief systems* and embracing multidimensional concepts. Clearing and balancing your emotions and biology. All gets processed though our meridian system and out through our biology. Aches and pains are our energetic blockages, stress and strain trying to release through our meridian and then the nervous system.

MERKABAH vehicle is our physicalized electromagnetic blueprint.

METATRON is our collective voice of consciousness in spirit and has been a go-between humans and the MULTIDIMENSIONAL realms. A spokesperson for all humans because our energies were so tied up on earth we weren't in a position to speak for ourselves. Ever since we left the Order of the Arc, Metatron has been THE SHOUD of human thoughts. Metatron was always present and consistent in representing us and converted human *inner space* or creativity into *coded light which congeals* energetically into physical dimensional realities. Metatron is NOT *going forward* as our voice in spirit. Metatron has transformed as we are doing.

In the new energy and consciousness on earth during the Quantum Leap of, 9-18-2007 **Yo-ham** is the transformation of Metatron into the physical, personal more melded state and new vibration or name of Yo-ham. "**You are.**" You are All That Is. You are that you are. Some had even a feeling of a metallic or electric energy, a scientific or a type of physics to the very name of Metatron

Yo-ham is our essence and joins in this triumphant discovery of life, purpose and of expression on earth.

MERKABAH are all our bodies, the invisible ones surrounding our physical core is our merkabah vehicle we use to enter into interdimensional realms. When our bodies cannot maintain the higher energies we will not reach them in this lifetime.

MIND CONTROL is a term used to label methods of extreme coercion that result in an individual's involuntary, robotic compliance. Trauma-based mind control is not a modern-day invention. The Egyptian Book of the Dead is a compilation of rituals explicitly describing methods of torture and intimidation (to create trauma), drugs, and casting spells (hypnosis) ultimately resulting in total enslavement of the initiate.

MISCREATE thoughts do create things so how easy would it be to miscreate. Miscreating means you are creating from darkness or negativity and a lot of grief for yourself. To wish someone dead or ill creates more karma than you can imagine. People that have not reached a level of mental and emotional control will miscreate. yet. Your thoughts need to always be in a state of unconditional love and total harmlessness. Once we are fully merged into the fifth dimension it will be impossible for us to inflict harm on any living creature. We will be keenly aware of the possibility of creating negative karma with others.

MULTIDIMENSIONAL LANGUAGE or THIRD LANGUAGE is the way the invisible realm, soul or our entourage communicates with humans. This communication happens slowly and naturally INSIDE us. It can be our OWN voice we hear, a **smell** or TASTE or the shivery feeling we get when our entourage is in agreement with something we have said, done or thought. *IT IS the feeling* that washes over us like a tingle, shiveries or a touch on the head or cheek or any place on the body. That feeling means we have reached a point of awareness that are feeling the *energy of compassion*. We are activating communication with our soul energy or any other member of our entourage. A spiritual interdimensional language that is **NOT linear** and crosses all of time and space.

When you present your soul or the invisible realm with questions, concerns or issues to increase your clarity or spiritual wisdom it is important to be AS PRESENT in the now moment as you possibly can. HEALING and GUIDANCE can be the **same thing**. Channeled guidance can relieve and release CONFLICTS within you *that block the flow of your wisdom*. Practice the guidance you get **WHEN you get** it or the guidance fades and diminishes. Blame will not get you desirable results. You are in lesson not victimhood. Speak with gratitude and softly to hear more.

Logic and reason found on the third dimension can **HIDE wisdom**. The entity wanting to communicate with you melds with your energy and through telepathy or whatever channel the human has open you get the information. The current energy of earth NOW allows communication IF you **WANT** to hear, sense or feel.

In the past, to communicate with the invisible realm took massive preparation to prepare the human biology for this kind of thing. We were too dense to feel the compassion of the invisible realm. Co-creation requires synchronicity. For synchronicity to happen in your life you need to LISTEN and DO as your soul or entourage are recommending you do. That is the only way you will meet those creating with you. Humans need to be an ACTIVE team member, no longer will ANYONE in the invisible realm do it for you.

Don't move too fast, answer with love and be patient. Feel the communication of compassion. All the tools a human may have mastered can leave or change but the cosmic flow of love and compassion is forever.

MYSTICISM is the unexplained science of the legion of light which is multidimensional and the third dimension is singular.

NEAR REALMS are the realms closest to the earth realm and that would include the fourth dimension and the mental realms. Near realms have entities without bodies including the earthbound and those not able to find the bridge of flowers or those that are addicted or too attached to the third dimension to leave and some are learning from the humans how to be spiritual.

NEW ENERGY 1987 was the start of new energy coming in. All ENERGY before that was older, denser energy. New energy can be INTEGRATED into Old Energy **reality**. New and old energy do not have to be independent or separate. BUT old energy is suspicious of new energy and within our biology isn't happy with what appears to be a foreign invasion.

The probabilities the new energy brought in were all delivered by 9-18-2007 and came into our reality in the form of energy bubbles and they are all around us now. We sense them as something different and strange. New energy "just is" and is working in your life right now.

New energy is undefinable with the current tools and resources we have. We have moved BEYOND the world of experience into the UNDEFINABLE expansional energy that moves **in and out of dimensions**. There is an infinite supply of energy available now. In oneness there are *no opposing forces* and IMAGINATION is used to create with. In new energy there will be compassion and unconditional love in a state of timeless serenity because of our higher vibration which eliminates pain and suffering. There is enough abundance and compassion for all. As creators we will feel FEAR and *self doubt* those emotions are real and the energies do not need to be considered **negative** they can work with YOU and for your creations.

New energy has a *consciousness* that directly corresponds to the consciousness of "I" and the energy keeps moving and flowing. Humans wanted AN answer. There are NO ANSWERS *because* **new energy is potentials**. A potential doesn't have to DEFINE itself as a truth. Potentials have **many** truth layers and many answers to A problem. The mind in particular wants to understand and analyze. Definition has opened to multiple definitions. Definition limits and new energy expands definition beyond definition. No more neat little compartments. 2 and 2 equals 4 and many MANY many more. In new energy the sum of any two parts always comes back to one. No right and wrong "it just is," without a value or moral parameters to keep tract of.

New energy has redefined the consciousness of old energy and has **allowed** the old energy to **expand AND RELEASE its old STRUCTURES and limitations** to join new energy in OPENED ENDED, free, BRILLIANTLY SIMPLE crystal clear expression.

LEVELS OF COMPASSION

New energy REDEFINES the awareness of old energy and in the process BREAKS or deconstructs old structures and limitations.

NEW ENERGY TOOLS and SKILLS to help you cope, prosper and see multiple perspectives. A full spectrum of vision is a good way to move forward in our evolution. There are no rights or wrongs.

DISCERNMENT is the art of making choices without judgment. Purposely choosing what is in our life is needed to alter our life in a constructive way. When it pulls at our heart it is ours. Anything less than that release without judgment it is there for another.

We have **PAST LIFE SUPPORT GROUPS** to keep us balanced. All our past lives surround us with the compassion and love needed to create mastery in us.

ENERGY is a tool or fuel and is created from nothingness. New energy **desire** moves us through the dimensions as our **desire** activates it.

Some **CRYSTALS** with the correct vibration can help translate communications to entities on other dimensions.

IMAGINATION is how we explore probabilities and when we send out for people or supplies in your imagination they come to you.

LAUGHTER cleanses and clears the energy. The breathe in between your laugh will pull in new potentials because you released old attachments. It switches your **point of perception** to change your reality and draw energy to you.

GRAY is the middle ground of the contrast of dark and light. Duality is what was needed to show us CONTRAST so we can SEE and KNOW our divinity. Our divinity or soul pulsing through us helps us create solutions in the density of earth.

A PERSONAL VORTEX is infinite energy moving in a circular motion without a beginning or end. Humans put it in finite form and try to hold it that way. To setup a personal vortex spin or think in a circular motion. Find a way to create a circular energy field around you to facilitate the changes you now face.

COLLECTIVE INTENTIONAL VORTICES Creating a vortex within a group also makes space for them in your lives as you interact with the earth on a collective basis. Unlike personal vortices, once a collective vortex is placed into motion it remains in that spot. These funnels will be used by the earth to anchor and distribute the crystal energy onto the planet. Some will turn to portals.

RIGHT ANGLES are the entrance between realities or dimensions. One dimensional reality is separated from another by **ninety degrees**. When you find your reality not to your liking stop and *turn ninety degrees* from where you are. You must discern which direction to turn. Even if this feels a symbolic gesture do it till you understand use of this universal truth.

SHIFTING PERCEPTION Is choosing an alternate or dimensional reality. When there are items in your life that drain you and can't be moved it is best to shift your perception to stop the ENERGY DRAIN by **thoughts**, *events* or HUMANS.

EXTERNALLY REBALANCE yourself by use of music, sights or sounds. A song that brings tears a movie that touches your soul.

PASSION and **JOY** our success in higher vibrations is directly related to the amount of joy and passion you can experience on a daily basis.

<u>**NHAHYU**</u> Nhahyu is an old Lemurian word. Nhahyu is a combination of **AWARENESS, feelings,** PERCEPTIONS

and **SENSATIONS.** The ability and skill to go into AND feel energies. We will FIND OURSELVES CALLED into consciousness situations to use this nonphysical ability, nhahyu. Our consciousness will be called in. Our presence alters things WITHOUT us doing anything physically or even being physically present.

<u>90%ER</u> The parts of the 90%er would include all the third dimensional terms used like spirit, holy ghost, angels, guides or higher self or the human's entourage. In my books I refer to the 90% as our SOUL even though there are different parts. I do not know names or descriptions of all the parts because they are multidimensional and not easily understood by a single dimensional human. I use the word soul when referring to any of the 90% to simplify and hopefully clarify what I am saying. All we need do is die or abandon our biology or go to sleep and the 10% and 90% reunite instantly.

Humans do have the "**street smarts of the Universe.**" Humans are the engines that generate the light and universal energy. Our 90% facilitates what the light and energy does after leaving us.

<u>NONRESISTANCE</u> has nothing to do with with ACTIONS. The effects of nonresistance are peace, tranquillity and serenity. Nonresistance IS LOVE and knowing each person Is God Also and deserves our respect and freedom to express themselves in their own unique way. Nonresistance is a freeing agent it is not passivity or escapism. We need to allow the threads of a circumstance to ease. Then take whatever action is necessary to remove the tangled situation from our life.

Our THOUGHTS ARE THINGS. Its quite a responsibility to know that our every thought CREATES.

With free will, we have the right to choose how we will think about our experiences and our feelings always follow. With **divine will your soul has nonresistance.**

NOW TIME *or* timeless space is the ENERGY of home and zero-point energy. It means to be in the present moment the past and future all at once. Space is CONGEALED time. The congealed time's VELOCITY is relative to *the speed of light* which determines the DENSITY of the congealed time or space. NOW time is circular.

As you take yourself off the *time line* by removing your experiences from it you see things the way they really are. The past is a memory and humans tend to store **NEGATIVE energy** in the past. The future is only potentials and **POSITIVE energy** that is in the future with our PASSION and excitement about potentials. Even good memories of the past are stored in the future.

There is a formula for **TIME** : The DENSITY of mass plus the rate at which it is VIBRATING equals its time frame. There are varying *time frames* IN EACH DIMENSION and they are circular. The now time frame is like a circle around us where all things past are known and future potentials are realized and known.

When the human SHIFTS their reality of time and their cells respond accordingly, our body lives in different dimensions at the same time. As rooms in a building we decide which reality we want to be in. Try not to use your brain too much sense and move through your heart and feelings. Release your old ways of managing and controlling things, people and yourself. Shift away from the mind to make room for the new energy of the heart.

LEVELS OF COMPASSION

NOW has **no judgments**. NOW is a quiet place where you can feel love washing through or over your entire being. NOW can last for a second or hours. In the NOW we have **NO needs or wants**. In the divine NOW moment there is a new vibration emanating out from within you ATTRACTING ALL APPROPRIATE things to you. Now energy is multidimensional not honoring linearity of time.

OLD ENERGY is the need to experience and have a low vibration. It needs *two opposing forces* to create with. It is confusing and challenging to maintain balance in the middle of these two opposing poles of energy. In **duality** we are exposed to deceit, self deception, corruption, greed, and decadence. Duality, opposition was encoded in our DNA. We setup this vibrational FRICTION on purpose to increase our wisdom and understanding. Generally speaking we made the ratio of energy in duality 1/3 to 2/3 dark and light and new awareness happened VERY slowly.

OMNI- PHYSICS is the science of all the potentials and their behaviors. Envision the potentials as bubbles that exist outside of physical reality waiting to be brought into physical reality. Each bubble on its own representing a different potential. As the humans brings things into reality through the energy tube the literal bubbles of potential gather together as atoms do in all the molecules of our scientific structures. They are attracted to what you are choosing in your life and begin to come in. Sometimes they cluster all around you in a state of potential waiting for expression in reality turning to matter, opportunity or concept finding their way to you.

ORDER means direction or a specific motive to energy. It can mean purpose. We served in the churches, secret organizations, as nuns, priests, rabbis and when we were asked to leave it caused deep wounds. The Order of the Crimson Circle is a common bond between evolved beings who have agreed to be here on Earth to move consciousness forward and some agreed to be teachers.

ORDER of the ARC or the committee was created and formed by angelic beings to resolve the energy impasse or STALLED energy of the universe. Earth was and continues to be the laboratory the universe watches. Opportunities were needed to work with time and space in a **VERY slowed** reality or very slowed vibration. They needed to understand the dynamics involved in making a CONSCIOUS choice and watching the results of that choice unfold and flow. They were observing the **EVOLUTION of the SOUL**.

OVER SOUL Each over soul creates 12 soul identities. Then each soul identity creates 12 incarnate identities, six male and six female. Thus each person is part of an incarnational family of 144 incarnates. The sacred mathematics of $12 \times 12 = 144$. When one life ends it is feed to another life energy, one of the threads. No energy is ever lost or wasted. Each of the 144 incarnates carries part of the 12-Strand DNA pattern within the genetic code. As the 144 incarnates progressively evolve with the planet through the six time cycles, the 12-Strand DNA imprint is progressively build up in the genetic code. There are an infinite number of over souls. All over souls exist for the purpose of the legion of light to explore Itself. Each over soul in existence represents a different aspect like the plant kingdom, or mineral kingdom, animal Kingdom, etc.

The animal kingdom over soul, for example has each animal innately connected to its own species over soul. Each one knows by knowing exactly what to do, how to do it, and when to do it. Each animal species is one over soul family.

All humans have similar descents we are a part of a specific energy stream that eventually chooses this reality. The soul-personalities who are a part of this energy stream are your original over soul family. Within your Over soul Family, you all existed in perfect harmony in a state of perfect communication, not only with your Over soul, but also with each other. Each member of the group has a function like no other, but each one is equally important to the whole.

Because of genetic manipulation, you have lost touch with the others that originated through your over soul lineage. A mixed genetic heritage is a deterrent to perfect alignment and communication with your own over soul. When the human race was created of mixed alien genetics, this ensured that people could not operate and function in perfect harmony with their over soul or with each other. And, with a reptilian brain stem, humans as they currently exist, will always have at least two genetic frequencies. Simply put, genetic engineering has taken place so that soul-personalities have no choice but to wear clothes (bodies) that do not match.

Once in the body, they are trapped by the genetics. Each soul-personality must first overcome the genetics before it is possible to even begin discovering their own frequency, much less that of their over soul and over soul family. a literal family tree of consciousness through which all humans are connected to each other, all other life forms, the universes, the cosmos and source.

PASSION is love expressed, expansive and open to all the many new realms. Passion is fuel. If you are not so sure what to do sit in a quiet moment and feel what your passion has to say. The answer of knowingness will come to you. When we attempt to control new energy passion with old human ways it will hurt us. Divine balance comes from within you along with all the wisdom you have gained from your past experiences and keep gaining or remembering in the now moment. The New Creators are the ones who remained here on earth in body and are able to call upon their divinity. They are creating, and will create a new environment, different science, expanded math and energy for themselves that will affect and help others who are wanting to evolve or become creators. The answers we seek are being found in different locations AND the location of answers is continually changing. When we are in the NOW moment there will be solutions that have never been available to us before. **Solutions** could not make their way through our FREE WILL and duality. Passion is **desiring the best outcome** in each and every endeavor you decide to take on.

PEACE is the ability to allow everything and everyone to be exactly as they are. Within real peace there is no need to be right or have a right way to be peaceful. The seeds of peace are a potential creation waiting to match the human vibration of peace. We envision peace as everyone satisfied and no hunger or pain. On a planet of free choice that cannot happen. We can be free of major wars. A one world government won't work because we need different leaders and governments to maintain profoundly *different ways of life*. Governments and communities will intertwine in very unique ways. Peace would need to be made of agreements to respect each others choice of how they wanted to live and exist.

No more *forcing others* from family members to countries.

There will always be disputes, hunger and situations where many need what others have. Neighbors will trade with neighbors. Neighbors will need and depend on each other.

PHOTON in quantum physics After the shift **PHOTON energy** will **REPLACE electricity.** Using photon energy starts in your AWARENESS. That is how you can work with it. The WILL to use photons and then your directing them accomplishes tasks. We are not limited by, but expanded by the use of photon energy it is VERY LIBERATING. This energy is FREE and available for taking. Photon particles are powerful energies that can **gather thoughts** and RETAIN MEMORY far greater than all OUR BRAINS. Photons know they are not a brain, they are LIGHT from the legion of light. The photon THINKS and is SELF DIRECTING in anyway it is needed. Each particle of photon energy can **think and evolve.**

The photon does not have a past or future. At a moments notice, photons vibrational ability can MANUFACTURE a *strand within the weave* to follow through a wavelength. Through the photon energy one can control EVERY **experiential** REALITY with the focus available in a matrix. Or control any energy field controlled by electromagnetic force.

The photon cell can transfer energy from one end of the universe to the other end without diminishing itself. Photon energy can raise and expand levels of awareness in the human by SHIFTING their PERSPECTIVE to a HIGHER perception. This would move and expand you in the direction you wanted to go.

SCIENTIST SAY

The **photon** is the elementary particle responsible for electromagnetic phenomena. The photon is the CARRIER of electromagnetic radiation of all wavelengths, including gamma rays, X-rays, ultraviolet light, visible light, infrared light, microwaves, and radio waves. The photon differs from many other elementary particles, such as the electron and the quark, in that it has zero rest mass so it travels in a vacuum at the speed of light. The photon has both wave and particle properties. Photons show wavelike phenomena. As a particle, it can only interact with matter by transferring the amount of energy

Apart from having energy, a photon also carries momentum and has a polarization. It follows the laws of quantum mechanics, which means that often these properties do not have a well-defined value for a given photon. Rather, they are defined as a probability to measure a certain polarization, position, or momentum. For example, although a photon can excite a single molecule, it is often impossible to predict beforehand *which* molecule will be excited. Photon as a carrier of electromagnetic radiation is commonly used by physicists. In theoretical physics, a photon can be considered as a mediator for any type of electromagnetic interactions, including magnetic fields and electrostatic repulsion between like charges.

PHYSICAL BODY is the GROUNDING force for all that we are on earth and this plane of AWARENESS. It carries our **physicalized electromagnetic blueprint**. Our biology has its own consciousness and is separate from the etheric mind, body and emotions. Each organ in the body has its own consciousness as does each organ, cell and tissue. In the physical body as everywhere else there are varying degrees of consciousness. Left to itself the biology follows its own instinctual wisdom transmitted from our spiritual awareness.

Sadly human negative emotions greatly affect our biology at the emotional level producing **MUSCLE tension** and disease. The aches and pains we have are energetic blockages we create from stress and strain that we need to release down our bodies meridian systems. Our biology needs to continually release OLD energy and breathe in the new energy which it does in a variety of ways. Literally we release old energy through the skin, the runny noses or runny eyes, our psychic energy and mental energies and ALL the places we have always rid our self of bodily waste. Our blockages represent the wear and tear on us from this life and past lives. A physical manifestation of things we are still wrestling with and trying to resolve within ourselves. Our bodies anchor our energetic layers that *FAN OUT* in ever-widening circles of *vibrating frequency*. Our auras TOUCH each other at six feet from our biology. As our auras become more sensitive it will become downright painful to have a disgruntled or unpleasant energy in your auric space. Your energetic bodies ARE GROWING more **dense and REAL** to humans as they connect to the higher frequencies.

<u>**PLAY**</u> is seen as something interesting and work is seen as arduous and necessary. Play is an activity OR work without a purpose.

<u>**PORTALS**</u> a DOOR through time and space. Portals have existed on Earth from the beginning and it was the early portals that spawned life on earth. Now portals are growing in size and number, some that have been in place for some time are changing. A portal opens a space in the time continuum to connect all dimensional realities simultaneously. When we start

sensing other dimensions the physical sensation is one of a gentle confusion or "fuzziness" or a flow or swirl of energy as we sense snippets. Sometimes you will see a dot or color get larger or open to another dimension or portal. Watch for unusual happenings as we start to see portals and the comings and goings of them. Portals range in sizes from a pinhole which is not too useful to the size of a large circle in a small room, maybe nine by nine foot which is a bit hard to handle. Portals are always round with no flat sides. Energy and entities go in and out of the portals. It opens and closes for a soul to travel in.

Learn to use what comes in and out of the portals for your benefit. A portal is a veil of interwoven energy. There is a gauzy covering on the opening of the portal to prevent heavier lower vibrating things and entities from entering. We use portals to connect to a different lifetime of ours to get reconnected with our other selves.

A portal moves like our soul does. They both connect to the stronger and higher vibration. Our seed of thought sends the message to the spiritual portal to open. Trust the feelings you are beginning to get as your vibrational communication starts getting stronger. Bring the energy through you but do not hold on to, let it keep moving. The new energy is coming in through **our consciousness** and through different portals that open according to the demands of CONSCIOUSNESS itself.

PRANA ENERGY is very potent BUT not powerful and works very, very quickly. Prana is everywhere and emanates from souled beings into the omniverse. It is radiated every moment of everyday by every human. The vast, vast, vast majority of all the prana floating around is unused. Earth herself and the beings who help take care of Earth use it often. It's yours and you can use it. Your essence, pran or prantay has a physics to it. Prana is the FLOW of **CONSCIOUSNESS** *into energy into this reality*. Prana can be transferred or captured in such a way that you can actually use it as an energy source in our third dimensional reality.

PRANA BREATHING is done by pulling down the breath through the crown chakra. Prana was what we existed on during our lifetimes in Lemuria. We used breath to oxygenate the system. Our energy pattern was sustained by prana. Imagine the golden particles of light entering through your crown chakra and move down through the pineal and thymus glands. Let it fill the whole biology. Holding this light for a few seconds exhale and release it through the heart chakra as you quiet your mind and relax the body and begin to slow down your breathing. And experience the feeling of love and light in being one with the creator. In the fifth dimension prana from the photon energy will be the main source of life. Prana breathing was the essence of survival. Over the years we learned how to use the lungs and mouth to breathe. When used properly, prana breathing allows one to move the molecular structure into a different level of understanding.

PROGRAMMING is coercive persuasion or the manipulation of a human to produce alter personalities, fragments, or entities for the purpose of mind control. Some programming is generic and used on a variety of individuals in different cults or groups in different locales. Some programming is specific to the cult or even the programmer or to a particular person being programmed.

Programming is a belief system forced on one that they adopt as their own and do not have conscious awareness of how it was forced on them.

The victim or survivor of programming can display an inordinate amount of alter personalities, with numerous back-up programs, mirrors, and shadows. Alters are often organized in a series of layers or levels. The deeper the level, the worse and more painful the memory is. Alters are divided into a light side (good) and a dark-side (bad) that are interwoven in the mind and that rotate on an axis. There are 7 levels, each having an internal programmer who oversees or is a "gatekeepers" who grants or denies entry into the different "rooms". Yes, that all goes on in the mind and can be graphed and charted.

The people interested in having a mind-controlled slave buy the child and have the parent train him or her. Later on, a handler may take over or the parent may continue. Females are turned into sex slaves, breeders, killers or trainers and are frequently couriers of one sort or another. Males are sex slaves and couriers also, as well as killers or handlers of mind-controlled people.

The most common, most compliant, and most defenseless victims are infants. Sometimes the fetus, and later the infant, is traumatized into a dissociated state, sometimes with a pin prick, when only a fetus. Electroshock and/or drugs are commonly used on older children. When a person is in a dissociated state, they are highly suggestible. It's easy to capitalize on the trauma implanted in the child's mind by Daddy or others.

Trainers in the main have stopped using trauma to induce altered brain states.

Current electronic technology makes torturing children obsolete. Programming success depends on altering the child's perception of his or her five senses, and computers are now used extensively. (Taylor, 1999) If you are over twenty years old and were trained as a mind-control slave, you would probably have the trauma-based dissociation used in ritual abuse.

QUANTUM HOLOGRAM is being in a state of timelessness. Only in an interdimensional state can we participate in the quantum hologram. On the other side of the veil you can FEEL the potentials for this planet. Those potentials vibrating highest are most likely to manifest. One potential waiting to match the humans vibration of creation would be the seeds of peace. Not the way humans see peace with everyone satisfied and no hunger or pain. That cannot happen on a planet of free choice and duality. But we can be free of major wars. Not a one world government because we need different leaders and governments for profoundly different ways of life. Peace on earth would need to be made up of an agreement to respect each others choice of existence.

We need to *stop forcing others* from family members to countries.

There will always be disputes, hunger and situations where many need what others have. Neighbors will trade with neighbors. They will need and depend on each other. There will be an intertwining of governments and communities in very unique ways. Business, ethical and spiritual is becoming more and more important.

Humans are interdimensional pieces of light, pieces of the legion of light. We are connected to the invisible realm in ways we cannot even imagine in a quantum state that serves us both.

QUANTUM MECHANICS or theory is a physical science dealing with the **behavior** of MATTER and ENERGY on the scale of atoms and subatomic particles. It can accurately predict the physical behavior of systems, including systems where Newtonian mechanics fails. The quantum realm is far smaller than protons and neutrons. Quantum scientists have shown that the thoughts and expectations of the experimenter caused the experiment's outcome! **We have a direct effect on the world around us.** Our thoughts are affecting the physical world we live in. The power of thought literally enables us to create our own reality.

Interdimensional energy is TIMELESS therefor there is **no PLACE**. There is no time on the other side of the veil and no past. On the Other side there is no struggle but there are challenges of energy balance. There is balancing and universal creation in the quantum state. Particles of light and matter behave differently when humans "watch" them. Energy follows thought "holographic creations" are made from waves of sound and light.

<u>**QUANTUM LEAP**</u> often means you must release a current set of beliefs and adopt new ones. Quantum leaps are achieved by enhancing the **WANTING part** and not the believing and allowing aspects. It requires exaggerated contrast causing dramatic propulsion of desire to produce startling results which are almost always temporary.

The balance of your beliefs will bring you back some. Before the quantum leap we flowed along in the grid and old consciousness just letting things happen being buffeted by the flow with no deliberate consciousness, choice or creatorship. The most recent quantum leap was September 18, 2007. After the leap the divine human says I AM what I Create, what I choose and what I experience.

Quantum leap celebration was a cycle of readjusting and making some deep types of changes **FROM within** ourselves.

<u>**REALITY**</u> on earth is agreement to what is, starting with probabilities and ending in mass. The reality of something is

the ability to place it in time and space an agreement. This can often have a few day lag time.

RESTIMULATION is the reactivation of something in your past. A simple system of stimulus response especially when the person tired or stressed.

RESONANT A resonant object whether mechanical, acoustic, or electrical, will probably have more than one resonance frequency, especially harmonics of the strongest resonance. It will "pick out" its resonance frequency while filtering out all frequencies other than its resonance.

***

CHAPTER 21
S through Z words and concepts

SACRED GEOMETRY is sacred to the observer of the geometric shapes. The term has been used to encompass the religious, philosophical and spiritual beliefs that have sprung up around geometry in various cultures during the course of human history. The ancients believed that the experience of sacred geometry was essential to the education of the SOUL. Math follows human consciousness.

SCALE OF EMOTIONS are based on the VIBRATION of the emotion.
The "NO EMOTION" or "UNCONSCIOUS human" or "NEGATIVE emotion" has within it; RESENTMENT and *antagonism* or BLAMING. Angry and acting out, or SELF hating or LIVES in anxiety and fear. The human can be in DENIAL or be *numb* or be DISSOCIATED or in grief. They can be in APATHY or near death. The soul may no longer even inhabit the body and the biology is on it's own.
ALL of the above are a very low and slow vibrations and as we move to the fifth dimension their pain will increase. When the human reaches for higher thoughts little by little they go in and out of awareness which is better for their well being than being unaware.
The HALF CONSCIOUS human functions emotionally in; Contentment or hopefulness or indifference and boredom

and are able to create some. As the human reaches for higher vibrating thoughts and get in sync with their 90%er, creation is faster and easier.

THE FULLY CONSCIOUS human functions emotionally in; Strong interest or joy or enthusiastic awareness. The 90%er and 10%er joined and functioning as one unit are in their eagerness and passion.

<u>**SECOND CIRCLE**</u> Everything outside of the First Circle. The realm in which we as humans live. The consciousness we are responsible for creating and shaping. Also referred to as the Second Creation.

<u>**SEED SOULS**</u> the first 500 souls that were the original prototypes of humanity here on earth. We all originated from one of those souls and all have memories that trace back to one of the original 500 Family of Light we are all descendants literally, you have a soul family that goes back to one, and then goes even further than that. As ethereal beings you had a unified consciousness, rather than separate in the physical body. Remembrances as one of the first 500 souls we will experience during our spiritual awakening at some point. As one of the first 500 beings we are considered royalty and referred to in the cosmos as the First Family of Light.

<u>**SELF LOVE** SELF ESTEEM or **worth** is a multidimensional</u> SPIRITUAL attribute and NOT a third dimensional, linear attribute.

<u>**SENDER**</u> is what the invisible realm calls the "senders of light" are already in place to be used after the great shift. They are humans in biology and operating on our earth plane

now. They can send a messages from one end of the world to the next. One sender sends and the next sender picks up the massage and does not **decipher** or CHANGE or **embellish** the message before they send it to the next sender.

When the sender receives the message it is DOWNLOADED for **anybody** to accept within that vicinity. The sender then UPLOADS any thoughts being experienced on the earth plane. All of the thoughts are gathered and put into an orderly fashion and sent to the next sender. It takes about four Senders to cover the entire United States.

The senders will locate ever living being on the planet within the first **eighteen** hours after the darkness arrives. Each individual will be in contact with a sender. Each human will HEAR and can **send** messages to and from the sender.

Senders will know the PHYSICAL shape you are in and the SPIRITUAL LEVEL you are on. Your spiritual level is important because each level has its own belief systems which will dictate your behavior and cooperativeness. The **SPIRITUAL level** you were at when you fell asleep during the three days of darkness. In the first few days senders will be sending **directions** and your IDENTITY because some of us will not remember who they are. Once you are under control of yourself you will seek and HOOKUP with other like minded humans to settle together and build communities.

During the three days of darkness PHOTON energies will be ignited on earth.

One of the things photon energy can do is enable you to exist on it for months without any sustenance whatsoever including water. Breathing the photon energy will sustain the human. You will look for those leaders among you to teach breathing if you do not know how.

SENSORY AWARENESS or your feelings ARE NOT little human emotion. Feelings are the method humans USE to **arrive at INTUITIVE knowledge** or divine wisdom. You can't go from third dimensional human knowledge, the brain to divine knowledge in one step. The multidimensional language process of sensing divine wisdom starts with you feeling it. Knowledge of YOUR larger SELF, your 90%er and ALL you are, come through your senses.

When we get a breakthroughs in awareness it is because we FELT the multidimensional language. The mind DID NOT suddenly get smarter. Anytime you have overwhelming feelings of compassion or knowingness and intuition it is your multidimensional language coming through YOUR feelings.

Sensory awareness can be VERY difficult to sense at times, but as you adjust and acclimate to allowing them to come through you discern what comes from your INSIDES and what is circling around in your environment. Many feelings are coming from the inside of you, your soul self has many feelings to share. It is becoming easier and easier to KNOW what is yours and what is not.

When you AVOID, **deny** or *suppress* your SENSORY AWARENESS there is a price to pay. Fun things like *mental disease*, HUMAN DEPRESSION, **anxiety**, issues of overweight or any of the ADDICTIONS.

When humans deliberately try to stop SENSORY AWARENESS they CRAVE excitement because they feel so dead. Feelings or senses are pulses of life and they are MEANT to be experienced. When we don't have sensory awareness we get irritable or start blaming. When a human feels less or nothing from their soul, they will create a crisis of one sort or another. They will spend money for a temporary thrill and then crash to enhance their HUMAN EMOTIONS to fill the void left by BLOCKING their multidimensional communication from the invisible realm and their soul

SEXUAL ENERGY When life force energy enters the physical body we call it sexual energy it is just SELF LOVE. Not necessarily *physical* or about what you would term *pleasure*. Sex can be enjoyed it is an energy exchange that is equal and balanced. There is always a fine line of balance. When you aren't in a place of self love you find yourself feeding off of others with physical or nonphysical sexual relations.

Unbalanced sexual energy in humans gets TWISTED, dark and **depressed.** Then we go feeding because we have been fed on. This inappropriately used sexual energy is a method of stealing energy from others and ENTRAPPING, **manipulating** and CONTROLLING them. When we **repress or deny** this UNBALANCED energy it builds a force this energy would NOT normally have. Let unbalanced sexual energy FLOW through you and release your belief systems around it.

SHAME will hold you back spiritually.

SHAUMBRA there are many layers of this. At its simplest level it means family. A group of humans going through the awakening process on a spiritual journey breaking through consciousness. The term shaumbra originated during the times of Yeshua Ben Joseph (Jesus) when people, frequently from the essences gathered for secret spiritual meetings. Loosely translated in old Hebrew, the first portion of the word is pronounced "shau-home" meaning home or family. The second portion is "ba-rah" meaning journey and mission. Together it is "shau-home-ba-rah" which means family on a journey and experiencing together. In biblical times a "shaumbra" was also a scarf or shawl worn by either male or female and was a distinctive crimson color that let the others know it was time to meet. The group of humans going through the awakening process first, the vanguard.

Shaumbra is a consciousness and energy one feels compatible with or not. Shaumbra are back with their extended family across Gaia at this time. They already **know their TRUTH** and are working to get in touch with their **OWN EMOTIONS** *which is a challenge* for them to do because they have been in service to others for so long and denying the self. In this process the self has gotten blurry and a bit hard to sense and honor.

Shaumbra come from many different angelic families and have spent more lifetimes on earth than any other group. These angels have not always been so "nice" to each other. They have stolen from and killed each other over and over again in many battles and bloody wars amongst themselves. They have trapped and stolen from each other each other. They have also loved and married and reproduced together over and over again.

Finally the realization came that the wars and battles were exercises in futility.

The Crimson Council and Crimson Circle were formed to develop a different way. To evolve awareness for the self and others if they choose to accept it. Shaumbra found when you care for and love **the self FIRST** and become sovereign with no need of anything from anyone else it is easy to get along with everyone.

Shaumbra are the leaders in consciousness. They are going into the new realms. Going deep within the self to open new corridors so others may also move into higher consciousness. Shaumbra will take on others issues and work on them as if they were their own. They resolve the issue within themselves and radiate that potential out to others that wish to follow that resolution. The internalized awareness has been put on the legion of lights store shelf for others to pick.

They are ending a six month cycle that's been taking place since the quantum leap, a cycle of readjusting and making some deep changes within,9-18-2007 until March or April 2008 when all the new potentials were dropped in. The next six month cycle April 2008 until september 2008 has to do with bringing the potentials into the third dimension. Bring some of these new tools and new energies into your life.

The work shaumbra does is not about them. Shaumbra internalizes awareness within themselves to expand it. They open up new ways and potentials for all of humanity to utilize. It is challenging work because they forget why they are doing it and no one thanks them for doing the new energy work. Mostly they are ridiculed by others who consider them "crazy" or bizarre. On the angelic realms they are understood for the work they tirelessly do with passion and compassion. They do it on behalf of all of those they truly love in humanity and the angelic realms.

SHIFT the great shift is about our movement to higher vibrations. Change is the only constant in this universe. As all of humanity shifts and changes each one will find their OWN way depending on how much their heart and thoughts can stretch and how much their body can clear their dense pockets of energy. The extent of your personal transformation depends on your awareness of the process and your ability to flow with it. Many will continue in their present mode of survival. Never realizing that they have been offered a new way to evolve spiritually.

The third dimension is included in the forth dimension and both third dimension and forth dimension are included in the fifth dimension. That would be why some people will **consciously and physically shift** and others will physically shift without awareness. The ones shifting without conscious awareness of the process will not fare as well as those consciously aware. Everyone and everything on Gaia is shifting to a higher vibration. Beyond this particular galaxy the shift **stretches and affects the entire body of the legion of light** which is "all that is." The easiest way to understand the fifth dimension is by understanding that the first three dimensions are **height, width and depth**. The two dimensions we are now forming new relationships with are **TIME** and **SPACE**.

SHIFTING PERCEPTION is choosing an alternate or dimensional reality. When there are items in your life that drain you and can't be moved it is best to shift your perception to stop the ENERGY DRAIN by **thoughts**, *events* or HUMANS that drain you. Your perspective is a CHOICE. Pick vibrant and full.

SHOUD A shoud is the collective energy and voice of each and everyone speaking as one voice. Similar to a channeling, where nonphysical beings communicate as one voice through a human. In a Shoud, the SPIRITUAL ESSENCE of each member of the group is collected and translated into one voice. The message of the group is then communicated back to the group by an entity via the human channeler. In simplified terms the audience is listening to their own collective inner selves.

SHIVERIES (my word) coming from the unseen world or our soul is a form of communication with us that we feel on different parts of our biology. They mean different things like hello, a pat on the back because you got it right or are moving in the right direction. It happens naturally and slowly inside us. It is the feedback feeling that may wash over us. It may feel like a tingle or a touch on the head. It feels like shiveries to me. That feeling means that we have reached a place where we can feel and experience the energy of compassion which activates communication and we feel the feedback of the soul energy or any of our other invisible parts.

You can ask what they are conveying. There has been a few times I have gotten VERY light headed, which did not go away until I said "thank you." Unseen world was grateful for something I had done, and they wanted me to know that.

SILICON Many forms of life contain silicon structures (biogenic silica), including microorganisms such as diatoms, plants such as horsetail, and animals such as hexactinellid sponges. It is present in the cell walls of various plants (including edible ones) to strengthen their structural integrity. Our carbon based bodies get threaded with silicon when we are in the void and as our awareness increases our silicon increases.

SOUL is our unique, individual, unified identity of the self, the COLLECTION of everything we have ever done, been or thought. Our soul understands every PROBABILITY and **potential** and all the shadow potentials. The soul is pure *positive energy*, TRUSTING, loving and adores the human. SOUL is in concert with the LEGION of LIGHT. The soul is androgynous, self contained and self sufficient. Our soul NEVER blames or JUDGES the human. Our divine self is the soul and cannot be defined or structured or controlled. **Humans PROJECT their shortcomings onto their soul.**

One soul has eleven different experiences of being a human. There are twelve dimensions. A point of perception is also a dimension. So, 1 soul and 11 different experiences of that soul, equals 12.

In my books I use the term soul to include what we call spirit, holy ghost, higher self, etc.... and all the other invisible aspects of ourselves. The soul is a very unique identity and expression of what we call God, the legion of light or Spirit. The soul is your *I AM, the overview of all that is visible and invisible*, a divine wholeness. Our soul cannot be defined or structured or controlled.

Our soul has not been able to, or wanted to come into a limited, overly structured and suppressive environment where the mind rules and reality is inflexible as it is in the third dimension. There are twelve dimensions of time and space in our soul. Eleven are a harmonic vibration of the first one or the current lifetime the one on top, that is why WE are the **master** of the others. All slightly different experiences and choices. The soul is an overview of all that you are, the entire system of "you", the "I AM", the higher self, the part in direct communication with the legion of light.

Soul is created by light-beings that are *primarily consciousness* which are formless, no shape. **Light-beings NEVER cease** to exist, but a SOUL CAN CEASE to exist. Soul encodes the DNA, evolves and grows. The light-beings or over souls are in themselves complete YET gain much knowledge through experiential entities for there is no duality in the over soul. The soul has those experiences. The light-being **DECIDES** the types of experiences it wants the soul to access.

<u>**SOVEREIGN SELF**</u> is a self sufficient onto itself with no dependency on others or mass consciousness or the planetary grids or the galactic grids or the cosmic grids. Our energetic meridians are woven into the outer dimensions and our nervous

system is wired into your inner dimensions. This total system connects our spiritual parts to our physical parts.

This system of connection by the energetic meridians is VITAL as we use it to clear our self of blocks to raising our vibration. The physical body must be clear enough to vibrate at the higher level or a full merge of the soul and its human. The clearer you are the more dimensions you can expand into being sovereign and having complete control over yourself.

We walk the path of ascension as a SOVEREIGN being and enter **the void alone**. To go to the next step of becoming enlightened we need to detach and grieve the loss of the little human. The first new relationship humans have in the new energy would **ideally be with their soul** which makes **a sovereign human.**

<u>SPIRIT</u> is the same as the higher self, awareness, life force, I am, expression of God. Spirit goes to earth THROUGH the Human to manifest "spirits" or the souls beliefs to see how they play out. Our energy as humans is always broadcasting our life in real time to all entities in the universe. Spirit is the single energy that exists throughout all of infinite reality. Spirit is found in all things, animate and inanimate. Spirit is where we all meet and experience oneness.

<u>SPIRITUAL BODY</u> is the fourth body out from the biology and has walls between the different dimensions now. The spiritual body is on a different plane and the walls go the length of the body and extend above and below or perpendicular to the earth. The spiritual body extends out about one half to one foot from the body and is amorphous and composed of clouds of color more beautiful than those of the emotional body. They are the same colors as those of the emotional body

but each color is infused with the rose light of love. The heart chakra of a loving person is full of rose light. When people are in love beautiful arcs of rose light connect their hearts and a beautiful rose color is added to the normal golden pulsation.

An immense amount of INTERACTION takes place between entities in their spiritual body. Great blobs of color and shape whisk across places between different humans. Some of these goings on are pleasant and some are not so pleasant. The spiritual bodies are interacting. You can feel the difference in the interactions when you focus on them. I am not talking body language but an actual energetic phenomenon that can be perceived.

SPIRITUALITY is everything that is NOT physical. Like *belief systems*, IDEAS and your higher self not in biology. Take responsibility to **take** ONLY what resonates with you and create from there. Our true power is the ability to create and the reason we placed ourselves at the front of the line at this time to come to earth.

SPIRITUAL SOUL GROUP each one of us has a group of souls we are SPIRITUALLY **connected to** a bit more than we are connected with the collective consciousness. This is a group we reconnect with for rejuvenation and activation in all dimensions. Spiritual families are different than our biological families in many ways they HOLD our **original vibration** and can help us to redirect our life when we are off course. The spiritual family or soul group can give you an accurate reflection of your divinity.

SPIRITUAL DEPRESSION is **not** caused by the MIND and the mind is NOT involved. When we grab the hand of soul and take THE LEAP OF FAITH, or go into the *dark night of the soul,* a spiritual metamorphosis or transmutation takes place. The transition from human to becoming a **divine human angel.** You will experience spiritual NUMBNESS and feel abandoned by the legion of light at this time. The irony is your soul is as close to you as it is possible to be. Your angels and guides leave your egg shaped aura to make room for the soul to move in. You are in between, in a dark hole moving from the caterpillar state to becoming a butterfly. This is zero point energy, a complete emptying of the OLD for the NEW to move in. The final surrender of your human beliefs and ways. Do the happy dance.

BREATHE it in and bring LOTS of compassion in for yourself. This depression has been building up for many lifetimes and is part of the ascension process. The first time ever we have done it while having a biology. The TEARS and more tears and stories come tumbling out. Depression and ascension are an interrelated process. You are dying, letting go of the old limiting story you created in third dimension and have built on for many many lifetimes. Release those stories so the energy can be transmute and made available to you in a new way.

When you breathe you start feeling, LIVING and waking UP. Spiritual depression generally lasts a year. During that time you will slip in and out of the void. Things and people start to go away. They are no longer a vibrational match to the new meld you have become. When we decide to move into this **interdimensional state** we see things through the *awareness of our soul and its immortal wisdom.*

When the human REJECTS the spiritual depression (SOUL) the human slips into a third dimensional depression. They LOOSE their divine, their soul, they will go back to human free will, and their guides and angels and a lower vibration.

Depression is used as a FUEL to ascension.

STRINGS OF VIBRATION are beautiful and always between all of the potentials. There are also strings between one person and another of how they met and what they do. Humans call that coincidence but the enlightened call it synchronicity. These strings of vibration represent **a system with RULES. The** strings of vibration are manifestation of potentials into realities based upon the vibration of the quantum attributes and this links into co-creation. Not necessarily planned but there is organization.

SYMBOLOGY or ENERGY symbols. As we expand our consciousness into other realms and move BEYOND the MIND we are going to get symbols that are not to be taken literally. Delve into the energy of the symbol and HOW that energy WORKS to get message for you. Use the symbols as directions to go or affirmations you are on the right track and not alone. Look for your knowingness in a holographic place. Answers will be there but not as words or pictures they are so subtle that the most enlightened human could miss the message. In YOUR **stillness** the ears will get attuned to hearing the truth present in a song or a tone you hear or sense. Words come later. FOR EXAMPLE: Cockroach as everlasting energy. Zucchini could be an energetic symbol for nurturing or feeding. Mathematics could suggest a type of mathematical structure that will enable it to function in this reality. Crop circles are symbols from the Order of the Arc as affirmations to humans they are in process of growing the human consciousness. War, chases, monsters and battle symbols could literally be releasing old energy within yourself. Spider can be patience things will get wrapped up eventually. Scorpion is possibly the energy of speaking your truth.

Debt can be a symbol of the extent you are holding onto past life karma incidences or indebted energy you are still holding onto. Debt is an illusion and sometimes is very emotional and painful taking the energy right out of you. Hands could be symbolically saying you are OR are not a hands-on person. Letting or not letting your energy flow out through your hands into creations in this reality.

Every insect even a tick, every animal, everything, is all interconnected and part of the workings of Gaia. Many of creatures of earth have to do with the continual process of renewal. When something is old and decrepit, the insects will come in, feed off of it, renew its energy so it can be born again. Don't get too stuck.

SYNCHRONICITY is energies that align with purpose. The situations in our life look like accidents or coincidence but they are not. Synchronicity is you at the right time and place with the potentials aligned that *you asked for*. Certainly NOT the way you asked for them. You have to take some action like accept an invitation or make a phone call or an electronic communication. You might need to put your body someplace as part of the synchronicity piece.

Understand the balance of things. Synchronicity works piecemeal and we are required to connect the pieces together for the whole thing to happen in a way you NEVER anticipated. Yes co-creation. And this is all done with divine timing NOT with third dimensional timing and that makes us crazy.

Our intuition is a product of synchronicity. A very real way of the invisible realm communicating with humanity. When we hear the intuition said in our voice it appears as though the human thought of it. They probably did not. Synchronicity is the system the creator uses to help us. The human IS very much a part of the system.

<u>10%er</u> The 10%er is the human which is only ten percent of a whole conglomerate. The "Little human" the 10%er does not always make soul too happy. We whine a lot and do not like change even when it is for the better. Giving up victimhood isn't easy. The human is NOT WHAT you are! It is only an aspect of our entireness. Humans are electrical, chemical and magnetic beings with our own magnetic field that creates our reality just before we step into it.

<u>2012</u> is the signpost in our timeline saying we are moving into a new energy that was foretold by the angels. There will be no significant spiritual happening in 2012, only the celebration that tells us, we have arrived.

<u>THIRD LANGUAGE</u> is a metaphor for our communication with our higher self or soul or our entourage. This communication happens slowly and naturally inside us. It can be our voice we hear, a smell or taste or the shivery feeling we get when our entourage is in agreement with something we have said or done. The third language IS feeling that washes over us like a tingle, shiveries or a touch on the head or cheek. That feeling means we reached a place where we can feel the *energy of compassion* activating communication with our soul energy or any other member of our entourage. A spiritual interdimensional language that is **not linear** and crosses all of time and space.

When you are presented with questions, concerns or issues from your soul to increase your clarity or light please be as present as you possibly can. Healing and guidance can be the same thing. Channeled guidance can relieve and release conflicts within you that block the flow of your wisdom. Practice the guidance you get when you get it or the guidance fades and diminishes. Blame will not get you desirable results. Speak softly and you will hear more. Logic and reason can hide wisdom.

<u>THOUGHT</u> is the fastest energy in the universe. To go to another dimension we can think and be there. Telepathy with thought is much faster than any vehicle. You can get there at the speed of thought. EACH thought is an **INDIVIDUAL ENTITY** expressed NOT in physical words but as **images HAVING vibration, COLOR, SHAPE and movement.** These entities (our thoughts) are grouped together by category and stored in the crystalline realms. So when we want information about anything we go to the crystalline realms and retrieve what we want. Any new awareness we might hit upon would go to the crystalline realms to be stored for others to have access to.

Thought has no wavelength, no space or time impinging on our physical universe that **does have** space, time, energy and matter. Thought is the perception of the present, compared to the past so one can draw conclusions for direct action in the now. The mission of thought is survival in the physical universe. **Thought controls ENERGY.** It is thought that causes everything structural and functional that happens in an organism.

Thoughts are THINGS and **emotions** are the energy behind thoughts.

Emotions shape our thoughts and the *two are inseparable.*

The rising frequencies around us is causing our short-term memory to slip. Embrace and enjoy our short-term memory is being affected by now time. Our long-term memory is more fully anchored in us because of our emotional ups and downs experienced this lifetime.

Our training as children was focused on navigating life in third dimension and not so much on the human heart. To be a divine creator we must be in **control of our thoughts** Our *thoughts define our emotions.* It is important to know that there is scale of emotion. That each emotion has its own vibration. That is why we need to control our thoughts.

To ascend the **mind** must be in charge of MATTER.

The LEAP of human consciousness is to achieve a *state of total love* while still being present in the physical body. Most humans do not realize that you can take control of your emotions. Controlling your emotions is a reachable goal now because of all the invisible realm help and the reconnecting of our DNA.

Thoughts of the same type of event are on a chain. Thinking of one of them will lead to you thinking of all the thoughts on that chain. Our memory is on a chain. Think one though and a similar one comes to mind and another and another. The smells of cooking triggers thoughts of other times you smelled that type of cooking.

THOUGHT CENTER A dimensional "thought center" can be found in space. A thought center is a collection point of all of the thoughts, good, bad and ugly there are on a particular subject.

So when humans rocket a thought out it might gravitate to a particular thought center which **ABSORBS any number of ideas**. The ideas are a collection of the coherent or **incoherent**. Discernment at a thought center is VERY useful. These collections of thoughts would represent all that has EVER been thought on a given subject. The center is a kind of focus for converging lines of thought about a given subject and that thought center or group of vortices would have links to all related subjects.

ANYONE and they do not need to be wearing biology, thinking deeply on a subject vibrates themselves to that thought center. If your biology restricts you in some way you can rise with a sympathetic vibration to that thought center and receive whatever you are capable of assimilating.

This influence is one reason many humans around the world grasp the same concept at the same time. It is known in the patent offices that practically identical inventions arrive simultaneously to be patented.

Emotion forms coalesce together creating enormous powerful **BLOCKS** of feeling and **float around almost everywhere**. An individual coming in contact with these blocks can be easily influenced by them. There are many on the earth in an emotional state of fear at this time and that energy coalesce together and comes back hitting the earth in waves. Remember it is only energy and you can take that energy and convert it to something constructive and compassionate.

THOUGHT FORM is an image that has taken PHYSICAL FORM with vibration, color and shape. A thought form is a temporary living entity of **intense activity** animated by THE ONE idea that generated it. If made of the finer kinds of matter it has great power and energy and can be used as a potent agency when directed by a **steady, strong willed entity**. The CLEARER and WELL FORMED the idea is the clearer and well formed the thought form associated with that idea is. We enhance these thought forms by focusing on the thoughts they represent. **Habitual thoughts** become very powerful, well formed forces affecting our lives. Human beings are *just beginning to develop* the mental body and use their intellects in clear ways.

A thought form is an **energy or consciousness** manifested either consciously or unconsciously by an individual or a group. A thought form may be benevolent or malevolent.

Within the mental body and its mostly YELLOW FIELD thought forms **can be seen**. The thought forms appear to be blobs of varying brightness and shape. These thought forms have additional colors superimposed on them *coming from the emotional body*. The color represents the person's emotion attachment to the particular thought form. The strength of the thought and emotion determines the size of a thought form and its duration as a separate entity. Duration depends on how much nurturing is generate by the repetition of the thought by its originator or others.

Every impulse sent out from the mental body of a human immediately cloaks itself in a temporary vehicle of the humans essence. The **quality of the thought** determines the COLOR it is. The type of thought determines its shape and a **clear thought has a well defined outline**. A glowing rose color is a wish to heal. Silver white would be a mental effort to strengthen and focus the mind. A yellow gold indicates intellect and has a darker dull tint if attached to lower negative goals.

Abstract ideas are represented by various geometrical forms. The merest abstraction in third dimension becomes a definite fact on the mental plane. When a human thinks of a concrete object like a pool or shed they build a tiny image of the object in matter in the mental body. These are so real they can be **moved about** and **rearranged by someone other than their creator**. The form can be seen by another that sees the invisible realm. The image floats around the upper part of that body generally in front of the face. When we think of another person a tiny portrait shows up.

A creator forms a concept of their creation out of the matter of their mental body and projects it into space in front of them keeping it before the mind's eye and copies it. A lecturer with weak thought forms confuses the audience. A clear cut speaker forces the mental bodies of the audience to try to reproduce her thought form.

THOUGHT WAVE has less defined action but reaches a wider circle and is very adaptable. A wave of compassion would arouse compassion in the recipient, but the object of compassion might well be different in both. In a thought form the object of compassion would be the same. A thought form carries a complete idea conveying the exact nature of the thought.

The constant pressure of the strong thought waves of a teacher gradually raises those of the pupil.

TIME is roundish, balloon like and not linear like the illusion we have lived with on earth. Time can be expanded or compressed to suit our need. Time speeds up as our consciousness increases and slows down when our awareness slows down. Basically there is no time. Time is an artificial creation by humans to help understand how to get from one moment to the next in their daily journey. Time is just a belief system we have divided energy into. In reality, and definitely in the other realms what we call time is a sequence of events that take place.

A series of choices or sequences that build one upon the other. But because the final choice has already been made the sequence of events is just us walking backwards through time.

There is a formula for **TIME** : The DENSITY of mass plus the rate at which it is VIBRATING equals its time frame. There are varying time frames IN EACH DIMENSION and it is *circular time*. The now time frame is a circle around us where all things past are known and future potentials are realized and known.

<u>TIMING</u> It is impossible to apply a third dimensional time frame to an interdimensional potential. The human gets very frustrated that the legion of light delivers things only WHEN YOU NEED THEM and not when you ask for them. The scenario of the synchronicity must be met with the energy of the moment.

Make *no assumptions about timing.*

<u>TRUTH</u> is always evolving you never find it except on some of the higher angelic realms. When you try to change the world with YOUR truth it try's to change you. Each vibrational level has different truths and beliefs. Truth unexpressed is not yet a truth. It is not important you speak the "perfect truth" only that the truth is your own and you are in INTEGRITY with what you say. Being in integrity with your truth is the only way that your truth can evolve. Other people have their truths. Learn to live with your truth and everyone else's truth for *no one person* holds all truth. Together we hold the larger truth. Each one of us comes in with a small piece. Find it and share it willingly not as the only truth, but as one that stands side by side with many other truths.

LEVELS OF COMPASSION

<u>UNIVERSE</u> what we call the universe or cosmos exists in **many DIMENSIONAL realities** simultaneously. The universe expands until it reaches the point where all the different realities intersect. As it reaches this point it continues with the same motion and collapses upon itself. It collapses until it reaches point zero again and then continuing with the same motion begins its expansion again.

<u>UNIVERSAL ENERGY</u> is the base energy that permeates EVERYTHING. This *unconditional love energy* has the highest vibration there is. UNIVERSAL ENERGY has a natural action of **blending** everything together. You could call it HOME or the legion of light or heaven or whatever name would please you. It is also referred to as cosmic intelligence and PERMEATES *all things and is infinite.* ALL the different energies come from a **base energy of love.** Even electricity or gravity are forms of love as is LIGHT a form of unique energy. Universal energy is even present in a vacuum with all other energy removed.

The nature of all energy is **CONSTANT MOTION.** *Observe the motion* so you can decide where you want to place YOURSELF. The higher your vibration the more important your placement is in that energy. Actions flowing *against* the **blending motion** of universal energy will cause a greater REACTION than it would have in the past. Now there is almost ZERO tolerance for MISDIRECTION of your energy.

Always observe the flow of universal energy and all of your actions, personally and in mass consciousness so you can **stay in HARMONY.** We are all part of each other and not separate in spite of the current illusion we are in. Thoughts and feelings in our heart are of increasing importance because they are being *radiated out.* There will be no SECRETS and there never is on the higher vibrational levels. **Secrets** are a product of duality and lower vibrations. We are moving into a dimension where we will ALL HAVE ACCESS to each other's thoughts and feelings, secrets and denials. Having balanced male and female energy is the first step to MATCHING the flow and vibration of universal energy. The Crystal Energy has been infiltrating into our reality providing a base for us all to move into a higher vibration as a unit. In the universal energy lower vibrating individuals *FEEL threatened and exposed*. If they cling to their old choices they suffer the worst. Putting your actions firmly in the flow of universal energy can be most painful or JOYFUL always your choice.

Typically we have judged and *found fault* with people vibrating at a different rate than ourselves. That behavior gave us a point of reference for the different levels people were on and also served to justify and hold us locked in the same level. In stead of attempting to change yourself or others *find a harmonic resonance* between the different levels. Once a single strand is in place connecting your level of vibration with their level of vibration **BOTH of you can see your similarities.**

<u>VEIL</u> "The veil", isn't someplace, its a dynamic energy that surrounds our very consciousness and every cell of the body. It distances us from ourselves, our invisible parts. "Lifting the veil" means turning on the light of REVELATION.

Your choice and intent to know more about what is real and what is not helps thin the veil. With increased light or awareness comes more RESPONSIBILITY and increased power and **new tools** to master. Once you become accustomed to and accept this new way of thinking, you take on more multidimensional qualities. The qualities that the veil has kept hidden.

LEVELS OF COMPASSION

VENUS TRANSIT is a delivery event of *compassionate feminine energy* to earth. This energy is to be picked up and used slowly so we can move into the next energy with INTEGRITY providing a compassionate balance to a planet that has not been balanced for eons. 2004, the tsunami and the venus transit. 2012, another venus transit.

VIBRATION the words **emotion** or **VIBRATION** or feeling have the same meaning to the invisible realm and are interchangeable. Every entity has a very specific energy balance a particular resonance or vibration. The true indication of your vibration LEVEL is what comes back to you. We are full of vibrations many serve us and many do not. A contradiction in our thoughts and behavior can keep us from what we desire. Focus on something not wanted lowers you vibration and ability to create and you cannot feel joy. A strong emotive response in the human is what the universe looks for and does not care if it is **negative** or POSITIVE. It is the *intensity* that counts. Whether it is passion or rage you feel in the moment, they both mean strong focused desire passing through you. Anything that affects your vibration affects your overall experience.

Vibration is the response of harmony or discord of all things to all things. is the magic of interdimensional math which is in a base-12. Zero is the POTENTIAL of all that ever was, is or can be. Zero is variable depending upon the equation. Zero removes what is not needed and reveals the solution

VOID or a Null Zone is established after there is an expansion outwards of energy which receives a blow or shock causing it to *COLLAPSE inwards upon itself.* The old established **energy patterns** (belief systems) **are now broken** and there is no way that they will ever return to the previous pattern. They have been IRREVOCABLY changed. The energy of a Null Zone feels *jagged and raw*. There is much hurt and pain, grieving for the "good old days" and cutting of MANY CORDS.

While in a void you find most EVERYTHING irritates you, even other people breathing is irritating. It's the shattering of a world or a belief system, a long-held desire, or sometimes an important relationship with yourself or another. You experience the FEELING with your **heart first**. LATER the brain processes the experience and all the changes. The old closely held belief gets shattered and you are liberated from its limits.

This would be similar to the feeling you would have after being in a hurricane or any natural disaster. This shattering creates the perfect foundation for the introduction of something ENTIRELY new to come in. The potential is enormous. Null Zones or voids **AMPLIFY** and ***destabilize*** **whatever inherent DISCORD is present** in the surrounding areas. They actually occur to help us *break free from old stagnant patterns and belief systems* giving us a unique opportunity for a *quantum leap* into a deeper sector of the unknown.

While in the void a lot of MENTAL and EMOTIONAL processing is done. The void is a **womb to birth the new** in our awareness. Generally voids last a few months or can be a few weeks. **The Void** is also the nothingness outside of All That Is. The consciousness we ventured into to discover *something* **new for our SOUL.**

<u>**VORTEXES**</u> can be seen in the spiraling motion of air or liquid around a center of rotation. Turbulent flow can make many vortices. A good example of a vortex is the atmospheric phenomenon of a whirlwind or a tornado or dust devil taking

the form of a helix, column, or spiral. Vortexes of energy have been forming on this planet since its beginning. As vortexes emerge from the earth and are joined with your own intentional vortex they become permanent vortexes and will anchor the Light in that location of the planet.

Your familiarity with vortexes would have you believe that they are stationary but once a vortex evolves into a portal, it is no longer bound to be stationary. Even now many vortexes that have created the high-energy spots on our planet are now beginning to turn into portals and move. Vortexes go up and have an airy smell. Simple vortexes like a tornado goes clockwise or counter clockwise.

WALKING BACKWARD IN TIME means stepping INTENTIONALLY into your future taking your creator powers with you. In the illusion of linear time you are moving in one direction but facing another. Whenever you find yourself in a difficult situation you can move forward in time to imagine and create an outcome that pleases you.

Now when the human says "I choose enlightenment" ascension or any of those things they have already arrived at them. Walking backward in time, they decide to ascend and just need to go through the steps to get there. This is the physics of the universe. You choose how to experience your own ascension and REINTEGRATION with your soul. It has already happened because you decided as a creator what you wanted to do. As you walked backwards you get to decide if you want to do it easy or hard. A series of choices build one upon the other because the final choice has already been made, the sequence of events is just walking backwards through time. Even if you need to pretend the confidence at first the soul confidence will build and offer you support that has never been there before.

You plan to go to the store. Then you go backwards through time to see what it was like to get there. This transcends time. We walk backwards in time all the time but we don't call it that. You CHOSE the potential and structure the steps building one upon the other to get there. We create everything around us in all the dimensions of time and space by walking backward in time.

WALL OF FIRE is a metaphor for "doorway" leading from Home into the void which is now our universe. The zone we crossed from the First Circle to the Second Circle.

WATER the earth is 71% **water**. 97% of water on earth is SALT WATER. Ground and the dirt of this planet is common ONLY to this planet. Water has FOUR states on earth. The visible and invisible state of solid, liquid, gas and the hidden part of water will be a new fuel.

Water is the **CONDUIT for interdimensional** energies. Its health and balance develops human consciousness and compassion. Water moves, rests and brings energies back into alignment and expands yet again. We drink the same water the dinosaur drank. *Understanding water* is most important to maintaining *your* HEALTH and the HEALTH of OUR WATER.

WATER CYCLES are the way Gaia balances herself. Her cycles take longer than a human life cycles to develop so we do not see the entire cycle. There are large and small water cycles and many small ones between the large ones. ICE AGES are part of water cycles. The last small ice age was in the 1200s to 1400s. Around 200 years long. Right now we have the *beginning of another ice age*. A cold time starts with the warming. Our PRESENT "global warming" is part of one of Gaia's WATER cycles happening naturally and normally. Water cycles vary in length from as short as 150 years or as long as 400 years. Gaia is starting a medium length water cycle that explains the reason for our changes of weather.

Humans are not responsible for the water cycles but this one is a little earlier than planned because of human help. The TEMPERATURE of the planet is dictated by how much water is on it. The water cycle of the planet is what controls the *temperature and the wind.* Part of the cycle is that it gets warm like it is now. We are at the beginning of a water cycle that will turn to a lower temperature eventually and that is typical, cyclical, and normal.

WATER CYCLE see **ICE AGE**

WEAVINGS OF REALITY are the grid systems and patterns and of the earth. After you understand the integration and acceptance of your divine self you will understand how this was all laid into a very beautiful orderly structure. It goes beyond mathematics and is very orderly. If you are trying to understand the grids to attain information you won't discover what you're looking for.

WISDOM comes from using all the knowledge you have accumulated from ALL your experiences. The experiences of all your parts and pieces, visible and invisible, that you have discerned to be wise. Using these wise bits of knowledge in a clear course of action is wisdom.

WORRY actually dramatizes events going on in your body, mind and the creative part of you and that DOES NOT SERVE

YOU. Worry is a MENTAL EXERCISE that drags down the **emotional body** to lower vibrations, enlarging your pockets of etheric baggage. Worry holds that thought TIGHT in your energetic field. Worry is a negative emotion and DRAINS your energy on all levels and *exhausts the physical body.*

Thoughts and emotions **require energy.** Worry CLOGS up the mental body by *dominating our awareness with negative thoughts.* Worry can FREQUENTLY PREVENT experiencing the NOW moment.

Worry ROBS the SPIRITUAL body of its **power** because you ARE DOUBTING yourself and your soul.

It is a question of your perception and what level you want to function at. Worry puts you in LACK, powerlessness, FEAR and doubt. Where you CHOOSE to put your **awareness** determines your feelings about life.

YESHUA BEN JOSEPH one of the actual names for Jesus, appropriate for the biblical times in which he lived.

YO -HAM is the transformation of Metatron into the physical, personal more melded state and new vibration or name of Yo-ham. **"You are."** YOU ARE ALL THAT IS. In the new energy and consciousness on earth THIS change took place during the Quantum Leap of 9-18-2007 **Yo-ham.** You are that you are. Yo-ham is our essence and joins us in our triumphant discovery of life, purpose and of expression on earth. With some humans choosing life and sovereignty and the energy of Yo-ham. Take a deep breath and allow the human to delight in the experience and feel this energy.

ZERO is the magic of interdimensional math which is in a base-12. Zero is the POTENTIAL of all that ever was, is or can be. Zero is variable depending upon the equation. Zero removes what is not needed and reveals the solution.

ZERO-POINT ENERGY is a measurement of UNIVERSAL energy at REST in whatever form it is CURRENTLY taking. Universal energy is **infinite** and exists in many dimensions. We are just becoming accustomed to living in zero-point energy. Initially it feels like being **held back or stuck** because of the lack of forward motion. Zero-point energy is the **most powerful point a person can attain**, meditation and many spiritual practices are all aimed at achieving it.

As a child might spin around we are actually making a personal vortex attempting to remember zero-point energy when we lived in all that is. This is the same secret that led to the formation of the Dervishes of Mevlevi know as the whirling Dervishes or the sacred practice of forming a portal from a vortex. A personal vortex can easily be created with **just a THOUGHT.**

When a vortex evolves into a portal there is a zero-point energy at the center of the vortex. The zero-point energy is **the PERFECT BALANCE of all energies** that have been used on earth since the beginning. Zero-point energy is NOT negative energy and positive energy that are canceling each other out.

JESUS—at zero point energy on the cross, being crucified seemingly at the point of death actually said "Where have You gone? Jesus felt a withdrawal of the invisible realm and all wisdom drained from his body. He felt the darkness and the void invade him. Just as he needed his entourage the most they were not there. He experienced a **multidimensional shift of energy** and taken to zero so he could ASCEND and then all the invisible realm and energy came back. The love of God poured into him with more power than he ever had before. That is the way of zero point energy. He blamed himself for a moment and questioned his faith.

MOTHER TERESA—at zero point energy died in sorrow because she was a linear human not understanding the shift of energy upon her. Years before her death her energy shifted and went to zero for a moment. A new frequency was begging her to change the way she did things so she could be JOYFUL. With more power and compassion than ever. She took that to mean she was abandoned and left alone SHE decided she lost her connection. God never did abandon her. GOD went away slightly to come back **STRONGER *with new attributes*.** She would have to go around the protocol she had been trained in and speak to the legion of light DIRECTLY. But she did as she always had done and died in sorrow. Her compassion was her gift right to the end.

Moving from 2007 to 2008, put the planet at zero-point energy. 2007 is a 9 symbolizing completion THE END. The last few months of 2007 was a winding down. A winding down of all OUR *gifts and tools we had depended on.* Our gifts were brought back to ZERO. That is the way of multidimensions. Allowing HUMANS to move into 2008 FRESH and clean. This IS NOT an upgrade, 2008 does not take an *old energy and add to it.* That is a linear third dimensional concept. Silly humans love to blame themselves because we are so conditioned to the "cause and effect" relationship of duality. When things don't go the way we THINK they should SPIRITUALLY we feel responsible. By the middle of January 2008 things will be RECONFIGURED, *renewed* and changed so you can reboot. All will come back in a NEW WAY.

***

www.ingramcontent.com/pod-product-compliance
Lightning Source LLC
Chambersburg PA
CBHW072226271025
34623CB00042B/1087